**Illustrator:**
Barb Lorseyedi

**Editor:**
Janet Cain M. Ed.

**Editorial Project Manager:**
Ina Massler Levin, M.A.

**Editor in Chief:**
Sharon Coan, M.S. Ed.

**Art Director:**
Elayne Roberts

**Associate Designer:**
Denise Bauer

**Cover Artist:**
Sue Fullam

**Product Manager:**
Phil Garcia

**Imaging:**
Alfred Lau
James Edward Grace

**Publishers:**
Rachelle Cracchiolo, M.S. Ed.
Mary Dupuy Smith, M.S. Ed.

# Alph
# Around
# the Year

**Author:**

*Phyllis Efoagui*

*Teacher Created Materials, Inc.*
P.O. Box 1040
Huntington Beach, CA   92647
**ISBN-1-55734-191-5**

*©1996 Teacher Created Materials, Inc.*          Made in U.S.A.

# Table of Contents

# Table of Contents *(cont.)*

# Table of Contents *(cont.)*

# Introduction

*Alphabet Around the Year* is a complete, classroom-tested, early childhood curriculum that is based on the alphabet. It is an integrated, whole-language program consisting of one- to two-week units focusing on each letter. The alphabet theme is connected to the content areas with activities in language arts (including language experience and writing suggestions), math, science, social studies, art, and cooking. As students explore each letter, they are provided with a variety of hands-on, developmentally appropriate experiences.

The letter units are primarily organized according to seasons and holidays. Basic topics, such as colors, animals, and patterns are presented in the fall. More complex subjects, such as astronomy, insects, and amphibians are covered in the winter and spring. The exciting year draws to a close with a study of dinosaurs, followed by the culminating activities.

The topics chosen for the letter units are intended to capture the curiosity of early childhood students. High-quality children's literature selections hold center stage in this curriculum. Imagination is used to spark a variety of creative writing that can be the product of a group or individual effort. A variety of math activities, such as counting, patterning, or numeration, are included in each unit. A bibliography that includes books and resources in technology related to the topics being studied is provided for each letter unit.

A bulletin board with a class tree made of crumpled brown paper bags is the focus for a variety of activities throughout the year. The products created by students are valued and prominently displayed on the tree. The art work and stories are changed monthly to correspond with the seasons and holidays. A monthly calendar can be included on the bulletin board, and it should be referred to each day when counting, or when discussing topics such as, the weather, holidays, seasons, days, and months.

A key picture associated with each letter of the alphabet is reproduced on poster board. It is first displayed when a letter is introduced. After the unit for a letter is completed, the key picture is placed on a wall as part of an alphabet line-up. Letters that have already been studied are reviewed at this time. By the end of the year, all 26 letters will be displayed in alphabetical order.

Students are encouraged to share objects from home which names begin with the Letter of the Week. These items can lead students to generate new ideas for study. Students may also bring additional books to read that are related to the topic of the week. Learning is an exciting endeavor, especially when students are invited to share in the process. Using this curriculum will enable students to discover the joy of learning.

# The Beginning of a Very Special Year

Welcome each student before school begins with a phone call or a letter on your own personal stationary, decorated with stamps, stickers, or clip art. Express how excited you are to meet your new students, and invite them to bring a teddy bear or another special stuffed animal friend when they come to school on the first day. Name a few of the wonderful activities you are planning for them during the year. Receiving a phone call or a letter from you will make them excited about coming to school and hopefully allay some of their fears.

On the first day of school, you may wish to give parents a copy of the Table of Contents (pages 2–4) which outlines how this curriculum is organized. In this way, parents can be encouraged to participate in their child's educational program.

Display a welcoming bulletin board in the hall or on your door. Write the students' names on teddy bear cutouts (page 8) or note paper, and scatter them over the bulletin board or door. Make a large tagboard bear by enlarging a pattern (page 8), and place it in the center. Cut out letters to create a title that shows the large bear saying, "Welcome to a 'Beary' Special Year!" Inside the classroom, have a table for students to display their teddy bears and other stuffed animals. Invite students to tell about these. After you take down the bulletin board, allow students to take home the teddy bear cutouts or note paper with their names.

Create an inside bulletin board featuring a class tree that changes each month. Make the tree from pieces of crumpled brown paper bag or brown tagboard that is cut and taped together. Students make new things for the tree each month as they learn about the changing seasons and different holidays. At the beginning of the year, scallop a large piece of green butcher paper or sheets of green construction paper to look like leaves and staple them to the tree. Students make apples to go on the tree for September. For October, take off the green leaves and have students make scary bats, owls, ghosts, and goblins for a haunted tree. For November, have students collect and trace leaves on one side of white finger paint paper. Have them cover the other side with red and yellow finger paint. Tell them to blend the paints in places to make the color orange. After the paint has dried, cut out the leaves and staple them onto and under the tree to make a gorgeous fall display. Invite students to make colorful candles for December and cut out winter birds for January. Hang on student-made heart creatures in February and shamrocks and leprechauns for March. Help them make dogwood or apple blossoms for April. Ask students to cut out green leaves from pieces of green construction paper for May. At the end of year, paint students' hands and press on handprints for a Friendship Tree. Add seasonal and holiday figures, as well as students' stories and artwork around the tree throughout the year. Place a calendar (page 9) beside the tree, and change it each month. Use the calendar to discuss topics, such as holidays, days of the week, numbers, weekly or monthly activities, and the weather. You may wish to use pieces of string and paper clips to hang students' seasonal artwork from the ceiling.

# The Beginning of a Very Special Year *(cont.)*

Use the following suggestions for an exciting first day of school.

### • *NAME TAGS*

Make teddy bear name tags for students (page 8) from laminated note paper, construction paper, or tagboard. Greet each child on the first day of school with a name tag.

### • *STUFFED ANIMALS*

Have a "Show and Tell" time when students can introduce their stuffed animals. Each student might like to tell the animal's name, how it came to live with him or her, where it sleeps, and his or her favorite thing to do with the animal. Be sure to have extra stuffed animals for students who forgot to bring theirs. These students can tell about the animals that stayed home. Then have students group the bears and other stuffed animals by common characteristics such as size, color, or type of animal. Make a real graph by lining up the stuffed animals, according to their groups. Count the animals in each line. Ask questions about the graph. Examples: *Which group has the greatest number? Which group has the fewest? How many animals are there of each color?*

### • *BEARS IN LITERATURE*

Spend the first two or three weeks of school reading bear books, such as *Winnie the Pooh's Friendship Book* by A.A. Milne (Dutton, 1994) or *Corduroy* by Don Freeman (Viking, 1976), and having students participate in additional bear activities *(Bears,* TCM267), especially if your school year begins in August. Show a *Winnie the Pooh* video (Walt Disney Home Entertainment) while you enjoy some bear-shaped cookies and milk or juice for snack.

### • *ANNOUNCING COLOR DAYS*

1. Send home the letter (page 16) announcing Color Days. Explain to students that during the next several days you will be celebrating Color Days. Tell them that each day they should wear or bring something that is the Color of the Day. The first day will be Red Day.

2. Introduce each Color Day by reading the appropriate page from *Hailstones and Halibut Bones* by Mary O'Neill (Doubleday, 1961). Discuss and name the things shown on each page. Then do activities (pages 10–14) involving each color on its special day. Write on the board using chalk that is that color. Students should tell what they are wearing or what they have brought that is that color. Ask students to make paintings using that color.

3. Create a Color Days bulletin board (page 17). Ask students to name things inside and outside that are the Color of the Day. On chart paper, using a marker that is the Color of the Day, list things that are that color (i.e., red apples, watermelons, cherries, etc.). Add to the list each day, and display it on the bulletin board. Cut a huge balloon from butcher or wrapping paper that is the Color of the Day. Each day have students cut and paste magazine pictures of things that are that color of the balloon. Display the balloons in a bunch on the bulletin board. Tape one end of a long piece of yarn to the bottom of each balloon. Gather the loose ends of the yarn and tape them into the hand of a large tagboard teddy bear (page 8). Make the title "Color Days."

# Bulletin Boards

Use the following teddy bear patterns to create the welcoming bulletin board as described on page 6.

# Bulletin Boards *(cont.)*

Use the following calendar to create a bulletin board as described on page 6. Change the tree and the calendar each month. Write the name of the month in the blank before the word *Calendar*.

| | | | | | | Calendar |
|---|---|---|---|---|---|---|
| **Sunday** | **Monday** | **Tuesday** | **Wednesday** | **Thursday** | **Friday** | **Saturday** |
| | | | | | | |
| | | | | | | |
| | | | | | | |
| | | | | | | |
| | | | | | | |
| | | | | | | |

# Color Days

**Note:** If your school year starts in August, you can extend the Color Days so each color is studied for more than one day or so that additional colors are included. You may also wish to spend additional time introducing the letters in alphabetical order.

## • *RED DAY*

1. On the chalkboard, draw some straight and curved lines. Show students how to used a curved line to make a circle. Write the word *circle* under the picture you have drawn. Invite students to find examples of objects in the classroom that are shaped like circles. Ask them to draw some imaginary circles in the air, using their fingers. Show some red construction paper. Write the word *red* on the chalkboard, using red chalk. Demonstrate how to cut out a circle from red construction paper. Cut pieces of red construction paper into fourths, and trace around the bottom of a can to make a circle on each. Provide students with the red construction paper and blunt pairs of scissors. Encourage them to make red circles by cutting along the lines you have drawn. Staple the red circles to the Class Tree (page 9) to make an apple tree for September.

2. Read aloud a book that includes the color red and/or information about circles. Examples: Any version of *Little Red Riding Hood; Red, Blue, Yellow Shoe* by Tana Hoban (Greenwillow, 1986); *Clifford, The Big Red Dog* by Norman Bridwell (Four Winds, 1973); *Round & Round & Round* by Tana Hoban (Greenwillow, 1983); *Shapes* by Rosalinda Kightley (Little, Brown & Company, 1986). See the bibliography (page 15) for additional suggestions.

3. Label a piece of poster board with the title "Seeds." Create a two-column chart with the headings: *Seeds We Eat* and *Seeds We Do Not Eat.* **Warning:** Before serving anything to eat, ask parents if their children have any food allergies or dietary restrictions. For a red snack, allow students to enjoy some watermelon or red apples. Wash and save some of the seeds. Ask students to bring other types of seeds from home. Help them decide in which column of the chart they should glue the seeds.

## • *YELLOW DAY*

1. Show some yellow construction paper. Write the word *yellow* on the chalkboard, using yellow chalk. Read aloud *Wild Wild Sunflower Child Anna* by Nancy White Carlstrom (Macmillan, 1991). Have students make sunflowers by using yellow crayons or markers to color small paper plates. Help them glue sunflower seeds in the centers of their flowers. Make stems for the sunflowers by stapling long green crepe paper streamers to one edge of each plate. Put some sunflower seeds in a bird feeder to attach to your classroom window or hang in a tree outside of it. Add some sunflower seeds to the seed chart described for Red Day.

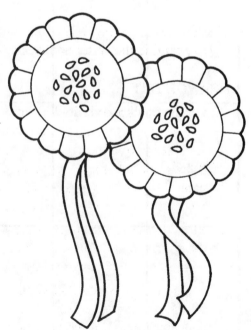

2. Use real lemons to make some lemonade for students. Save some seeds for the seed chart and others for planting. For a yellow snack, allow students to eat some lemon pudding. Then invite them to finger-paint with the pudding on wax paper or paper plates. Encourage them to draw circles and write their names.

# Color Days *(cont.)*

- **YELLOW DAY** *(cont.)*

    3. You may wish to read aloud some books that include the color yellow. See the bibliography (page 15) for suggestions.

    4. Read *School Bus* by Donald Crews (Scholastic, 1990). Use the bus pattern (page 18) to make a Big Book. Enlarge the pattern by making it into an overhead transparency and projecting it onto the desired material. Trace two copies of the pattern on yellow tagboard for the covers of the book. Write the title "Our Bus Book" on the front of one tagboard bus. Laminate both tagboard buses. Use large white paper to trace the bus pattern for each student. You may wish to have parent volunteers or older students help you do this. Give students the white bus patterns, and let them draw wheels, doors, and windows with faces looking out. Have them color their buses yellow. If they ride buses to school, have them write their bus numbers on the patterns. Discuss bus safety rules. Invite students to dictate a sentence that tells a bus rule they have learned or what they like about buses. Write the sentences on their buses. Place students' buses between the tagboard covers. Punch two holes in the tops and bind the book with metal rings. Put two stick-on plastic hooks on your classroom door or in the library center. Attach a sign above the Big Book that says, "The latest edition from [your name] Publishing Company!" (Punch the holes in future Big Books the same distance apart so they will fit on the hooks.)

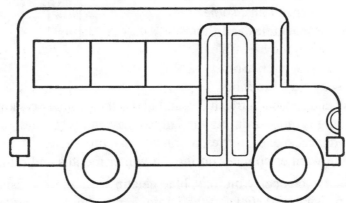

    5. Pour water into a clear glass. Add some red and yellow food coloring to the water. Ask students to examine the water and name the color they will be learning about tomorrow.

- **ORANGE DAY**

    1. On the chalkboard, draw a variety of rectangles. Point out that they all have four straight sides, two long and two short, and four corners. Write the word *rectangles* under the pictures. Invite students to find examples of objects in the classroom that are shaped like rectangles. Ask them to draw some imaginary rectangles in the air, using their fingers. Show some orange construction paper. Write the word *orange* on the chalkboard, using orange chalk. Demonstrate how to cut a piece of orange construction paper into rectangles of different sizes.

    2. Show a real aquarium or some pictures. Cut pieces of blue construction paper in half, showing the rectangular shapes. Give each student one half. Ask students to imagine that these blue rectangles are aquariums, and have them glue orange fish-shaped crackers onto their papers.

    3. For an orange snack, serve orange sections, cantaloupe, orange sherbet in orange ice cream cones, or orange slushies. Slushies are made by mixing a 6-ounce (177 mL) can of frozen orange juice concentrate with three cans of cold water in a blender. Remember to wash and save the orange seeds for the seed chart (page 10).

# Color Days (cont.)

- **BLUE DAY**

1. Take the class outside, and have students look at the sky. Be sure they do not look directly at the sun. Point out how the sky touches the ground as they look in all directions. Ask questions such as: *What color is it? What is in the sky during the daytime? What is in the nighttime sky? What color is the sky at night?* Return to the classroom. Provide each student with a piece of white construction paper. Write the word *blue* on the chalkboard. Direct students to paint the tops of their papers blue. When the blue paint dries, they can paint the sun in their skies. Tomorrow, tell them to paint the bottom half green. When the green paint dries, invite students to paint red, yellow, and orange flowers in the green grass.

2. Read *Blueberries for Sal* by Robert McCloskey (Viking Penguin, 1976). Talk about the fall and the changes that will occur during this season. Point out that people and animals store up food to prepare for the winter ahead. In many places, it is too cold in the winter to grow food. During the warmer months, some people can and freeze vegetables and fruits from their gardens. Then they are able to enjoy these foods in the winter. Some animals also have ways to store food.

Squirrels hide nuts and acorns in tree holes and under the ground so they will have food for the winter. Bears eat large amounts during the fall, so they can hibernate, or sleep, during the winter. Chipmunks, groundhogs, snakes, turtles, and frogs also hibernate. Many birds migrate or fly south to find food in warmer climates during the winter months and return in the spring.

3. For a blue snack, serve blueberry muffins, blue gelatin with gummy fish, or freeze blue juice or punch in small cups with craft sticks. While enjoying the snack, teach the nursery rhyme "Little Boy Blue." You may also wish to read aloud some books that include the color blue. See the bibliography (page 15) for suggestions.

4. Pour water into a clear glass. Add some blue and yellow food coloring to the water. Ask students to examine the water and name the color they will be learning about tomorrow.

- **GREEN DAY**

1. On the chalkboard, draw a variety of *triangles*. Point out that they all have three straight sides and three corners. Write the word triangles under the pictures you have drawn. Invite students to find examples of objects in the classroom that are shaped like triangles. Ask them to draw some imaginary triangles in the air, using their fingers. Show some green construction paper. Write the word *green* on the chalkboard, using green chalk. Demonstrate how to cut a piece of green construction paper into triangles of different sizes. Cut pieces of green construction paper into fourths, and trace a triangle pattern on each. Provide students with the green construction paper and blunt pairs of scissors. Encourage them to make green triangles by cutting along the lines you have drawn. Tell them to pretend that the triangles are trees. Have them glue the "trees" onto their paintings from Blue Day.

# Color Days *(cont.)*

- ***GREEN DAY*** *(cont.)*

    2. For a green snack, serve honeydew melon, green grapes, and/or green vegetables. Save some seeds for the seed chart (page 10). While enjoying the snack, you may wish to read aloud some books that include the color green. See the bibliography (page 15) for suggestions.

    3. Pour water into a clear glass. Add some red and blue food coloring to the water. Ask students to examine the water and name the color they will be learning about tomorrow.

- ***PURPLE DAY***

    1. Show some purple construction paper. Write the word *purple* on the chalkboard, using purple chalk. Read *Harold and the Purple Crayon* by Crockett Johnson (Weston Woods, 1955). Reproduce page 21 for students. Ask them to draw "Purple Adventure" pictures.

    2. Have students learn "Little Jack Horner." You may also wish to read aloud some books that include the color purple. See the bibliography (page 15) for suggestions.

    3. For a purple snack, serve some plums, saving the seed for the seed chart (page 10) and mix one quart of milk (0.95 L) and a 6-oz. (150 g) can of frozen grape juice in a blender. If you prefer, you can pour grape soda over vanilla ice cream in individual glasses and stir.

- ***BLACK DAY***

    1. Show some black construction paper. Write the word *black* on white construction paper, using black chalk or marker.

    2. Teach students "The Cat and the Fiddle." Use dark colors to create a picture to illustrate the nursery rhyme. Ask: *Does the picture show a daytime or nighttime scene? What is in the night sky?* Use white crayon to draw a moon and some stars. Paint the picture with a thin black wash to make it look like nighttime. Learn "Little Miss Muffett." Have students draw black spiders on white construction paper. Discuss how many legs a spider has (8), and have students practice counting spider legs on their drawings. Learn "Baa, Baa, Black Sheep." Model for students how to make a sheep by dipping cotton balls in black paint then gluing several cottonballs in an oval shape and drawing a head, legs, and a tail on a piece of construction paper. Have them make their own sheep. Discuss the uses of wool.

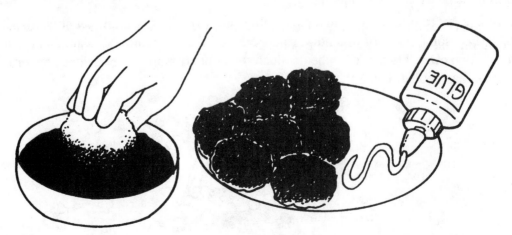

    3. Have students make "Ants on a Log" for snack by spreading peanut butter on carrot sticks and putting raisins on top. While enjoying the snack, you may wish to read aloud some books that include the color black. See the bibliography (page 15) for suggestions.

# Color Days *(cont.)*

### • *BROWN DAY*

1. Show brown construction paper. Write the word *brown* on the chalkboard, using brown chalk. Read *Brown Bear, Brown Bear, What Do You See?* by Bill Martin, Jr. (Holt, 1983). Make a bear-shaped Big Book (page 19). Write the title on the front. Assign each student a color with which to a draw a picture of something he or she sees that is that color. Below each drawing write: "I see a _____ looking at me." Have students tell you what to write in the blank.

2. Mix equal parts of soap flakes and water in a jar. Shake until the mixture is thick. Add brown tempera paint, and shake again. Use white construction paper to reproduce the bear pattern (page 20) for students. Have them paint their bears with the mixture. Once the pictures are dry, help students glue on wiggley eyes, pom pom noses, red rick-rack mouths, and sequin buttons. Display them around the Class Tree (page 9).

3. On the chalkboard, draw a square. Point out that it has four straight sides that are the same length and four corners. Write the word *square*. Invite students to find objects in the classroom that are shaped like squares. Bake brownies in square pans, cutting them into squares. Ask what makes the brownies brown. Have students tell other ways they enjoy chocolate.

### • *PINK DAY*

1. Show students some pink construction paper. Write the word *pink* on the chalkboard, using pink chalk.

2. Encourage students to brainstorm a list of things that are pink.

3. Invite them to enjoy some pink lemonade, while you read aloud some books that include the color pink. See the bibliography (page 15) for suggestions.

### • *WHITE DAY*

1. Show some white construction paper. Write the word *white* on the chalkboard, using white chalk. Take the class outside to look at white clouds. Ask: *What shapes do you see?* Once inside mix equal amounts of soap flakes and water in a jar. Shake until the mixture is thick. Add white tempera paint, and shake again. Allow students to use light blue paper and the mixture to finger paint the shapes they saw outside.

2. Have a popcorn picnic. Spread a clean white sheet on the floor, and let students sit around the edge. Pop some popcorn in a hot-air popper, with the top removed, placed in the center of the sheet. **Warning:** Do not let students touch the popcorn popper or the hot popcorn. When the popcorn has cooled, invite them to eat some.

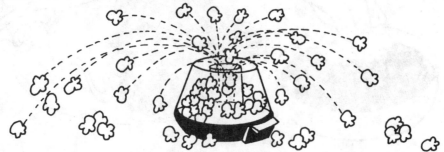

3. Have students learn "Mary Had a Little Lamb" and "Humpty Dumpty." Give students white oval-shaped pieces of paper. Let them draw Humpty Dumpty on the ovals. They can draw a wall on another piece of paper and glue Humpty on the wall.

# Bibliography

## Colors

Aylesworth, Jim. *Old Black Fly.* Holt, 1992.

Courson, Diana. *Let's Learn About Colors, Shapes, & Sizes.* Good Apple, 1986.

Crews, Donald. *Ten Black Dots.* Greenwillow, 1986.

de Paola, Tomie. *The Legend of the Bluebonnet.* Putnam, 1983.

de Paola, Tomie. *The Legend of the Indian Paintbrush.* Putnam, 1988.

Drescher, Henrik. *The Yellow Umbrella.* Broadway, 1987.

Ehlert, Lois. *Color Farm.* Lippincott, 1990.

Ehlert, Lois. *Color Zoo.* Lippincott, 1989.

Ehlert, Lois. *Planting a Rainbow.* HBJ, 1988.

Giganti, Paul, Jr. *Each Orange Had 8 Slices.* Greenwillow, 1992.

Goodall, John S. *Little Red Riding Hood.* McElderry, 1988.

Grimm, Jacob and Willhelm. *Snow White.* Farrar, Straus, and Giroux, 1974.

Hale, Sarah Josepha. *Mary Had a Little Lamb.* Scholastic, 1990.

Hest, Amy. *Purple Coat.* Aladdin, 1986.

Hoban, Tana. *Red, Blue, Yellow Shoe.* Greenwillow, 1986.

Imershein, Betsy. *Finding Red Finding Yellow.* HBJ, 1989.

Jeunesse, Galimard and Pascale de Bourgoing. *Colors.* Scholastic, 1991.

Kowalczyk, Carolyn. *Purple is a Part of a Rainbow.* Childrens Press, 1985.

Kropa, Susan. *Sky Blue, Grass Green.* Good Apple, 1986.

McMillan, Bruce. *Growing Colors.* Lothrop, 1988.

Munsch, Robert. *Purple Green and Yellow.* Firefly Books, 1992.

Steig, William. *Yellow & Pink.* FS&G, 1984.

## Shapes

Allington, Richard L. *Shapes.* Raintree, 1985.

Buddle, Jacqueline. *Fun with Sizes & Shapes.* Lawrence Science, 1988.

Dodds, Dayle Ann. *The Shape of Things.* Candlewick Press, 1994.

Forte, Imogene. *I'm Ready to Learn About Shapes.* Incentive Publications, 1986.

Griffiths, Rose. *Circles.* Gareth Stevens, 1994.

Hoban, Tana. *Shapes, Shapes, Shapes.* William Morrow, 1986.

Moss, David. *Shapes.* Outlet Book Company, 1989.

Pienkowski, Jan. *Shapes.* S&S Trade, 1989.

Rogers, Paul. *Shapes Game.* Holt, 1990.

Ross, Shirley and Cindy McCord. *Shape Creatures.* Monday Morning Books, 1987.

Taulbee, Annette. *Shapes & Colors.* Schaffer Publications, 1986.

Thomson, Ruth. *All About Shapes.* Gareth Stevens, 1987.

Worth, Bonnie. *Muppet Babies Shape Machine.* Checkerboard Press, 1988.

Yenawine, Phillip. *Shapes.* Delacorte, 1991.

# Announcing Our Color Days

Dear Parents,

We will celebrate colors during the first ten days of school. Please encourage your child to wear something in the Color of the Day. A schedule of the day, date, and color is shown below.

| Day | Date | Color Day |
| --- | --- | --- |
| | | Red Day |
| | | Yellow Day |
| | | Orange Day |
| | | Blue Day |
| | | Green Day |
| | | Purple Day |
| | | Black Day |
| | | Brown Day |
| | | Pink Day |
| | | White Day |

Thanks for your help!

Sincerely,

_____

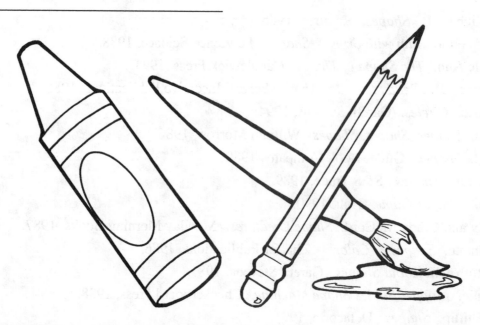

# Color Days Bulletin Board

## Color Days

| | | |
|---|---|---|
| Red: apple, wagon, . . . | | |
| Yellow: sun, . . . | | |
| Orange: pumpkin, . . . | | |
| Blue: sky, . . . | | |
| Green: grass, . . . | | |
| Brown: bear, . . . | | |
| Purple: plum, . . . | | |
| Black: spider, . . . | | |
| Pink: pig, . . . | | |
| White: snow, . . . | | |

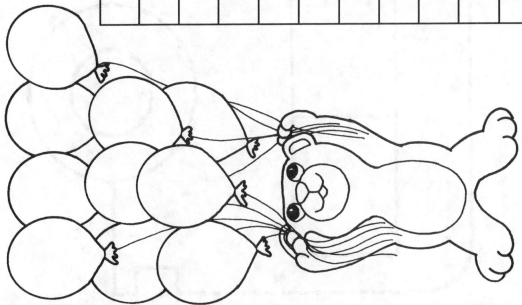

# Yellow Bus Big Book

Create a Big Book, using the directions on page 11 and the pattern shown below.

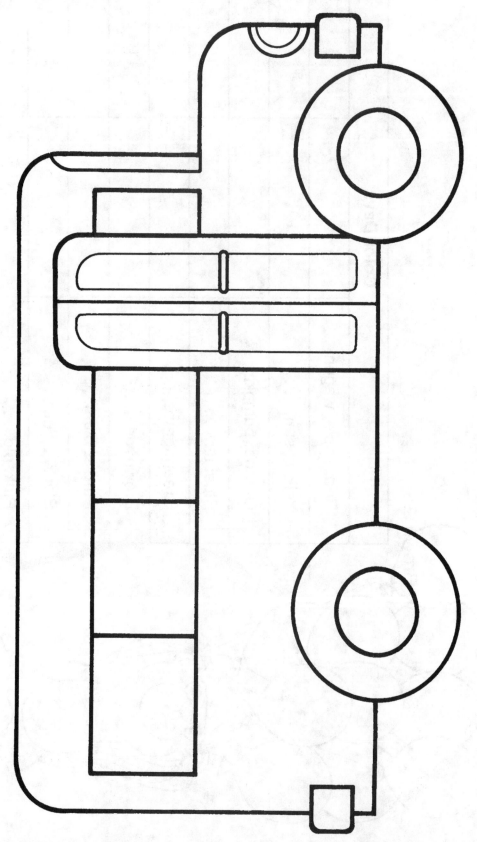

# Brown Bear Big Book

Create a Big Book, using the directions on page 14 and the pattern shown below.

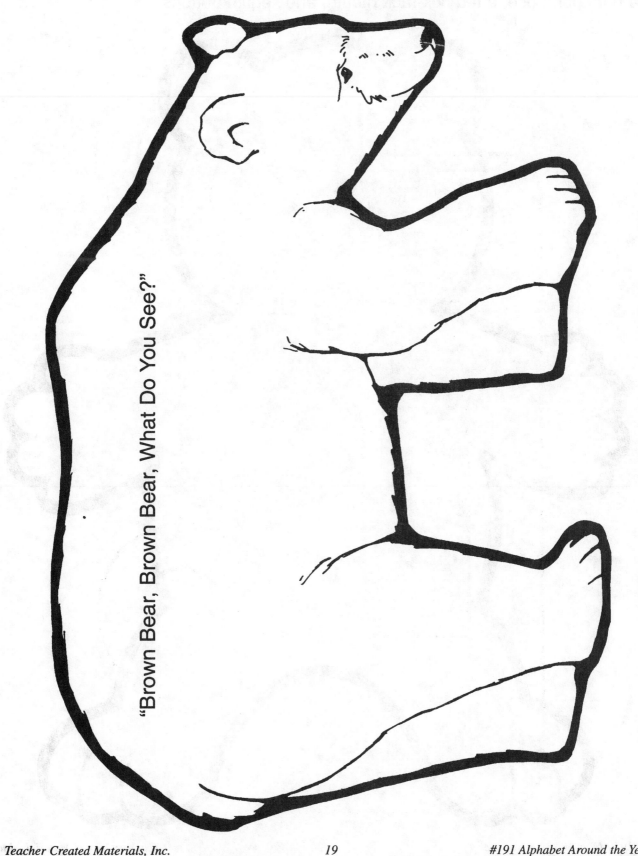

"Brown Bear, Brown Bear, What Do You See?"

# Make a Brown Bear

**Directions:** Paint the bear brown.  Let the paint dry.  Then glue on wiggley eyes, a pom pon nose, a red rick-rack mouth, and sequin buttons.

# My Purple Adventure

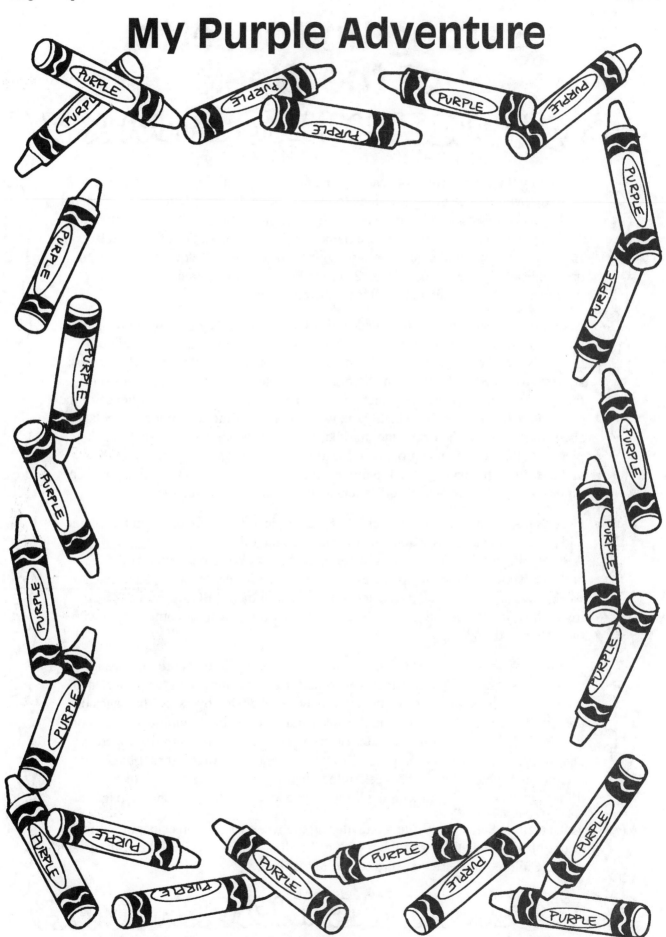

# Setting Up for Letter of the Week

Beginning the second week of school, send notes home to parents (page 25) to tell them that you will be doing activities to learn about a different letter of the alphabet each week. A few letters will be studied for more than one week. Ask parents to help their children find things whose names begin with the Letter of the Week. Explain that students should bring those things to school for Show and Tell on the date you specify. Send notes (page 25) each Friday, telling parents which letter your class will be learning about during the next week.

According to the directions provided in this book, make a key picture showing the uppercase and lowercase letters for each Letter of the Week. As you study each letter, display the key picture. Each morning, as you do the calendar activities, ask students to name the Letter of the Week. Encourage them to brainstorm a list of things whose names begin with that letter. On Mondays, review the sequence of the entire alphabet and discuss whether the letter studied during the previous week should be placed at the beginning, middle, or end of the alphabet. Attach that key picture to the wall in an approximate location. (As you add key pictures to the alphabet line-up, you may need to move some of the ones you have already placed on the wall.) Then review all the letters students have learned so far.

Create an ABC Booklet for each child. Fold 13 pieces of white paper in the center and staple. Add a construction paper cover with the title "_____'s ABC Book," writing the student's name in the blank. Write one letter of the alphabet, showing both the uppercase and lowercase forms, on each page. Each week, have students locate the Letter of the Week in their ABC Booklets. Then invite them to cut out and glue or draw pictures of things whose names begin with the Letter of the Week.

You may wish to make an ABC Big Book for the class. To create the front and back covers, glue wallpaper samples onto poster board, allow the glue to dry, then laminate. Place 26 pieces of white paper between the two covers for the pages of the Big Book. Punch two holes in the sides and bind the book with metal rings or pieces of thick yarn. Write one letter of the alphabet, showing both the uppercase and lowercase forms, on each page. Provide students with magazines, blunt scissors, and glue. During the week, allow them to cut out and glue pictures of things whose names begin with the Letter of the Week on the appropriate page.

Make a class dictionary. Write words during the week whose names begin with the Letter of the Week. Illustrate them with a sketch or a sticker. Combine with metal rings. Children may use the words to write stories.

# Letter Worksheets

Use the suggestions provided below and on page 24 to create worksheets that students can use to practice each Letter of the Week. Have students cut out and glue pictures of things whose names begin with the correct letter as described below. As an alternative, you may wish to create puzzle pictures for which students color the Letter of the Week after searching for it among the letters they have already learned.

**A a** — An Alligator in an apron ate an apple.
(Place **A a** pictures on the apple.)

**B b** — Brown Bear baked bread for the blue birds.
(Place **B b** pictures on the birds.)

**C c** — C Ornaments on a Christmas Tree
(Place **C c** pictures on the tree as ornaments.)

**D d** — A Dozen Dancing Dinosaurs
(Place **D d** pictures on the dinosaurs.)

**E e** — Eleven Elegant Easter Eggs
(Place **E e** pictures on the eggs.)

**F f** — Five Friendly Floating Frogs
(Place **F f** pictures on the frogs.)

**G g** — Goats wearing glasses are grazing in the green grass.
(Place **G g** pictures on the goats.)

**H h** — Happy Heart House
(Place **H h** pictures on the hearts.)

**I i** — Ice Skater Eating Ice Cream
(Place **I i** pictures on the ice cream.)

**J j** — Jumping Jolly Jack-O'-Lanterns
(Place **J j** pictures on the jack-o'-lanterns.)

**K k** — Kittens and Kangaroos Flying Kites
(Place **K k** pictures on the kites.)

**L l** — Leprechaun Picking Lucky Shamrocks
(Place **L l** pictures on the shamrocks.)

# Letter Worksheets *(cont.)*

**M m** — Mischievous Mice with Monsters
(Place **M m** pictures on the mice and monsters.)

**N n** — Nurse Eating Nuts
(Place **N n** pictures in a bowl to look like nuts.)

**O o** — Octopus in the Ocean
(Place **O o** pictures on the octopus.)

**P p** — Patch of Plump Pumpkins
(Place **P p** pictures on the pumpkins.)

**Q q** — Quiet Queen's Quilt
(Place **Q q** pictures on the squares of the quilt.)

**R r** — Rabbits Racing through Roses
(Make the roses from **R r** pictures.)

**S s** — Seven Smiling Snowmen
(Make hats for the snowmen from **S s** pictures.)

**T t** — Tap-dancing Turkey with a Top Hat
(Make feathers for the turkeys from **T t** pictures.)

**U u** — A Unicorn Using an Umbrella
(Make the umbrella for the unicorn from **U u** pictures.)

**V v** — A Variety of Vegetables
(Make vegetables from **V v** pictures.)

**W w** — Wiggly Worms in a Watermelon Patch
(Place **W w** pictures on the watermelons.)

**X x** — **X** marks the spot for a treasure hunt.
(Color the **X x** pictures—or
words ending in **X**—to find a treasure.)

**Y y** — Yaks Using Yo-Yos
(Place **Y y** pictures on the yo-yos.)

**Z z** — A Zippy Zebra in the Zoo

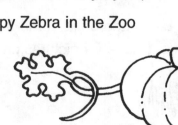

# Notes to Parents

_____
(Date)

Dear Parents,

This year, we will be learning about the letters A–Z. Each week, we will have Show and Tell, or sharing time. Please help your child find something that has a name beginning with the Letter of the Week and have him or her bring it to school for Show and Tell. Examples include bringing a stuffed bear for **B** week or a candle for **C** week. On Fridays, I will send you a note telling which letter we will be studying during the next week. Thanks for all your help!

Sincerely,

_____

---

_____
(Date)

Dear Parents,

Next week will be _____ Week. We will be learning about this letter using the key picture of _____. Please remember to help your child find something that has a name beginning with this letter. Talk about the object at home so your child will be able to tell about it at school. Thanks for your help!

Sincerely,

_____

# The Letter A

## • *LETTER OF THE WEEK*

Display the key picture of An Apple in an Apron (page 31). Refer to it each day. During the week, have students make the letter **A** using a variety of materials such as apple seeds or apple prints, tiny acorns, animal crackers, etc.

## • *ALPHABET*

Read aloud some books about the alphabet. See the bibliography (page 15) for suggestions. Show students the entire alphabet, including uppercase and lowercase forms of the letters. Together, count the letters in the alphabet. Ask a volunteer to find the letter **A**. Have students note that it is the first letter. Ask what letter comes after **A**. Ask a volunteer to identify the last letter. Ask what letter comes before the letter **Z**. Point out the letters that appear in the middle of the alphabet, both the uppercase and lowercase forms. Ask which ones look almost the same and which ones look very different. Ask students why it is important to study the alphabet. Lead them to conclude that it is important because knowing the letters and sounds they represent can help them read words. Make letters out of ropes made from clay or sugar cookie dough. If they are made from cookie dough, bake according to the directions and then sprinkle the cookies with sugar sprinkles. You may wish to have students make their initials or the Letter of the Week.

## • *APPLES*

1. Read *Johnny Appleseed* by Steven Kellogg (Scholastic, 1988). Ask students to bring apples sometime during **A Week**. Compare all the apples according to color, size, shape, and weight. Make a graph by lining up the apples according to color. Ask: *Which color has the greatest number? Which color has the least?* Arrange the apples according to size from the largest to the smallest. Have students count them. Divide the class into small groups. Give two apples to each group. Ask students to estimate which of their two apples weighs more. Then have them compare the apples on balance scales. Ask them to guess how many crayons, paper clips, or other small objects will equal the weight of one apple. Then let them check their responses.

2. Use the apples to make applesauce on September 26 in celebration of Johnny Appleseed's birthday. (You may wish to prepare the applesauce the day before.) As you peel and cut the apples open, allow students to guess how many seeds are in each. Ask: *Does each apple have the same number of seeds?* Have students glue some seeds on the seed chart (page 10). Save the rest of the seeds for later activities. Allow students to taste some raw apple. **Warning:** Before serving any food, be sure to ask parents if their children have any food allergies or dietary restrictions. Peel, core, and dice the apples into a crock pot as early as possible in the morning. Add a little water, cover, and cook on high all day. During the last hour or after the apples have softened, add sugar, cinnamon, and allspice to taste. Remove the cover, and finish cooking the apples. Write *allspice* on the chalkboard and have a volunteer point to the letter **a**. Spoon the applesauce into cups, and allow it to cool. Invite students to eat it with animal crackers. Ask: *How many animals can you name?*

# The Letter A *(cont.)*

• *APPLES (cont.)*

3. Give each student some washed and dried apple seeds in a reclosable plastic bag. Together, practice counting skills and simple addition and subtraction facts using the apple seeds. A quick check will tell you who needs additional practice. Encourage students to take their bags of seeds home and practice with family members. You may wish to provide outlines of apples drawn on construction paper on which students can glue some seeds.

4. Read *The Seasons of Arnold's Apple Tree* by Gail Gibbons (HBJ, 1984). Talk about autumn and the changes that occur. Find the first day of autumn on the calendar. Together, count the number of days until then. Have volunteers name the colors of autumn leaves.

5. Let students make booklets entitled "The Seasons of My Apple Tree." Make four identical patterns of a tree trunk and limbs on a half sheets of paper. Use the name of a season (Autumn, Winter, Spring, Summer) to label each. Reproduce the patterns so that each student gets a copy for each season. Allow students to use crayons to show how the tree will look during each season. Have them draw their favorite thing to do during each season and dictate sentences for you to write below the trees. Fold and staple a construction paper cover over each student's pages, and write the title on the front.

• *AUTUMN*

On the first day of autumn, read *The Tiny Seed* by Eric Carle (Scholastic Big Book, 1987). Take students on a walk to collect fallen seeds, leaves, etc. Display these items. Encourage students to bring in additional autumn items such as pumpkins and gourds for the display. Invite them to make red, orange, yellow, and brown leaf rubbings. Use acorns as math manipulatives. Ask students if they see any signs that autumn is coming.

• *AVOCADO*

Allow students to examine an avocado. Ask a volunteer to name it. Then ask why its nickname is the "alligator pear." Encourage students to guess what is inside. Then ask: *How many seeds do you think are inside an avocado? Is it large or small?* Cut it open, remove the seed, and show it. Peel the avocado, and allow students to taste it. Ask if they like it. Stick three toothpicks into the middle of the seed at equal distances apart. Use the toothpicks to suspend it in a glass of water. When it sprouts, plant it in soil, put it in a sunny window, and water it. Periodically have students measure it as they watch it grow into a tree.

• *ANIMALS*

1. Collect and show pictures of farm animals. Have students identify them and match the mothers and their babies. Ask: *Where do they live? What do they eat? What products do we get from them? What are the babies called?* Create a farm mural bulletin board using the patterns on pages 32 and 33. Draw in fences. Add a barn and a house.

2. Cut out a barn from a brown paper bag. Provide magazines and blunt scissors for students to cut out pictures of farm animals. Have them make a collage on the barn.

# The Letter A *(cont.)*

- **ANIMALS** *(cont.)*

3. Use two small plastic baskets, labeling one "Farm Animals" and the other "Zoo Animals." Have students sort plastic animals into the baskets.

4. Allow students to create imaginary animals using blocks. Put *Farm* and *Zoo* labels in a basket with additional strips of paper, markers, and tape so that they can label their block creations. You may wish to have students record their invented animals by sketching them in a "Block Book." To make the books, use drawing paper for the pages and construction paper for the covers.

5. Review animal nursery rhymes: "Little Boy Blue," "Baa, Baa, Black Sheep," "Little Bo Peep," and "Mary Had a Little Lamb" Take students to a nearby farm to see the animals and how we actually get eggs and milk. Ask: *What coverings do animals have on their bodies—fur or feathers?*

6. Explain that pets are tame animals that live in our homes or yards. Point out that, like people, they need food, water, shelter, and love. Ask: *What pets do you have? How do you care for them? What do they give you?* (friendship, love) Make a dog-shaped Pets Big Book entitled "Our Pets," using the pattern provided on page 34. Enlarge the pattern by making it into an overhead transparency and projecting it onto tagboard for the covers of the book. Write the title on the front. Laminate both pieces of tagboard. Have students draw their pets and dictate sentences about how they like to spend time with their animals. If any students do not have pets, ask them to draw pets they would like to have and tell how they think they would enjoy spending time with those animals. Punch two holes in the tops and bind the book with metal rings. Hang the book on the stick-on plastic hooks on your classroom door or in the library center.

7. Invite students to share photographs of their pets.

8. For more activities related to Zoo Animals, see pages 278–292. During your study of animals, you may wish to include those that live in the ocean. See pages 157–175 for information about ocean animals.

- **ANIMALS GAME**

Make a file-folder game for every two or three students according to the following directions. Glue Farm Animals (page 35) onto the front of a neon-colored file folder. Inside the folder, glue Pets (page 36) on the left side and Wild Forest Animals (page 37) on the right side. On the back of the folder, glue Jungle Animals (page 38). Allow the glue to dry. Use a craft knife to cut slits along the short lines marked on pages 35 and 37. Carefully slide small paper clips through the slits. Reproduce the animal patterns (pages 39–41), one set per file folder. Ask parent volunteers or older students to color the animals. Glue the pictures onto tagboard, laminate, cut them out, and place each set in a reclosable plastic bag. Have students mix up their set of pictures, and then sort and clip the animals to their folders under the correct headings. Place the games in a learning center so that students can play them when time allows.

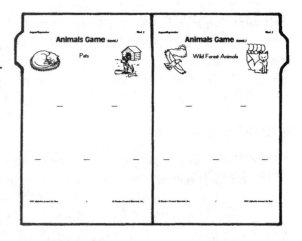

# The Letter A *(cont.)*

## • *ALFALFA SPROUTS*

Obtain alfalfa seeds from a health food store. Put one tablespoon (15 mL) of seeds in a wide-mouthed quart-size (0.95 L) jar. Pour water into the jar until it is about half full. Cover it with a piece of cheesecloth folded into fourths and secured with a rubber band. Soak the seeds overnight and carefully pour off the water the next morning. Lay the jar on its side and cover with a towel. Watch the sprouts grow for four days, rinsing and draining the seeds twice each day. Uncover the jar and put it in the sun on the fourth day so the seeds will turn green. Refrigerate the jar overnight and eat the alfalfa sprouts for lunch on a salad or sandwich. Don't forget to have students add some alfalfa seeds to the seed chart (page 10).

## • *ART*

Take students on a field trip to an art museum. Discuss the importance of not touching anything before you go. If possible arrange for a guide. Ask students to find portraits (people), landscapes (outside scenes), seascapes (water scenes), still life (inanimate objects), and sculptures (three-dimensional figures/designs). After returning to the classroom, let students paint their favorite kinds of art. Put construction paper frames around the paintings, and display them in a "Class Art Gallery." You may also wish to have students make and display clay sculptures.

## • *ALIKE AND DIFFERENT*

Discuss how groups of things, such as people, are alike and how they are different.

## • *AGE*

Have students learn how old they are. Have them practice writing their ages.

## • *ANT FARM*

Fill a jar with some dirt. Collect ants to observe. Cover the outside with black paper and top with a piece of cloth or an old stocking secured with a rubber band. Leave the ants undisturbed for several days. Remove the paper so students can watch the ants at work. Feed them honey mixed with water and small pieces of fruit every 3 to 4 days. Return the ants to their habitat when your study is completed. Commercial ant farms can be purchased at hobby stores.

## • *ACORN SQUASH*

Compare acorns with acorn squash. Use your favorite recipe to cook some acorn squash for students to taste. Have them add some seeds from the squash to the seed chart (page 10).

## • *AUSTRALIA*

Use a world map to show students where Australia is. Write to the following address to ask for information to share with your class: Australian Tourist Commission, 489 Fifth Avenue, New York, NY, 10117.

# Bibliography

## Books

Balian, Lorna. *The Aminal.* Abingdon, 1985.

Beller, Janet. *A-B-C-ing: An Action Alphabet.* Crown, 1984.

Booth, Eugene. *On the Farm.* Raintree, 1985.

Darros, Arthur. *Ant Cities.* Harper & Row, 1987.

Fass, Bernie. *Old MacDonald Had a Farm.* Clarus Music, 1985.

Fowler, Allan. *Cubs and Colts and Calves and Kittens.* Childrens Press, 1991.

Fowler, Allan. *Horses, Horses, Horses.* Childrens Press, 1992.

Fowler, Allan. *How Do You Know It's Fall?* Childrens Press, 1992.

Fowler, Allan. *Thanks to Cows.* Childrens Press, 1992.

Hammond, Lucille. *Polly's Pet.* Western, 1984.

Higham, Jon A. *Aardvark's Picnic.* Little, Brown and Company, 1987.

Hinds, P. Mignon. *Baby Calf.* Longmeadow, 1988.

Kanno, Wendy. *The Funny Farm House.* ARO, 1984.

Krementz, Jill. *Holly's Farm Animals.* Random House, 1986.

Lear, Edward. *A New Nonsense Alphabet.* Bloomsbury, 1988.

MacDonald, Suse. *Alphabatics.* Bradbury, 1986.

Mahy, Margaret. *17 Kings and 42 Elephants.* Dial, 1987.

Mayer, Mercer. *There's an Alligator Under My Bed.* Dial, 1987.

McPhail, David. *Emma's Pet.* E.P. Dutton, 1985.

Nakatani, Chiyoko. *My Day on the Farm.* Crowell, 1986.

Patterson, Bettina. *My First Wild Animals.* HarperCollins, 1989.

Pfloog, Jan. *Wild Animals and Their Babies.* Western, 1987.

Rockwell, Anne and Albert B. *Cub and Zebra: An Alphabet Storybook.* Harper & Row, 1987.

Rothman, Joel. *The Antcyclopedia.* Publication Development Company, 1988.

Seuss, Dr. *Dr. Seuss's ABC Book.* Beginner Books, 1960.

Van Allsburg, Chris. *Two Bad Ants.* Houghton Mifflin, 1988.

## Technology

*An Alphabet of Animals.* (Video); 13 min. Coronet/MTI Film and Video, P.O. Box 2649, Columbus, OH 43216; 1-800-321-3106.

*Animals at Night.* (Video); 8 min. Troll Associates, Catalog Sales Dept., 100 Corporate Dr., Mahwah, NJ 07498; 1-800-929-8765.

*Learn About Animals* by Learningways, Inc. (Software); MAC; Available from Sunburst, P.O. Box 100, Pleasantville, NY 10570; 1-800-321-7511.

*Three Little Chicks.* (Video about three chicks hatching and playing); 8 min. Troll Associates, Catalog Sales Dept., 100 Corporate Dr., Mahwah, NJ 07498; 1-800-929-8765.

*What's It Like to Be an Astronaut?* (Cassette); Troll Associates, Catalog Sales Dept., 100 Corporate Dr., Mahwah, NJ 07498; 1-800-929-8765.

# An Apple in an Apron

Enlarge the following key picture by creating an overhead transparency of this page and projecting it onto poster board. Then trace each part to make a red apple, green leaf, brown stem, and white apron. Cut out the poster board pieces and glue them together. Allow the glue to dry. Use a black marker to draw on the facial features. Then laminate the apple. Refer to the key picture each day, especially when you discuss the calendar (page 9). At the end of the week, tape the apple to a wall as part of an alphabet line-up.

# Farm Animals Bulletin Board

Enlarge the patterns below and on page 33 to create a farm bulletin board.

# Farm Animals Bulletin Board (cont.)

# Pets Big Book

Create a Big Book, using the directions on page 28 and the pattern shown below.

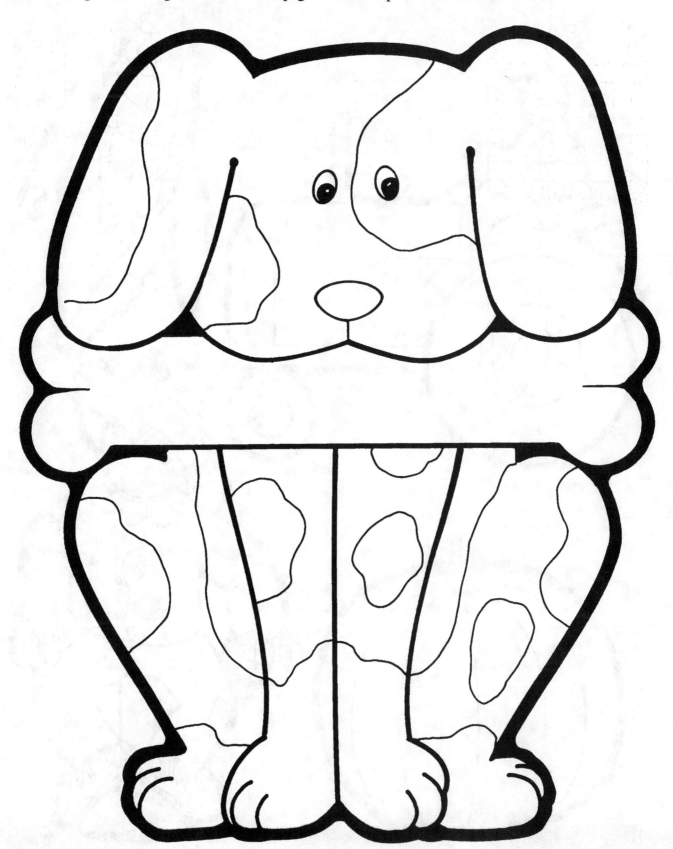

# Animals Game

## Farm Animals

-----          -----

-----          -----          -----

# Animals Game *(cont.)*

Pets

-----

-----

-----

-----

-----

# Animals Game *(cont.)*

## Wild Forest Animals

-----  -----

-----  -----  -----

# Animals Game *(cont.)*

## Jungle Animals

-----                -----

-----         -----         -----

# Animals Game (cont.)

Use the animal patterns below and on pages 40 and 41 for the Animals Game described on page 28.

# Animals Game (cont.)

# Animals Game *(cont.)*

# The Letter M

## • *LETTER OF THE WEEK*

Display the key picture of the Musical Mouse (page 57). Refer to it each day. During the week, have students make the letter **M** using a variety of materials such as macaroni, miniature marshmallows, markers, etc.

## • *MARVELOUS ME*

1. Read any of Mercer Mayer's books about "me," especially *All By Myself* (Western, 1983) and *When I Get Bigger* (Western, 1983). Additional suggestions are provided in the bibliography (page 43). Have students make "Marvelous Me" books. Topics for drawings on each page might include having students tell about their families; the city in which they live; their favorite colors, foods, and toys; the name of their school and teacher; their favorite things to do at home, at school, and with friends; the things they want to learn about in school; the things they can do now that they could not do when they were babies; what they cannot do now but they will be able to do when they grow up; what makes them feel happy, sad, mad, and afraid; what they like to do during different seasons. Reproduce the "Marvelous Me" boy and girl book cover patterns (page 44) and the inside pages (pages 45-50). Cut the pages in half along the dashed line. Provide additional pages with other topics if desired. Arrange all the pages in order, and staple each book together. Encourage students to draw self-portraits on the front of their books.

2. Display a collection of Mercer Mayer's books. Have students practice doing things that Little Critter says he can do in *All By Myself:* button buttons, zip zippers, tie shoes, pour water in glasses or cups in a plastic pan, practice staying in the lines when coloring, and putting toys away when playtime is over. Surprise students with a sticker or special treat one day when they have done a good job of cleaning up.

3. Put a big sneaker cutout in the housekeeping center for students to sign when they can tie their shoes by themselves. Add a birthday cake and a house cutout (pages 51-52) for students to sign after they learn their birthdates and home addresses. These cutouts will an add extra incentive as well as enable you to quickly determine who still needs help with these skills.

## • *MY FAMILY*

1. Share one of the following stories with the class: *The Berenstain Bears Are a Family* by Stan and Jan Berenstain (Random House, 1991) or Mercer Mayer's *The New Baby* (Western, 1983), *Just Grandma and Me* (Western, 1983), *Just Grandpa and Me* (Western, 1985), *Just Me and My Puppy* (Western, 1985), *Just Me and My Little Sister* (Western, 1986), *Just Me and My Little Brother* (Western, 1991). Ask students to tell what a family is and what the word related means. Have them tell about their families: who the members are that live with them, who the members are that do not live with them, who the oldest and youngest are, where they live, what they like to do together, and how they help each other.

2. Have each student draw a picture and dictate a story about his or her family.

3. Ask students to draw pictures of themselves doing something just like their parents do.

# Bibliography

## Books

Adoff, Arnold, ed. *My Black Me: A Beginning Book of Black Poetry.* Dutton, 1994.

Aliki. *My Feet.* HarperCollins, 1990.

Aliki. *My Five Senses.* HarperCollins, 1989.

Aliki. *My Hands.* HarperCollins, 1990.

Butterworth, Nick. *My Grandma is Wonderful.* Candlewick Press, 1992.

Butterworth, Nick. *My Grandpa is Amazing.* Candlewick Press, 1992.

Butterworth, Nick. *My Mom is Excellent.* Candlewick Press, 1994.

Dorling Kindersley Editors. *My First Look at Clothes.* Random House, 1991.

Dorling Kindersley Editors. *My First Look at Home.* Random House, 1990.

Hayes, Sarah. *Eat Up, Gemma.* Lothrop, Lee and Shepard, 1988.

Hooker, Ruth. *At Grandma and Grandpa's House.* Albert Whitman, 1986.

Hutchins, Pat. *My Best Friend.* William Morrow, 1993.

Johnson, Angela. *When I Am Old with You.* Orchard, 1990.

Koehler, Phoebe. *The Day We Met You.* Bradbury, 1990.

Lester, Alison. *My Farm.* Houghton Mifflin, 1994.

Loewen, Iris. *My Mom is So Unusual.* Pemmican, 1991.

Maccarone, Grace. *My Tooth is About to Fall Out.* Scholastic, 1995.

Mayer, Gina and Mercer. *This Is My Family.* Western, 1992.

Mayer, Mercer. *Just Me and My Mom.* Western, 1990.

Mayer, Mercer. *Just Me and My Puppy.* Western, 1985.

Mayer, Mercer. *Just My Friend and Me.* Western, 1988.

Pearson, Susan. *My Favorite Time of Year.* HarperCollins, 1988.

Quinlan, Patricia. *My Dad Takes Care of Me.* Firefly Books, 1987.

Westman, Barbara. *I Like the Music.* Harper & Row, 1987.

Wildsmith, Brian. *My Dream.* Oxford University Press, 1986.

Ziefert, Harriet. *My Tooth is Loose.* Viking Penguin, 1994.

## Technology

*Birthday Buddies.* (Video about a bear's special birthday present for his grandfather); 8 min. Troll Associates, Catalog Sales Dept., 100 Corporate Dr., Mahwah, NJ 07498; 1-800-929-8765.

*Kidsongs: What I Want to Be.* (Video with kids singing about their goals for the future); 30 min. Perma-Bound Books, 617 E. Vandalia Rd., Jacksonville, IL 62650; 1-800-637-6581.

*Riki Levinson's Family Album.* (Video includes *I Go with My Family to Grandma's*); 15 min. SRA, P.O. Box 543, Blacklick, OH 43004; 1-800-843-8855.

*Teddy Finds a Family.* (Software about the importance of belonging to a family); PC; National School Products, 101 East Broadway, Maryville, TN 37804; 1-800-251-9124.

*You and Your Five Senses.* (Videotape/Videodisc by Disney Educational Products); 13 min. Available from Coronet/MTI Film and Video, P.O. Box 2649, Columbus, OH 43216; 1-800-321-3106.

# Marvelous Me Book

Marvelous
Me
Book

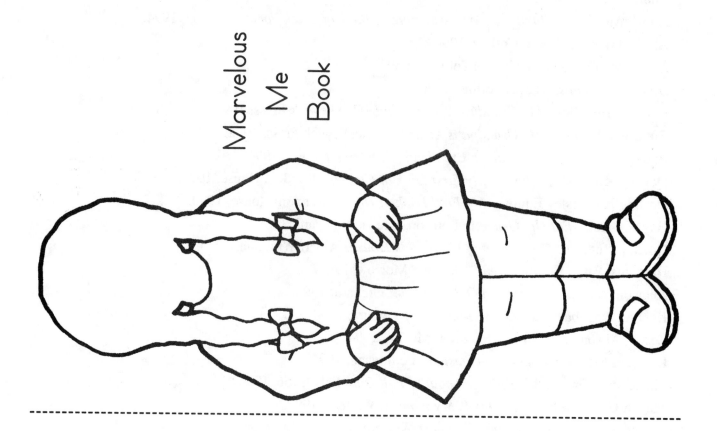

Marvelous
Me
Book

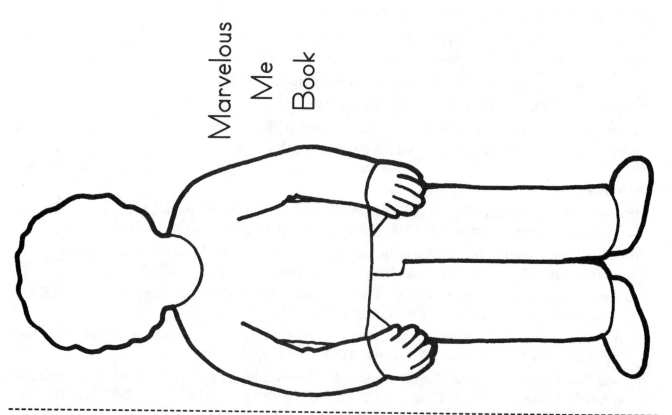

# Marvelous Me Book *(cont.)*

This is my home. We live in

_____
(city, state)

3

My name is _____

This is me when I was a baby.

1

# Marvelous Me Book *(cont.)*

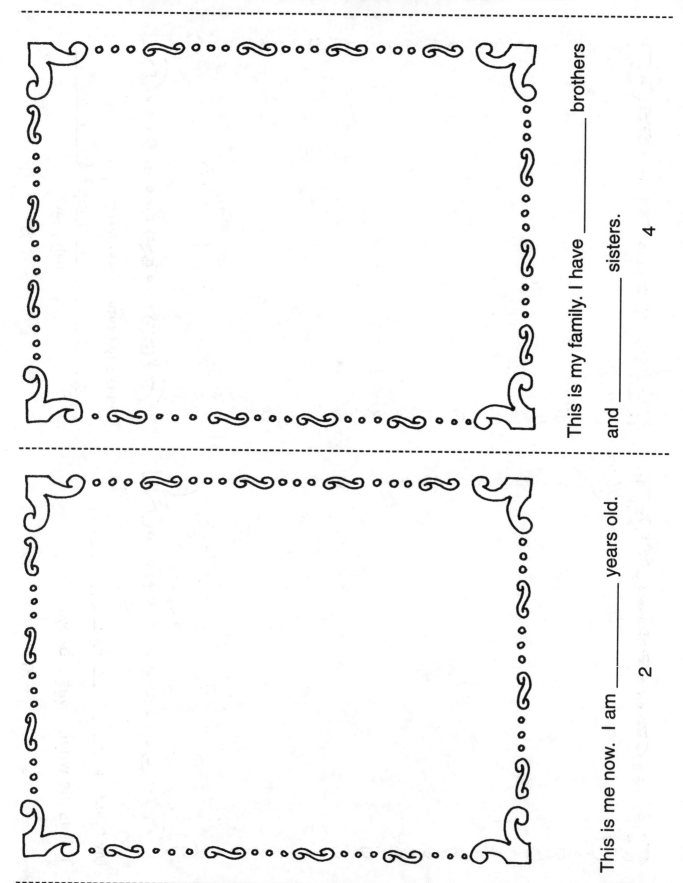

This is my family. I have _____ brothers

and _____ sisters.

4

This is me now.  I am _____ years old.

2

# Marvelous Me Book *(cont.)*

My favorite colors are _____

This is a special picture using my favorite colors.

7

This is my school. I go to school at _____

This year I want to learn about _____

5

# Marvelous Me Book (cont.)

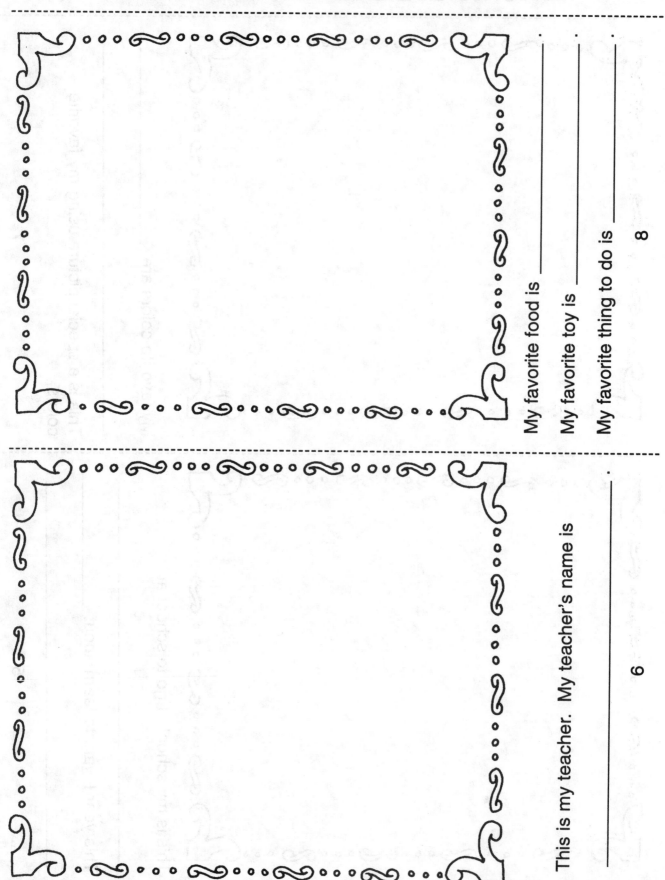

My favorite food is

My favorite toy is

My favorite thing to do is

8

This is my teacher.  My teacher's name is

6

# Marvelous Me Book (cont.)

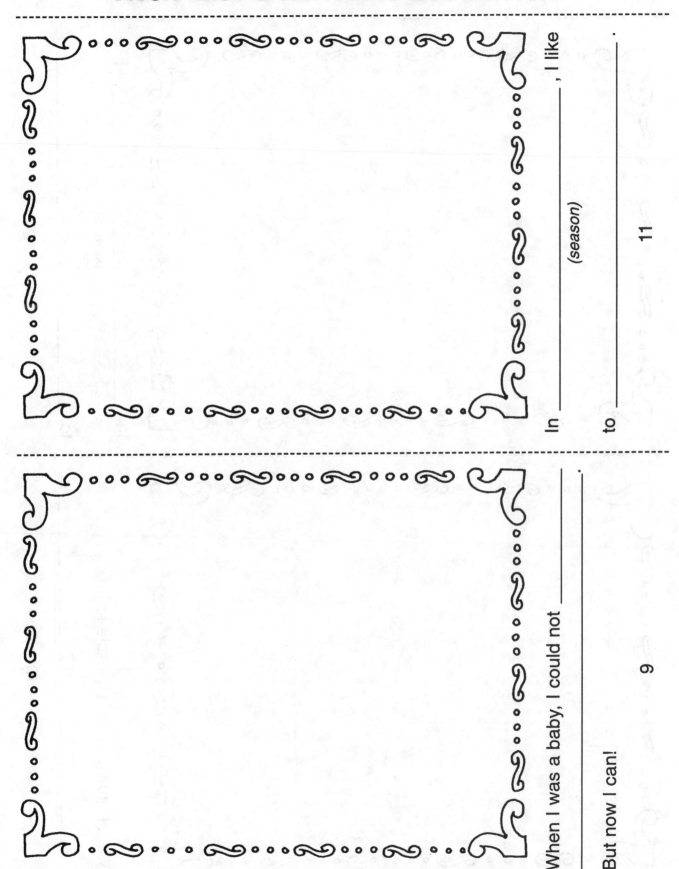

In _____ , I like

(season)

to _____ .

11

When I was a baby, I could not _____

But now I can! _____ .

9

# Marvelous Me Book *(cont.)*

In _____ , I like
    *(season)*

to _____ .

**12**

When I grow up, I will be able to _____ .

**10**

# House

Enlarge the following pattern by creating an overhead transparency of this page, then projecting and tracing it on poster board. Color the poster board house, and write "I know my home address!" in large letters above the door as shown. Laminate the picture. Allow students to sign the house with water-based markers when they have learned their home addresses.

# Birthday Cake

Enlarge the following pattern by creating an overhead transparency of this page, then projecting and tracing it on poster board. Color the poster board birthday cake, and write "I know when my birthday is!" in large letters at the bottom of the cake as shown. Laminate the picture. Allow students to sign the cake with water-based markers when they have learned their dates of birth.

I know when my birthday is!

# The Letter M

## • *OCTOBER*

Reproduce the Monstrously Scary Owl pattern (page 60) for students. Have students cut out, color, and attach the wings. Then place their owls on the Class Tree (page 9). Students may also enjoy making other Halloween creatures, such as bats, goblins, and ghosts, to add to the tree.

## • *LETTER OF THE WEEK*

Display the key picture of the Musical Mouse (page 57). Refer to it each day. During the week, have students make the letter M using a variety of materials such as macaroni, miniature marshmallows, markers, etc.

## • *MICE*

1. Read one or more books about mice. Suggestions are provided in the bibliography (page 56). Have students make a mouse-shaped Big Book. To do this, enlarge the Mischievous Mice pattern (page 58) by making it into an overhead transparency and projecting it onto the desired material. Trace two copies of the pattern on tagboard for the covers of the book. Write the title "Mischievous Mice" on the front. Laminate both tagboard mice. Provide a sheet of large white paper for each student. Tell students to imagine that they are taking an autumn walk and come across a mouse playing outside of a house. Have students draw pictures that show the house and what the mouse is playing. If desired, they can include themselves in the picture, playing with the mouse. Encourage them to dictate a sentence or story. Write the sentences below their pictures. Place students' pages between the tagboard mice. Punch two holes in the tops and bind the book with metal rings. Staple on a tail made from braided black yarn. Hang the book on the stick-on plastic hooks on your classroom door or in the library center. As an alternative, have the class make a mole-shaped Big Book.

2. Read aloud *Mouse Paint* by Ellen Stoll Walsh (HBJ, 1989) and *Country Mouse and City Mouse* by Pat McKissack (Childrens Press, 1985). Provide students with mouse-shaped light gray paper, and have them draw pictures of what they think mice might do while people are sleeping. Ask: *What adventures do they have?* Write students' dictated responses. Put the mice on a bulletin board entitled "Mischievous Mice." If available, use a mouse footprint stamp to put different colored tracks between the mice.

3. Read aloud *The Bremen Town Musicians* by Janet Stevens (Holiday House, 1992). Ask students what the musicians are. If possible, invite a music teacher or music specialist to visit your class for a discussion about different musical instruments. Show real instruments or look at pictures of some. Play a variety of recordings for students to hear how different instruments sound. Display some sheet music and allow them to practice drawing notes.

4. Make a mouse-ears headband (page 59) for each student. Show students how to play "Musical Mice," a variation of Musical Chairs. Encourage them to wear their mouse-ear headbands while playing the game.

5. You may wish to have your "Musical Mice" experiment with rhythm band instruments while you play some music.

# The Letter M *(cont.)*

- ### *MICE (cont.)*

  6. Write a group story about "Musical Mice." Ask: *What instruments do they play? What adventures do they have? How do they work together to solve their problems?* Make a Big Book, using the pattern provided on page 57. To enlarge the pattern, make it into an overhead transparency. Then project and trace two copies on gray tagboard for the front and back covers of the Big Book. Write the title "Musical Mice" on the front cover. Laminate both tagboard mice. Use large white paper to write the story as students dictate it. Write only part of the story on each page, so small groups can work together on the illustrations. Coordinate the art by helping students decide what to draw. After it is completed, place the story pages between the covers, punch two holes in the tops, and bind the book with metal rings. Share the book with the class. Then hang it on the stick-on plastic hooks on your classroom door or in the library center.

  7. Have students learn "Hickory Dickory Dock" *(Nursery Rhymes: Book Two,* TCM561).

- ### *MONTHLY MOON PHASES*

Read aloud any of the following books about the moon: *Owl Moon* by Jane Yolen (Philomel, 1987), *Papa, Please Get the Moon for Me* by Eric Carle (Picture Book Studio, 1986), *Goodnight Moon* by Margaret Wise Brown (Harper & Row, 1947), and *Wait Till the Moon Is Full* by Margaret Wise Brown (Harper & Row, 1948). Ask parents to have their children look at the moon at night. Make a chart that shows how it changes during each month.

- ### *MAGNIFYING GLASSES*

Read *All About Magnifying Glasses* by Melvin Berger (Scholastic, 1993). Put a tray of plastic magnifying glasses in a science/discovery center for students to take around and explore the room. Ask: *How do the magnifying glasses change what we see?*

- ### *MUDPIES*

Put water in the sandtable and allow students to make mudpies and other mud delicacies.

- ### *"M" FOODS FOR YOUR MOUTH*

Ask: *What can you put in your mouth? What things should you never put in your mouth?* Lead students to conclude that they should only put food, cleaned and cooked as necessary, and their toothbrushes in their mouths. Have them brainstorm a list of some "M" foods as you write them on the chalkboard. Examples: milk, macaroni, muffins, store-bought mushrooms, marshmallows, meatballs, marmalade, and melon. Ask parents if their children have any food allergies or dietary restrictions. Then allow students to sample some of the "M" foods they listed.

- ### *MEDICINE*

Stress that students should not take any medicine, including vitamins, unless it is given to them by their parents or doctors. "Mr. Yuk" stickers are available from poison control centers. Inform parents that these stickers can be placed on things at home that should never be put into children's mouths. Have students make Yuk and Yum Magnet Monsters (pages 55 and 61).

# The Letter M *(cont.)*

## • *MONSTERS*

1. Create a life-size monster from butcher paper. Put it on the outside of the door with a sign that says, "Our class monster!" written in spooky-looking letters.

2. Read aloud the following monster books by Mercer Mayer: *There's Something in My Attic* (Dial, 1988) and *A Monster Followed Me to School* (Western, 1991). The monsters in these books are humorous rather than frightening. Then read Maurice Sendak's *Where the Wild Things Are* (Harper & Row, 1963). Additional suggestions are provided in the bibliography (page 56).

3. Provide students with several different colors of butcher and/or construction paper; decorating supplies, such as yarn, stickers, buttons, and sequins; and glue. Instruct them to cut or tear some of the paper into small pieces. Have them glue the paper scraps and decorating supplies onto separate, whole pieces of paper to create their own monsters. When the glue is dry, tell students to draw the monsters' features using markers and cut them out. Suspend the monsters from the ceiling using paper clips tied to pieces of string. Write stories about the monsters.

4. Put "M-M-M-Monsters Story Stamps" (Educational Insights) in the writing center. Students can use the stamps when creating pictures and then dictate stories about the monsters.

## • *MARBLE MONSTER MASKS*

Create a mask for each student using the following directions. Place a piece of paper in a box. Dip some marbles in tempera paint. Place the marbles in the box and have a student roll them around on the paper. Remove the marbles and the paper. Cut out a mask shape when the paint is dry. Allow the student to decorate his or her mask with yarn, glitter, sequins, etc.

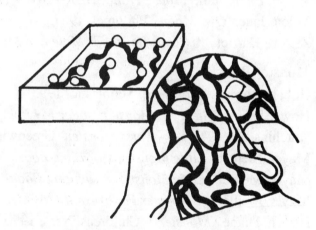

## • *MONSTER MASH*

In a bowl, mix equal amounts of peanut butter, honey, nonfat dry milk, and quick rolled oats. Refrigerate the mixture overnight. Then decorate it with candy coated chocolates.

## • *MARSHMALLOW MONSTERS FOR A MARVELOUS MONDAY*

Invite students to create monsters by joining large and small marshmallows with toothpicks. Tell a story about the monsters, then allow students to eat them!

## • *MAGNET MONSTERS*

Read *Mickey's Magnet* by Franklyn M. Branley and Eleanor K. Vaughn (Scholastic, 1988) and *All About Magnets* by Stephen Krensky (Scholastic, 1992). Show some magnets and how they attract different objects. Color and laminate two tagboard Magnet Monsters (page 61) for each group. Glue each monster onto one side of a magnet. Tape the other side of each magnet onto a small plastic basket. Divide the class into small groups. Provide each group with a tray of objects, some that will attract to a magnet and some that will not, and two small plastic baskets, one with The Yum Monster and the other with The Yuk Monster. Allow students to experiment with the objects and magnets. Have them place those that attract in The Yum Monster's basket and those that do not attract in The Yuk Monster's basket. You may wish to have each student make Magnet Monsters to take home.

# Bibliography

**Mouse and Moon Books**

Aesop. *The Lion and the Mouse.* Troll, 1981.

Branley, Franklyn. *The Moon Seems to Change.* HarperCollins, 1987.

Brown, Margaret Wise. *Goodnight Moon.* Harper & Row, 1947.

Carle, Eric. *Papa, Please Get the Moon for Me.* Picture Book Studio, 1986.

Fowler, Allan. *So That's How the Moon Changes Shape.* Childrens Press, 1991.

Ivimey, John W. *Three Blind Mice.* Clarion, 1987.

Lundell, Margo. *The Wee Mouse Who Was Afraid of the Dark.* Platt and Munk, 1990.

McDonnell, Janet. *Mouse's Adventure in Alphabet Town.* Childrens Press, 1992.

Numeroff, Laura Joffe. *If You Give a Mouse a Cookie.* Harper & Row, 1985.

Stevens, Janet. *The Town Mouse and the Country Mouse.* Holiday, 1987.

Thurber, James. *Many Moons.* HBJ, 1990.

Ungerer, Tomi. *Moon Man.* Delacorte, 1991.

Walsh, Ellen Stall. *Mouse Paint.* HBJ, 1989.

Yolen, Jane. *Owl Moon.* Philomel, 1987.

Ziefert, Harriet. *A Clean House for Mole and Mouse.* Scholastic, 1989.

**Monster Books**

Hoban, Russell. *Monsters.* Scholastic, 1993.

Howe, James. *There's a Monster Under My Bed.* Atheneum, 1986.

Hutchins, Pat. *The Very Worst Monster.* Greenwillow, 1985.

Mayer, Mercer. *Little Monster's Bedtime Book.* Western, 1978.

Mayer, Mercer. *Little Monster's Counting Book.* Western, 1978.

Mayer, Mercer. *A Monster Followed Me to School.* Western, 1991.

Namm, Diane. *Monsters!* Childrens Press, 1990.

O'Keefe, Susan H. *One Hungry Monster.* Little, Brown and Company, 1989.

Sendak, Maurice. *Seven Little Monsters.* Harper & Row, 1977.

Sendak, Maurice. *Where the Wild Things Are.* Harper & Row, 1963.

Willis, Jeanne. *Monster Bed.* William Morrow, 1987.

**Mud Books**

Impey, Rose. *Joe's Cafe.* Little, Brown and Company, 1990.

Knutson, Kimberly. *Muddigush.* Macmillan, 1992.

**Technology**

*Jolly Monsters.* (Video about two monster friends); 8 min. Troll Associates, Catalog Sales Dept., 100 Corporate Dr., Mahwah, NJ 07498; 1-800-929-8765.

*Monkeys.* (Video); 8 min. Troll Associates, Catalog Sales Dept., 100 Corporate Dr., Mahwah, NJ, 07498; 1-800-929-8765.

*Mouse Soup.* (Video about a mouse who outwits a weasel); 12 min. SRA, P.O. Box 543, Blacklick, OH 43004; 1-800-843-8855.

*Muppetville* by Jim Henson and Sunburst Corp. (Software); MAC/IBM/Tandy 100/Apple II family; Available from Sunburst, P.O. Box 100, Pleasantville, NY 10570; 1-800-321-7511.

# Musical Mouse

Enlarge the following key picture by creating an overhead transparency of this page and projecting it onto gray poster board. Trace and cut out and laminate the mouse pattern. Braid some black yarn and staple it onto the mouse for a tail. Refer to the key picture each day, especially when you discuss the calendar (page 9). At the end of the week, tape the mouse to a wall as part of an alphabet line-up.

# Mischievous Mice

Create a Big Book, using the directions on page 53 and the pattern shown below.

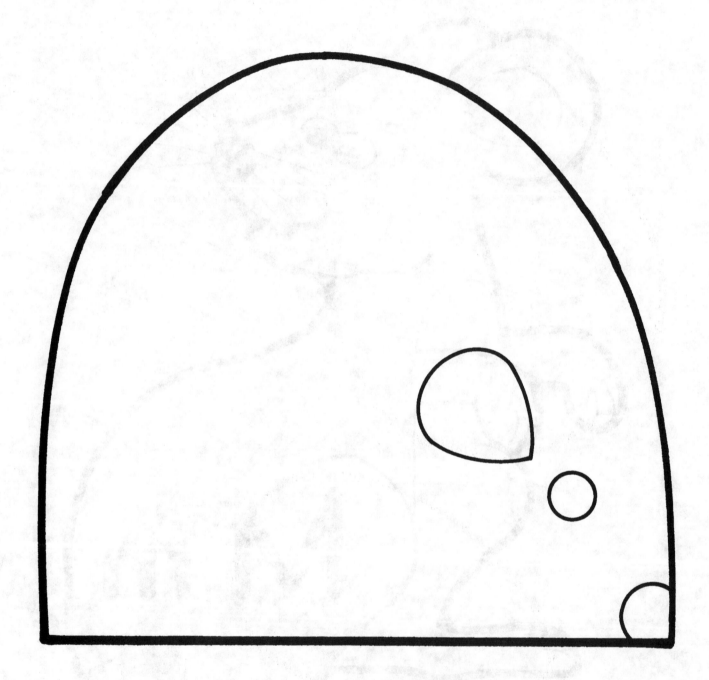

# Mouse-Ears Headband

**Directions:** Make two outer ears. Make two inner ears. Glue an inner ear to each outer ear. Make a headband. Staple the ears to the headband.

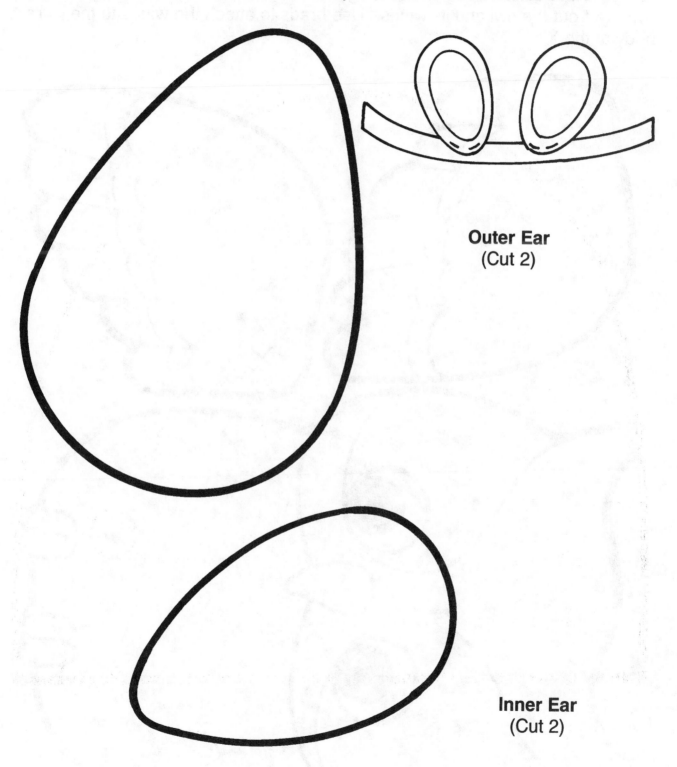

**Outer Ear**
(Cut 2)

**Inner Ear**
(Cut 2)

# Monstrously Scary Owl

**Directions:** Use white to color in the rings around the owl's eyes. Use brown and yellow to color stripes on the wings. Use brown to color the rest of the owl. Cut out the owl and its wings. Use brads to attach the wings to the owl's body at the X's.

# Magnet Monsters

**Directions:** Color the monsters.  Cut them out.  Glue each monster to a magnet.

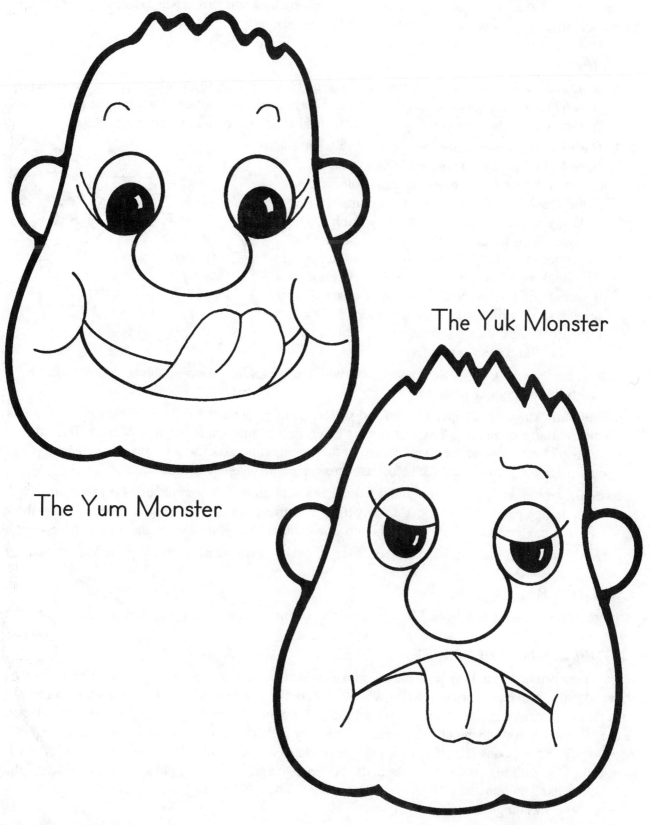

The Yuk Monster

The Yum Monster

# The Letter P

### • LETTER OF THE WEEK

Display the key picture of the Plump Pumpkin (page 66). Refer to it each day. During the week, have students make the letter **P** using a variety of materials such as popcorn, pasta, peanuts, pumpkin seeds, pine cone bits, paint, paper, pencils, potato prints, pretzels, etc.

### • PUMPKINS

1. Read *Pumpkin Pumpkin* by Jeanne Titherington (Mulberry, 1986). Enlarge the pictures shown on page 67 to make a set of six sequence cards. Have students practice arranging the cards in the correct order. Then reproduce page 67 for students and have them make the booklets.

2. Have students investigate a pumpkin. Ask what color and shape it is. Invite students to find things in the room that have the same color and shape. Have them describe how the pumpkin feels and smells. Ask how much they think it weighs. Then weigh it. Have students predict the circumference. Help them cut a length of string they think will fit around the pumpkin. Record the length of each student's string on a chart. Stretch some string around the pumpkin, and measure it. Ask students to determine who came closest to the correct circumference.

3. Ask students how they could make noise with the pumpkin. Allow students to experiment by carefully thumping and shaking it.

4. Put pumpkin-shaped paper and red and yellow paint at an easel. Tell students to mix the paints to make orange pumpkins. Teach students "Peter, Peter, Pumpkin Eater" (TCM303). Have them draw pictures of what they would keep in their pumpkins. Ask them to dictate sentences. Cut out and paste the pictures and dictated sentences on the painted pumpkins.

5. Make a pumpkin patch. Stuff small lunch bags with crumpled newspaper. Tie at the top. Paint with orange paint. When dry, glue on yellow construction paper faces. Tie green curling ribbon vines at the top. Line them up on the top of a cabinet. Label it "The Pumpkin Patch."

6. Make pumpkin muffins, pancakes, cookies, or cake. Invite students to eat pumpkin seeds.

### • PINEAPPLE

Explore a fresh pineapple using all five senses. Cut off the top and plant it in potting soil.

### • PETER PAN POPCORN PARTY

Have a popcorn or pizza party with pink lemonade. Watch the video *Peter Pan* (GoodTimes Home Video, 1990). Make popcorn pumpkins which are caramel popcorn balls, tinted orange, with candy corn faces. Alternate recipe: Melt one pound (450 g) orange confectioner's candy coating at half power in the microwave for one minute. Stir until thoroughly melted. Mix in 9 to 10 cups (2.25-2.5 L) of popcorn. Two teaspoons (10 mL) of oil may be added to facilitate mixing. Line a 1-cup - (250 mL) measuring cup with plastic wrap. Press in the popcorn mixture. Wrap in plastic and form into slightly flattened balls. Unwrap and allow to dry. Use icing to add candy corn faces.
Makes about 15 pumpkins.

# The Letter P *(cont.)*

## • PEPPERONI POLKA-DOT PIZZAS

Roll out refrigerated biscuit dough until it is flattened but remains fairly thick. On top, spread canned pizza sauce and sprinkle mozzarella cheese and diced pepperoni. Add parmesan cheese if desired. Bake according to the directions on the biscuit package.

## • PIZZA COOKIES

Mix chocolate chip cookie dough, as directed on the back of the chocolate chips' bag. Spread the dough in two pizza pans. Sprinkle the top with coconut, candies, additional nuts, and/or chocolate chips. Bake at 350° F (173° C) for 20–25 minutes.

## • PEANUTS

1. Buy a bag of whole roasted peanuts. Talk about how they grow and how many there are in the bag. Then count them. Have students guess how many peanuts are inside each shell. Ask if they think each shell has the same number of peanuts.

2. Help each student count out ten peanuts to shell and eat. Caution them again not to eat the shells. Tell them to find out if there are the same number of peanuts in each shell.

3. Make some peanut butter in a blender using peanuts and a little peanut oil or margarine. Allow students to spread the peanut butter on carrots, bananas, apples, celery, or crackers. **Note:** Check for food allergies or dietary restrictions.

4. Use balance scales to compare the weight of Styrofoam® peanuts to real peanuts.

## • PUPPETS

Introduce puppets into the dramatic play area. Discuss how to use them. Encourage students to act out stories that they know as well as ones they create. Puppets can be made from old socks, mittens, paper lunch bags, tongue depressors, paper plates, yarn, buttons, paper, fabric, etc.

## • PIGS

Read *The Wonderful Pigs of Jillian Jiggs* by Phoebe Gilman (Scholastic Big Book, 1988). Have students compare/contrast the pigs that she made. Have them write stories about their favorite pigs and create their own pigs from paper and/or fabric.

## • PRINCIPAL

Invite the principal to visit your classroom to tell about his or her job or to read aloud a story.

## • SWEET POTATO

Put a sweet potato in water. Place it in a sunny window and have students watch the vine grow.

# The Letter P *(cont.)*

**• *PANSIES***

Select a spot outside to make a "Kindergarden." Have students pull the weeds, dig up the dirt, and add some fertilizer. Plant some pansies. Add some pine straw or bark mulch to keep out the weeds. Watch periodically throughout the year. In some areas, they will grow during the winter.

**• *PATTERNS***

1. Read *Harriet's Halloween Candy* by Nancy Carlson (Carolrhoda, 1982). Buy bags of assorted wrapped candies. Invite students to choose two kinds of candies and lay them on the table. Show students how to make a pattern by repeating the same types of candies in the same order. Have them create their own simple patterns. Then invite them to reproduce each other's patterns.

2. Ask students to save candy wrappers. Cut strips of orange tagboard 4" (11 cm) wide. Make patterns by gluing on folded wrappers. Have students reproduce and continue the patterns using additional candy wrappers.

3. Make patterns with 2 to 3 interlocking cubes, pattern blocks, crayons, flannel board shapes, etc. Allow students to copy the patterns.

**• *PEACHES, PEARS, AND PLUMS***

Read *Each Peach Pear Plum* by Janet and Allen Ahlberg (Penguin Books, 1986) to introduce or review nursery rhymes and fairy tales. Invite students to illustrate their favorite ones. Then have them say a nursery rhyme, while you write it, or dictate a sentence or two about the fairy tale.

**• *PASTA***

Dye different kinds and shapes of pasta in reclosable plastic bags with one tablespoon (15 mL) of rubbing alcohol and about 12 drops of food coloring in each bag. Close the bags and gently shake. Add more food coloring if necessary. Dry the pasta overnight on wax paper. Mix all of the pasta together. Allow students to sort it by shape and color, as well as make pasta patterns.

**• *PLAY WITH DOUGH***

Have students play with dough to practice making letters and shapes.

**• *PENNY***

Give each student a penny to examine. Have them make rubbings of the pennies. Count the pennies together. Emphasize that a penny is worth one cent. Ask students how many pennies they would need if they wanted to buy a piece of candy that costs five cents.

**• *PARACHUTE***

Obtain a parachute and do parachute activities for physical education classes or ask your P.E. teacher to do parachute activities with your class. Allow students to experience the fun.

# Bibliography

**Books**

Ahlberg, Janet and Allan. *Each Peach Pear Plum.* Penguin Books, 1986.

Carlson, Nancy. *Harriet's Halloween Candy.* Carolrhoda, 1982.

de Paola, Tomie. *The Popcorn Book.* Holiday House, 1984.

Gilman, Phoebe. *The Wonderful Pigs of Jillian Jiggs.* Scholastic Big Book, 1988.

Hoban, Tana. *Push Pull, Empty Full: A Book of Opposites.* Macmillan, 1972.

Johnston, Tony. *The Vanishing Pumpkin.* Scholastic, 1983.

Kasza, Keiko. *Pig's Picnic.* Putnam, 1988.

Kellogg, Steven. *The Mystery of the Flying Orange Pumpkin.* Dial, 1983.

King, Elizabeth. *The Pumpkin Patch.* Dutton, 1990.

Kroll, Steven. *The Biggest Pumpkin Ever.* Scholastic, 1984.

Lobel, Anita. *Potatoes Potatoes.* Harper & Row, 1984.

McEwan, Chris. *Pinocchio.* Doubleday, 1990.

Munsch, Robert N. *Purple, Green, and Yellow.* Annick, 1992.

Nordqvist, Sven. *Pancake Pie.* Morrow, 1984.

Rockwell, Anne. *Apples and Pumpkins.* Scholastic, 1989.

Rockwell, Anne. *Pots and Pans.* Macmillan, 1993.

Seker, Jo Ann and George Jones. *Rhythmic Parachute Play,* (activity book and 2 tapes). Kimbo Productions, Long Beach, NJ.

Testa, Fulvio. *If You Take a Pencil.* Dial, 1985.

Titherington, Jeanne. *Pumpkin Pumpkin.* Mulberry, 1986.

Walt Disney Editors. *Peter Pan.* Warner Brothers, 1986.

Westcott, Nadine Bernard. *Peanut Butter and Jelly.* Dutton, 1987.

Zagwyn, Deborah Turney. *The Pumpkin Blanket.* Celestial Arts, 1990.

**Technology**

*Halloween Party.* (Video showing Halloween costumes, games, and treats); 8 min. Troll Associates, Catalog Sales Dept., 100 Corporate Dr., Mahwah, NJ 07498; 1-800-929-8765.

*Peter and the Wolf.* (Software with story narration by Jack Lemmon, illustrations, and orchestra music); CD-ROM for MPC and MAC; Troll Associates, Catalog Sales Dept., 100 Corporate Dr., Mahwah, NJ 07498; 1-800-929-8765.

*Peter's Adventures.* (Software for three adventures that let young students learn about colors, numbers, and other topics); CD-ROM for MAC or WIN; Troll Associates, Catalog Sales Dept., 100 Corporate Dr., Mahwah, NJ 07498; 1-800-929-8765.

*Preschool Parade.* (Software that teaches colors, shapes, patterns, the alphabet, etc.); CD-ROM for MAC and MPC; Discis; Available from Educorp, 7434 Trade Street, San Diego, CA 92121; 1-800-843-9497.

*Putt-Putt Joins the Parade* by Humongous Entertainment. (Software for basic reading and problem-solving skills); CD-ROM for MAC and WIN; Available from Sunburst, P.O. Box 100, Pleasantville, NY 10570; 1-800-321-7511.

# Plump Pumpkin

Enlarge the following key picture by creating an overhead transparency of this page and projecting it onto poster board. Then trace each part on poster board to make an orange pumpkin, green leaf, and brown stem. Cut out the poster board pieces and glue them together. Allow the glue to dry, then laminate the pumpkin. Refer to the key picture each day, especially when you discuss the calendar (page 9). At the end of the week, tape the pumpkin to a wall as part of an alphabet line-up.

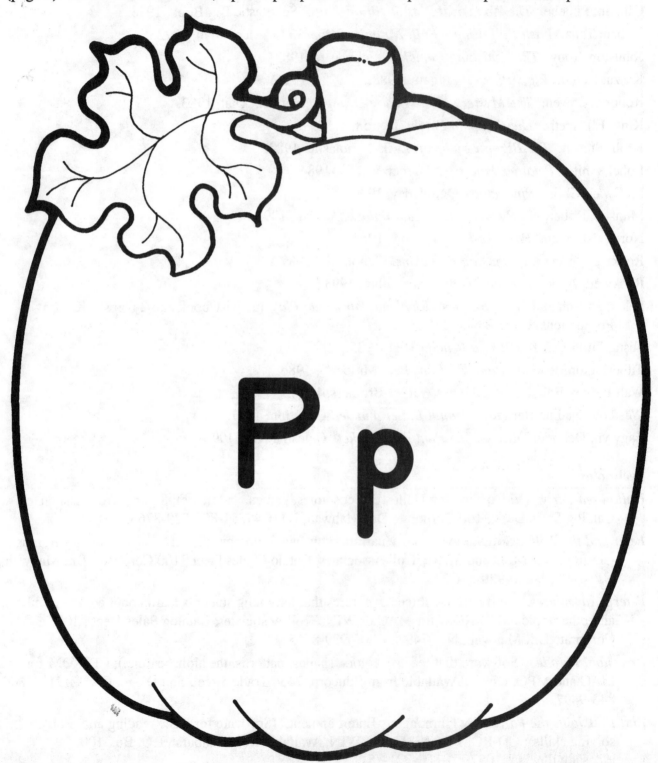

# A Pumpkin Booklet

**Directions:** Color, cut apart, and make the booklet shown below.

1. Plant the seed.

2. A green vine grows on the ground.

3. A yellow flower blooms.

4. The little orange pumpkin grows.

5. The pumpkin gets big.

6. Cut a jack-o'-lantern.

# Pet Pig

**Directions:** Cut out and glue the pig onto construction paper. Then color and decorate it using different materials such as lace, fabric, trims, ribbon, yarn, flowers, glitter, and spangles.

# The Letter J

## • *LETTER OF THE WEEK*

Display the key picture of A Jolly Jack-O'-Lantern (page 72). Refer to it each day. During the week, have students make the letter **J** using a variety of materials such as jewels (sequins, colored stones, or glitter), junk, jelly beans, etc.

## • *JACK-O'-LANTERN*

1. Obtain a pumpkin to make a jack-o'-lantern. Ask: *What do you think is inside the pumpkin? How many seeds do you think are in there? Are they large or small?* Cut the pumpkin open. Let each student use a hand to scoop out some seeds. Ask: *How does the inside feel? How does it compare to the feel of the outside?* Together, count the seeds. Scoop out some of the pumpkin. Put part of what you scooped out in each of two reclosable plastic bags, and store them in the refrigerator. Save the contents of one bag for later use. Cook the pumpkin from the other bag in a microwave with a little water until it is soft. Mash it or put it through a food processor. When it is cool, offer students the opportunity to taste it. You may wish to make pumpkin pies, muffins, bread, cookies, pudding, or a cake.

2. Let each student vote on how the jack-o'-lantern should look by drawing either a happy or a scary face. Make a pictograph with the pictures. Have students determine which type of face was more popular. Cut the jack-o'-lantern to look like the winning face. Put a flashlight inside. Turn out the lights and read a jack-o'-lantern story such as Janet Craig's *Joey the Jack-O'-Lantern* (Troll, 1988) or *Magic Pumpkin* by Bill Martin and John Archambault (Holt, 1989).

3. Ice a round cake with orange frosting and make a face on it with candy corn or chocolate chips for a jack-o'-lantern cake to serve on Halloween.

4. On the day after Halloween, compare the jack-o'-lantern to the refrigerated pumpkin. Discuss the differences and the changes that have occurred. Recycle your jack-o'-lantern by crushing it for use as mulch. Ask students what will happen to the pumpkin on the ground.

## • *JAPAN*

Use a world map to show students where Japan is. Write to the following address to ask for information to share with your class: Japan National Tourist Organization, 630 Fifth Avenue, New York, NY 10111. Compare and contrast lifestyles in the United States with those in Japan. Try to eat rice with chopsticks.

## • *JOBS*

1. Have students brainstorm a list of some jobs that people have. Ask: *Where do we find people doing these jobs? What special skills do people need for each job?*

2. Take students to visit a variety of places in your community. These experiences will give them a first-hand view of people doing different jobs. Possible destinations include the police station, fire department, post office, library, stores, and restaurants.

3. Collect an assortment of job-related props, such as hats, badges, uniforms, doctor and nurse kits, a cash register, toy money, empty food containers, menus, and restaurant order pads, for students to use in a dramatic play center.

# The Letter J *(cont.)*

## • *JOBS (cont.)*

4. Read one or more books about jobs. See the bibliography (page 71) for suggestions.

5. Provide magazines and blunt scissors for students to cut out pictures of people at work. Ask them to identify the jobs being done in the pictures. Then have them use the pictures to create a class collage.

6. Invite parents to tell your class about their jobs. Students can draw pictures to show what their parents do. Collect students' drawings and make them into a Big Book entitled "Mommies and Daddies at Work." Punch two holes in the tops and bind the book with metal rings. Hang the book on the stick-on plastic hooks on your classroom door or in the library center.

## • *JELLYFISH*

Tell students that jellyfish is a type of ocean animal. If possible, show students pictures of different types of jellyfish. Then have students make their own jellyfish (page 164).

## • *JUNGLE*

Have students identify various jungle animals (pages 255–261 and page 38). Read aloud Rudyard Kipling's *The Jungle Book* (Simon, 1992) or watch a video (Walt Disney Home Video, 1967) of the story. Use jungle animal cookie cutters to cut congealed gelatin for students to eat as a snack.

## • *JUMP*

1. Encourage students to practice jumping. Together, do jumping jacks and the broad jump. Allow students to try jumping rope. Have them learn some jump rope rhymes.

2. Have the class play "Jump the River" by laying two ropes parallel to each other with about a foot (30 cm) in between. After everyone has had a turn jumping over them, move the ropes further apart to make the river wider.

3. Teach students "Jack Be Nimble" (*Nursery Rhymes: Book Two*, TCM561) and practice jumping over an unlit candlestick.

## • *JUNK FOOD*

Read *The Berenstain Bears and Too Much Junk Food* by Stan and Jan Berenstain (Random House, 1985). Have students brainstorm a list of some junk foods. Ask: *Why are some foods called junk food?* Caution students to eat only small amounts of candy. Then have them brainstorm a list of some healthful foods.

## • *JAM/JUICE SNACK: JAMBOREE!*

1. Ask parents if their children have any food allergies or dietary restrictions. Give each student a cup of juice. Invite students to taste different flavors of jam, such as blueberry, strawberry, blackberry, raspberry, and grape, on crackers or bread. Have them vote for their favorite flavors and make a graph using this data.

2. Read aloud *Bread and Jam for Frances* by Russell Hoban (Harper & Row, 1964) and *Jamberry* by Bruce Degen (Scholastic Big Book, 1983).

# Bibliography

**Books**

Allen, Julia. *My First Job.* ARO, 1987.

Berenstain, Stan and Jan. *The Berenstain Bears and Mama's New Job.* Random House, 1984.

Berenstain, Stan and Jan. *The Berenstain Bears and Too Much Junk Food.* Random House, 1985.

Brehner, Carolyn. *Job for Wittilda.* Dial, 1993.

Carlstrom, Nancy. *Jesse Bear, What Will You Wear?* Macmillan, 1986.

Carroll, Lewis. *Jabberwocky.* St. Martin's Press, 1993.

Craig, Janet. *Joey the Jack-O'-Lantern.* Troll, 1988.

Degen, Bruce. *Jamberry.* Scholastic Big Book, 1983.

Fischetto, Laura. *The Jungle is My Home.* Viking Penguin, 1993.

Hoban, Russell. *Bread and Jam for Frances.* Harper & Row, 1964.

Kellogg, Steven. *Jack and the Beanstalk.* William Morrow, 1991.

Kipling, Rudyard. *The Jungle Book.* Simon, 1992.

Kipling, Rudyard. *Just So Stories.* Harper, 1991.

Lord, John V. and Janet Burroway. *The Giant Jam Sandwich.* Houghton Mifflin, 1987.

Merriam, Eve. *Daddies at Work.* Simon and Schuster, 1989.

Merriam, Eve. *Mommies at Work.* Simon and Schuster, 1989.

Ormerod, Jan. *Joe Can Count.* William Morrow, 1993.

Peet, Bill. *Jennifer and Josephine.* Houghton Mifflin, 1984.

Peet, Bill. *Jethro and Joel Were a Troll.* Houghton Mifflin, 1987.

Rodriguez, Anita. *Jamal and the Angel.* Crown Publishers, 1992.

Walt Disney Editors. *The Jungle Book.* Warner Books, 1986.

**Technology**

*I'm a Little Jealous of That Baby.* (Video of how Jennifer copes with a new baby sister); 12 min. Pied Piper/AIMS Multimedia, 9710 De Soto Ave., Chatsworth, CA 91311; 1-800-367-2567.

*Jasper's Hospital Experience.* (Video of Jasper the puppet going to the hospital); 20 min. Pied Piper/AIMS Multimedia, 9710 De Soto Ave., Chatsworth, CA 91311; 1-800-367-2567.

*Joey the Jack-O'-Lantern.* (Cassette with ten paperbacks); Troll Associates, Catalog Sales Dept., 100 Corporate Dr., Mahwah, NJ 07498; 1-800-929-8765.

*Jo-Jo Joins the Reading Circus.* (Software for basic reading skills); PC; National School Products, 101 East Broadway, Maryville, TN 37804; 1-800-251-9124.

*Jorinda and Joringel.* (Cassette and four paperbacks); Troll Associates, Catalog Sales Dept., 100 Corporate Dr., Mahwah, NJ 07498; 1-800-929-8765.

*Junk Food Man.* (Video shows how to choose healthful snacks); 10 min. Pied Piper/AIMS Multimedia, 9710 De Soto Ave., Chatsworth, CA 91311; 1-800-367-2567.

# A Jolly Jack-O'-Lantern

Enlarge the following key picture by creating an overhead transparency of this page and projecting it onto poster board. Then trace each part to make an orange pumpkin and yellow features. Cut out the poster board pieces and glue them together. Allow the glue to dry. Then laminate the jack-o'-lantern. Refer to the key picture each day, especially when you discuss the calendar (page 9). At the end of the week, tape the jack-o'-lantern to a wall as part of an alphabet line-up.

# My Jar

**Directions:** What is in your jar?  Write a story to tell about it.

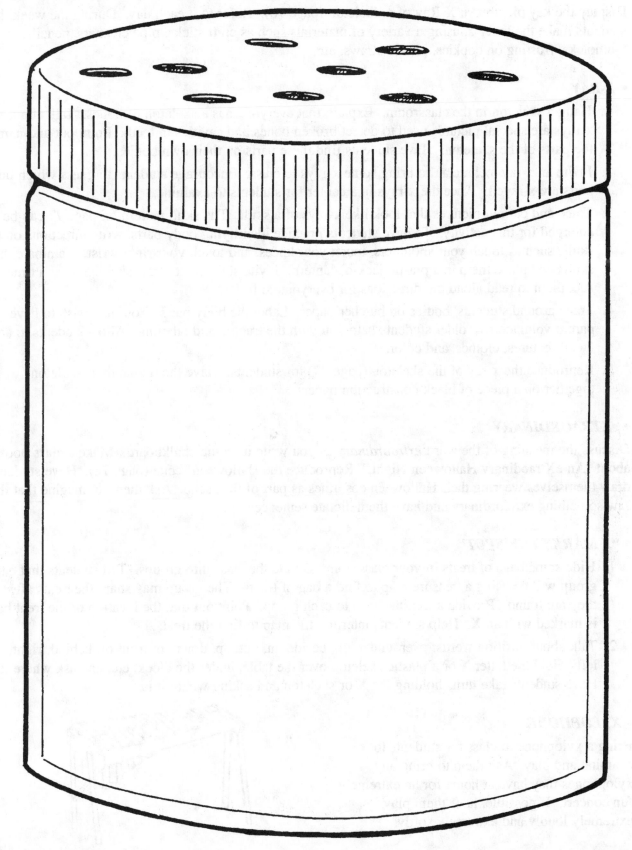

# The Letter X

## • *LETTER OF THE WEEK*

Display the key picture An X-Ray of a Skeleton (page 76).  Refer to it each day.  During the week, have students make the letter **X** using a variety of materials such as craft sticks, pipe cleaners, pencils, toothpicks, frosting on cookies, plastic straws, etc.

## • *X-RAY*

1.  Hang a skeleton in the classroom.  Explain that everyone has a skeleton of bones.  Talk about how x-rays are special pictures used to detect broken bones and cavities in teeth.  Point out and name the parts of the skeleton.  Have students find these parts on their own bodies.

2.  Invite an x-ray technician to bring some x-rays to class.  Encourage students to guess which body parts are x-rayed.  Place the x-rays in a center for students to examine.

3.  Trace and cut out pictures that look like x-rays of a skull.  The skull pattern on page 77 can be enlarged for this activity.  To have students practice identifying body parts, write directions on the skulls such as touch your shoulders, touch your knees, and touch your right wrist.  Laminate the skulls and place them in a plastic jack-o'-lantern.  Invite students to draw skulls, one at a time.  Ask them to read aloud the directions for everyone to follow.

4.  Trace around students' bodies on butcher paper.  Label the body parts.  You may wish to have parent volunteers or older students help you with the tracing and labeling.  Allow students to add facial features, clothes, and color.

5.  Reproduce the x-ray of the skeleton (page 77) for students.  Have them glue their skeletons together on a piece of black construction paper.

## • *eXTRAORDINARY*

Discuss the meaning of the word *extraordinary* as you write it on the chalkboard.  Make a class book about "An eXtraodinary Halloween Night."  Reproduce the Halloween scene (page 78).  Have students draw themselves wearing their Halloween costumes as part of the scene.  Ask them to imagine that they saw something extraordinary and have them dictate sentences.

## • *"X MARKS THE SPOT"*

1.  Hide some bags of treats in your classroom.  Divide the class into groups.  Tell students that each group will be using a treasure map to find a bag of treats.  The group may share the treats after they are found.  Provide a treasure map to each group.  Point out that the location of the treat bag is marked with an **X**.  Help students interpret the map to find the treats.

2.  Talk about position words: over, under, on, beside, in, out, up, down, in front of, behind, right, left.  Hold the letter **X** or a plastic skeleton over the table, under the clock, etc. and ask where it is.  Have students take turns holding the **X** or skeleton and asking where it is.

## • *XYLOPHONE*

Bring a xylophone to class for students to examine and play.  Ask them to bring any xylophones they have at home for an extremely fun concert.  If possible, have them play extremely loudly and extremely softly.

# Bibliography

## Books

Bailey, Donna. *All About Your Skeleton.* Steck-Vaughn, 1990.

Balestrino, Phillip. *The Skeleton Inside You.* HarperCollins, 1989.

Bishop, Pamela R. *Exploring Your Skeleton.* Franklin Watts, 1991.

Broekel, Ray. *Experiments with Air.* Childrens Press, 1988.

Broekel, Ray. *Experiments with Light.* Childrens Press, 1986.

Broekel, Ray. *Experiments with Straws and Paper.* Childrens Press, 1990.

Broekel, Ray. *Experiments with Water.* Childrens Press, 1988.

Broekel, Ray. *Your Skeleton and Your Skin.* Childrens Press, 1984.

Hall, Katy. *Skeletons! Skeletons!: All About Bones.* Scholastic, 1991.

Hanel, Wolfram. *Extraordinary Adventures of an Ordinary Hat.* North-South, 1994.

Johnson, Jimmy. *Skeletons: An Inside Look at Animals.* Random House, 1994.

Lionni, Leo. *Extraordinary Egg.* Knopf, 1994.

Martin, Bill, Jr. and John Archambault. *Here Are My Hands.* Holt, 1985.

McDonnell, Janet. *XYZ Adventure in Alphabet Town.* Childrens Press, 1992.

Peterson, Cris. *Extra Cheese, Please!: Mozzarella's Journey From Cow to Pizza.* Boyds Mills, 1994.

Poffenberger, Nancy. *Instant Fun with Bells and Xylophones.* Fun Publishing Co., 1986.

## Technology

*How It Moves.* (Videotape/Videodisc that explains use of bones, joints, ligaments, and muscles); 10 min. Coronet/MTI Film and Video, P.O. Box 2649, Columbus, OH 43216; 1-800-321-3106.

*Learning About the Human Body.* (Software that gives an inside look at the body); CD-ROM for MAC; Sunburst, P.O. Box 100, Pleasantville, NY 10570; 1-800-321-7511.

*Science Explorers.* (Software includes a learning lab about skeletons); Apple/MS-DOS. Scholastic Inc., 2931 E. McCarty St., Jefferson City, MO 65101; 1-800-541-5513.

*Xavier in India.* (Videotape of children exploring Benares, India); 18 min. Pied Piper/AIMS Multimedia, 9710 De Soto Ave., Chatsworth, CA 91311; 1-800-367-2567.

## Teacher Created Materials

*Hands-On Minds-On Science: Our Bodies* (TCM618)

*The Human Body Lesson Card Pack for GeoSafari* ® (TCM1150)

*My Body Thematic Unit* (TCM584)

# An X-Ray of a Skeleton

Enlarge the following key picture by creating an overhead transparency of this page and projecting it onto white poster board. Trace and cut out and laminate the skeleton. Allow the glue to dry, then laminate it. (As an alternative, you may prefer to purchase a metal or cardboard Halloween skeleton to glue on black poster board with the white poster board letters and laminate.) Refer to the key picture each day, especially when you discuss the calendar (page 9). At the end of the week, tape the skeleton x-ray to a wall as part of an alphabet line-up.

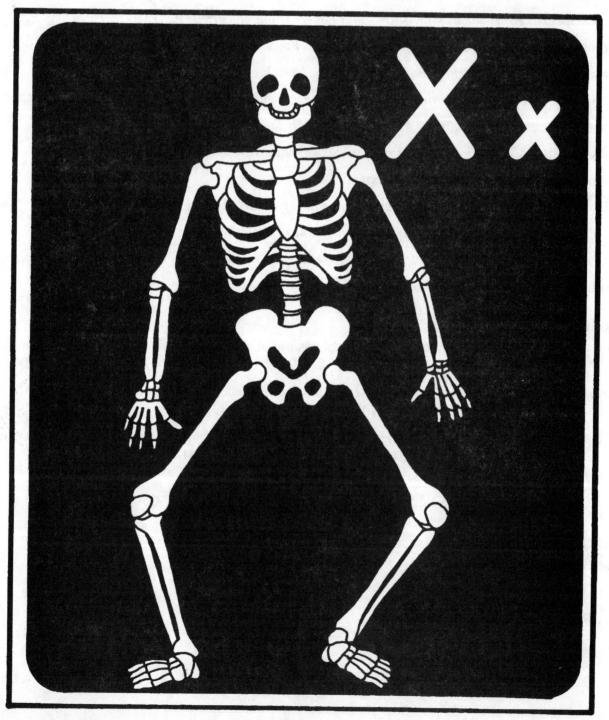

# Skeleton

**Directions:** Cut out the parts of this x-ray. Match the letters to put the x-ray of the skeleton together. Glue the parts in place on a piece of black construction paper.

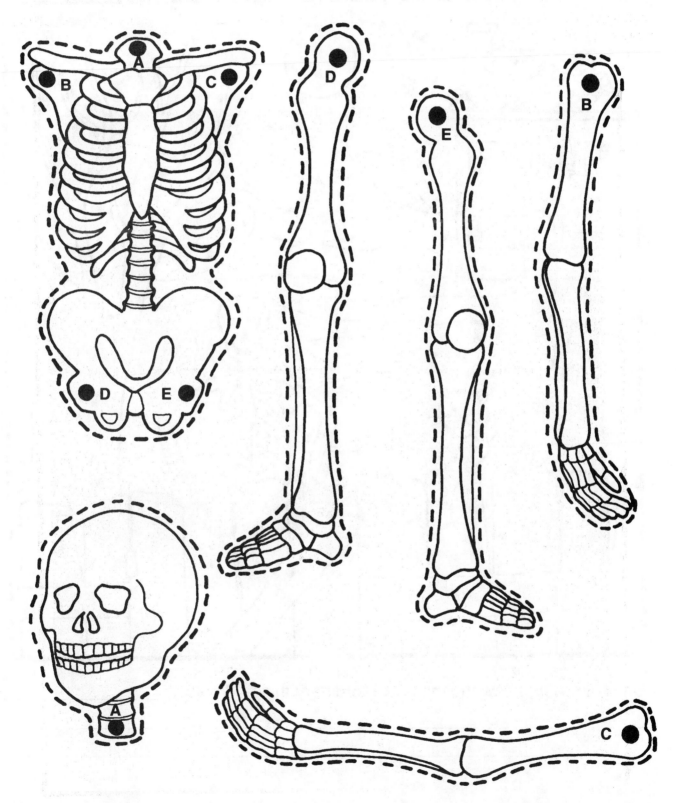

# Trick-or-Treat

**Directions:** Color the picture.  Then tell what extraordinary thing you saw on Halloween.

On Halloween, I saw the most extraordinary thing.  It was _____

_____

_____ .

# The Letter I

## • NOVEMBER

1. Draw some autumn leaves on finger paint paper. Turn the paper over and have students spread yellow finger paint all over it. Sprinkle on a little powdered red tempera paint or finger paint. Use your fingers to blend it in slightly so that there are shades of yellow, red, and orange. After the paint is dry, help students cut out the leaves. Then staple the leaves to the Class Tree (page 9).

2. Color a copy of the Pilgrims and Native Americans (page 91) for the Class Tree/Calendar bulletin board (page 9). Use tan or light gray construction paper to cut out longhouses (page 108). Use brown construction paper to cut out Pilgrim log cabins. Use marker to draw the doors and windows. Add these to the bulletin board. Just before Thanksgiving, you may wish to add long tables with harvest foods on them. Provide each student with a copy of The First Thanksgiving (page 92) to color. Display the pictures on the bulletin board.

## • LETTER OF THE WEEK

Display the key picture of An Ice Skater Eating Ice Cream (page 82). Refer to it each day. During the week, have students make the letter I using a variety of materials such as icicles made from Christmas tree tinsel, or ink fingerprints, chocolate syrup on ice cream, etc.

## • ICE CREAM

1. Have an "Ice Cream Election" on Tuesday, Election Day. Use brown and white construction paper to cut out shapes that look like scoops of chocolate and vanilla ice cream. Make a ballot box with a slit at the top through which the scoops can be deposited. The voting booth can be a large box, another classroom, or just outside the classroom door. Instruct students to decide whether they prefer chocolate or vanilla ice cream. Tell them to vote for the one they like better by putting either a brown or a white "scoop" in the ballot box. When everyone has voted, make a pictograph by taping the ballots (brown and white "scoops") to chart paper.

Together, count to see how many votes each flavor received. Determine which was more popular.

2. If vanilla wins, have students make "Ice Cream Igloos." To do so, put scoops of vanilla ice cream on a cookie tray and freeze. Help students use chocolate cake decorator's icing in a tube to draw lines on the scoops so that they resemble igloos. Refreeze them before serving. If chocolate wins, just serve it. Allow students to enjoy the ice cream treat as you discuss the election results. Remind them that they are being served the winning ice cream flavor, whether or not it is the one they voted for. Point out that there is only one winner of an election. Relate the ice cream voting to real elections. Explain that the person who gets the most votes serves as president, governor, mayor, etc. for everyone, whether or not any particular individual voted for that person.

## • ICE PAINTING

Freeze half of a straw in an ice cube. For each student or pair of students, pour some powdered tempera paint or finger paint on freezer paper. Invite students to paint using the ice cube.

# The Letter I *(cont.)*

## • *INITIALS*

1. Show students how to make initials out of cookie or pretzel dough.
2. Invite students to write their initials using glue sprinkled with powdered gelatin.
3. Have them write their initials on small pieces of wood using colored glue.
4. Use alphabet cookie cutters for students to make their initials from congealed gelatin, raw cookie dough that is rolled out, or clay that is rolled out. If you make cookie dough, students can make cookies and spread canned icing on them after they have baked and cooled. Point out that icing also starts with the letter **I**.

## • *INCH*

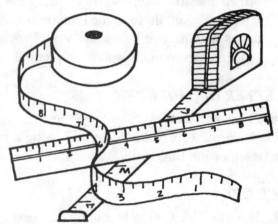

Read aloud *Inch by Inch* by Leo Lionni (Astor-Honor, 1962). Show students what an inch measurement looks like on 12-inch (30 cm) rulers, yardsticks or meter sticks, and tape measures. Allow students to use these tools to measure objects and people in inches. Keep a record and have students remeasure the same objects and people in the spring. Ask: *What grew? What did not grow? How much did you grow?*

## • *GOVERNMENT OF INDIA TOURIST BUREAU*

Use a world map to show students where India is. Write to the following address to ask for information to share with your class: Government of India Tourist Bureau, 30 Rockefeller Plaza, New York, NY 10112.

## • *IMAGINATION*

Write the word *imagination* on the chalkboard. Discuss what imagination is. Ask students to brainstorm a list of things they like to imagine themselves doing.

## • *ICE SPORTS*

Ask students to brainstorm a list of ice sports as you write them on the chalkboard. Examples include ice skating, ice fishing, and ice hockey. Have students vote for the ice sport they would like to do. Make a table and a graph to show the results of the vote.

## • *ISLAND*

Use a map to show students some islands. Ask: *What is an island? How do people get from an island to the mainland?* If you are on an island, ask students what they like and dislike about living there. If you are not on an island, ask them what they think they would like and dislike about living there.

## • *INSECTS*

Read aloud a book about insects. Suggestions are provided in the bibliography (page 81). Have students imagine that they are insects. Ask them how their life would be different. Walk around your school to look for insects. Remind students to observe rather than touch.

# Bibliography

**Books**

Arvetis, Chris. *What Is an Iceberg?* Checkerboard Press, 1987.

Barrett, Norman. *Poisonous Insects.* Watts, 1991.

Berenstain, Stan and Jan. *The Berenstain Bears and the Big Election.* Random House, 1984.

Cobb, Vicki. *The Scoop on Ice Cream.* Little, Brown, 1985.

Cocca-Leffler, Maryann. *Ice-Cold Birthday.* Putnam, 1992.

Dale, C. *Ivy.* Scholastic Big Book, 1993.

Dorling Kindersley Editors. *Insects and Crawly Creatures.* Aladdin, 1991.

Gans, Roma. *Danger—Icebergs!* HarperCollins, 1987.

Goble, Paul. *Iktomi and the Berries: A Plains Indian Story.* Orchard, 1989.

Goble, Paul. *Iktomi and the Boulder: A Plains Indian Story.* Orchard, 1988.

Goble, Paul. *Iktomi and the Buffalo Skull: A Plains Indian Story.* Orchard, 1991.

Goble, Paul. *Iktomi and the Ducks: A Plains Indian Story.* Orchard, 1990.

Herman, Gail. *Ice Cream Soup.* Random House, 1990.

Hobson, Phyllis. *Making Ice Creams, Ices, & Sherbets.* Storey Communications, Inc., 1984.

Jaspersohn, William. *Ice Cream.* Macmillan, 1988.

Keller, Holly. *Island Baby.* William Morrow, 1992.

Keller, Stella. *Ice Cream.* Raintree, 1989.

Lioni, Leo. *Inch By Inch.* Astor-Honor, 1962.

Maccarone, G. *Itchy, Itchy Chicken Pox.* Scholastic, 1992.

Mattern, Joanne. *Insects.* Troll, 1991.

McDonald, M. *Insects Are My Life.* Orchard Books, 1995.

Parker, Steve. *Insects.* Dorling Kindersley, 1992.

Ryder, Joanne. *White Bear, Ice Bear.* Morrow, 1989.

Waber, Bernard. *Ira Says Goodbye.* Houghton Mifflin, 1988.

**Technology**

*An Alphabet of Insects.* (Video); 12 min. Coronet/MTI Film and Video, P.O. Box 2649, Columbus, OH 43216; 1-800-321-3106.

*Champ on Ice!* (Video about Champ the bear); 8 min. Troll Associates, Catalog Sales Dept., 100 Corporate Dr., Mahwah, NJ 07498; 1-800-929-8765.

*Learn About Insects* by Learningways Inc. (Software); MAC; Available from Sunburst, P.O. Box 100, Pleasantville, NY 10570; 1-800-321-7511.

*Pretty Insects.* (Video about collecting and studying butterflies); 30 min. National School Products, 101 East Broadway, Maryville, TN 37804; 1-800-251-9124.

*Why We Need Reading: The Piemaker of Ignoramia.* (Video by LCA used to motivate young readers); 12 min. Coronet/MTI Film and Video, P.O. Box 2649, Columbus, OH 43216; 1-800-321-3106.

# An Ice Skater Eating Ice Cream

Enlarge the following key picture by creating an overhead transparency of this page. Project and trace it onto white poster board. Use paints to color the picture. Then laminate the ice skater. Refer to the key picture each day, especially when you discuss the calendar (page 9). At the end of the week, tape the ice skater to a wall as part of an alphabet line-up.

# The Letter T

## • *LETTER OF THE WEEK*

Display the key picture, The Tasty Tom Turkey (page 89).  Refer to it each day.  During the week, have students make the letter **T** using a variety of materials such as tree twigs, toothpicks, tea leaves, tissue paper triangles, etc.

## • *TRANSPORTATION / TRAVEL*

1. Explain that transportation is how you travel, or move, from one place to another.  Have students brainstorm a list of some different modes of transportation.  Have them cut and glue pictures from magazines to make a class collage, or divide a bulletin board into three sections (land, air, and water) and have them glue transportation pictures in each.

2 Read a book about transportation.  See the bibliography (page 88) for suggestions.  Point out all the words related to transportation, such as travel, train, truck, traffic, turn, ticket, and tunnel that begin with the letter t.  Show pictures of traffic signs, and talk about what they mean. If possible, purchase fabric with a community printed on it.  If not, draw a map of your community on a shower curtain or a piece of oilcloth.  Include roads, stores, schools, parks, lakes, railroads, airports, and houses.  Place the map in a center with small cars, trucks, boats, airplanes, trains, and traffic signs.  Talk about why we need traffic signs and laws. List safety rules on a chart.  Discuss what happens when laws and rules are not followed.

3. Discuss the Pilgrims.  Begin by using a world map to show students where England and America are.  Then explain that the Pilgrims were a group of people who lived in England in 1620.  They did not like the king's rules.  They decided to come to America so they could make their own rules and have the freedom to live as they wanted.  (Point out that the word *Pilgrim* means someone who takes a long trip.)  Tell students that the Pilgrims arrived at Plymouth Rock, Massachusetts, just as winter arrived.  The first thing they did was to make some rules which they called the "Mayflower Compact."  They agreed to follow these rules and remain together for safety reasons.  Ask: *What might some of these rules have been?  What rules do we have at school to keep us safe?*  After the Pilgrims found a place to live, they built a large common house.  Later they built individual houses.  Many died during the long, cold winter.  When spring came, those who survived began to plant gardens.  Some friendly Native Americans helped them.  One Native American named Squanto taught the Pilgrims how to plant crops such as corn, beans, squash, and pumpkins.  He taught them how to fertilize their crops by putting fish heads in the soil while planting.  Squanto also taught them how to hunt, fish, and find nuts and berries.  With the Native Americans' help, the Pilgrims survived.  In the fall, the Pilgrims had a celebration to thank God for the harvest.  In appreciation for their help and friendship, the Native Americans were invited to join with the Pilgrims in this harvest feast celebration which lasted for three days.  This is known as the first Thanksgiving.  Today, we remember how our country began as we give thanks at this time for all that we have.

   Compare modern methods of transportation to those used by the Pilgrims.  Ask: *If you moved to a new home today, how would you get there?*  Reproduce the picture of the *Mayflower* (page 90). Explain that the Pilgrims traveled on a ship called the *Mayflower*.  Ask: *How do you think it moved?*  Point out that each family could only bring a few belongings such as guns for hunting, axes for cutting trees, and some clothes.  The children probably brought only one toy.  Ask: *Which toy would you bring?*  Then allow students to color the picture.

# The Letter T *(cont.)*

## • *TRANSPORTATION / TRAVEL (cont.)*

4. Make a pictograph that shows how students get to school. Have each student draw a picture of his or her method of transportation on an index card. Ask students to write their names on their cards. Have them tape their cards in the appropriate section on the graph. Ask: *How do most students get to school? Which type of transportation is used the least?*

## • *TEPEE*

Reproduce the Tepee (page 109). Discuss this traditional type of Native American home. Allow students to color the picture.

## • *THANKSGIVING FEAST*

1. Make your own Thanksgiving feast. Be sure to ask parents if their children have any food allergies or dietary restrictions. Make some cranberry sauce using the recipe on the cranberry package. The difference between homemade and canned cranberry sauce is unbelievable! Then fill a small seeded pumpkin with peeled and diced apples, sweet potatoes, butternut squash, raisins, and nuts. Sprinkle with brown sugar and/or honey and cinnamon. Put the top back on the pumpkin and bake at 350° F (175° C) for 1½ hours. Allow the mixture to cool before serving.

2. Reproduce the Pilgrims and Native Americans (page 91) and The First Thanksgiving (page 92). Invite students to color these pictures and add them to the Thanksgiving mural. Help students make Pilgrim hats (pages 97 and 98) to wear as they enjoy the feast.

## • *THANKSGIVING WREATH*

Discuss what it means to feel thankful for something. Lead students to conclude that if they feel thankful, they are glad. Invite volunteers to name things for which they are thankful. Possible answers include family, home, food, clothes, friends, and pets. Give each student a large, thin, white paper plate. Ask students to draw pictures of what they are thankful for in the center of their plates. Have each student dictate a sentence telling what they are thankful for as you write it on the plate below the picture. Provide small squares of red, yellow, and orange tissue paper. Show students how to center and wrap a square of tissue paper around the eraser end of a pencil, dip it in some glue, and use the pencil to press the tissue paper onto the rim of the paper plate. Tell them to continue in this manner until the rim of the paper plate is completely decorated to look like a wreath. Attach the wreaths to a bulletin board entitled "We Are Thankful."

## • *TEACHING TURKEY*

Color, cut out, and laminate a turkey's head and body (page 94). Make tail feathers of various colors (page 95). Write a letter of the alphabet on each feather, some uppercase and some lowercase. Have students pick feathers from the pile. If they can name their letters, they can put their feathers on the turkey. If not, they must put their feathers back in the pile. You may also wish to have students put the letters in alphabetical order. Students can match letters and put the feathers on the turkey as well.

# The Letter T *(cont.)*

- **TURKEY ART**

  1. Have students make pine cone turkeys using the directions on page 96. Display the turkeys in the discovery center with collected signs of fall: gourds, Indian corn, small pumpkins, winter squash, fall leaves, and seeds collected on a fall walk outside. Remember to have students add to the seed chart (page 10) whenever possible.

  2. Allow students to make handprint turkeys using the directions on page 96. Add the turkeys to the farm bulletin board (pages 32 and 33), add a barn and create a turkey farm bulletin board, or attach them to the Thanksgiving bulletin board (page 79).

  3. Encourage students to draw pictures and dictate stories about what they would do if they were a turkey at Thanksgiving time. Add these to the turkey display.

- **TREES**

  1. Read aloud a book about trees, leaves, or seeds. See the bibliography for suggestions (page 88). Then take a walk outside to look for signs of fall. Ask: *Can you find a tree with yellow leaves? red leaves? orange leaves? brown leaves? green leaves?* Explain that pine and cedar trees, among others, are called evergreens because they remain green all year long. Look for tiny trees that have sprouted. Ask: *Can you find the parent trees?* If possible, bring some sweetgum, sycamore balls, and pine cones to school for students to examine. Shake out the seeds. Obtain closed pine cones that have just fallen from the trees. Allow students to watch them open and release their seeds. Add as many types of seeds to your chart (page 10) as possible. Bring back some colorful fall leaves and seeds for the discovery center. Use some for sorting and matching. Help students notice that leaves from the same tree can be different sizes.

  2. Have the class take care of a tree on the school grounds. Have students observe and record any changes. Allow students to make bark rubbings of the trunk. Bring some fallen leaves from the tree to the classroom for students to examine. Press some of the leaves in phone books or old catalogs for a couple of weeks. When they are dry, have students tape the pressed leaves to paper. Ask students to make leaf people by drawing heads, arms, and legs and write stories about them.

  3. Have students make leaf rubbings using different fall colors. To do this, have them put the leaves under paper and rub crayons on their sides over the leaves. This activity can also be done with bark on tree trunks.

  4. Have students brainstorm a list of things that trees give us. Make a chart or a class collage. Ask: *Who lives in trees? What happens when there is a forest fire? What can we do to prevent them?*

  5. Make a Big Book entitled "Trees." Draw two copies of a leaf pattern on red or orange tagboard. Write the title on the front, and laminate the tagboard leaves. Have students use leaf-shaped yellow paper to draw pictures of trees and dictate sentences describing their importance. Place students' leaves between the tagboard covers. Punch two holes in the tops and bind the book with metal rings. Hang the book on the stick-on plastic hooks on your classroom door or in the library center.

# The Letter T *(cont.)*

- ***TREES*** *(cont.)*

    6.  Draw and reproduce a tree pattern for students. Talk about what trees look like during the different seasons. Take students outside to observe how the trees look. Ask them to describe what they see. After returning to the classroom, have them use brown to color the trunk and branches of the tree. Provide small squares of red, yellow, brown, and orange tissue paper. Have them create fall leaves using the squares of tissue paper as described for the Thanksgiving Wreath project (page 84). You may wish to repeat this project and have students decorate their trees with tissue paper to show the different seasons.

- ***TASTE***

Provide a variety of foods to let students taste different sweet, salty, bitter, and sour things. Ask: *What do you like? What don't you like? Should you eat something that tastes or smells spoiled? Why not?* Have students brainstorm a list of some things that they should not put in their mouths. Illicit the response that if it is not food, they should not put it in their mouths. Stress that medicines and vitamins should only be given by an adult. Show students pictures of some poisonous household substances. Emphasize that these things should **never** be put in anyone's mouth. Ask students to help their parents by making sure younger brothers and sisters never get hold of these products. Reproduce the Yuk Monster (page 61), making several copies for each student. Have students color and cut out the Yuk Monsters. Then allow them to take the Yuk Monsters home so they can be taped onto containers of poisonous substances.

- ***T-SHIRTS***

Ask parents to send old white T-shirts for students to decorate in this art activity. (Undershirts or sweatshirts can be substituted.) Take students on a walk and collect fallen leaves with interesting shapes. After returning to the classroom, have them put newspaper inside their shirts to prevent the paint from bleeding through to the other side. Mix one part fabric or textile medium to two parts acrylic (water-based) paint. (These products can be purchased at art supply or craft stores.) Help each student with the following steps: Apply a thin, even coat of paint to the front of a leaf. Place the leaf, paint side down, on the shirt. Place a small piece of newspaper over the back of the leaf. Gently, but firmly, rub on the newspaper to transfer the paint to the shirt. Carefully remove the newspaper and the leaf. The leaf veins should be imprinted in a beautiful design. The leaves may be reused and overlapped to create the desired effect.

- ***TIME***

    1.  On the chalkboard, write *Time: yesterday, today, tomorrow.* Have a volunteer locate the letter **t** in each of these words. Ask: *What did you do yesterday? What are you going to do today? What will you do tomorrow?*

    2.  Discuss their daily routine/schedule. Ask a variety of questions about time such as, *What time do you go to bed at night?* or *What time do you get up in the morning?* Show students what these times look like using a clock with moveable hands.

# The Letter T *(cont.)*

## • *TWEEZERS*

Develop fine motor coordination by putting tweezers in the discovery center. **Warning:** Caution students to be careful when working with the tweezers. Collect several different kinds (or colors) of small objects. Encourage students to pick up the objects with the tweezers and sort them into egg carton cups, according to like characteristics.

## • *TULIPS*

Have students plant tulips and other spring bulbs. Sprinkle with fertilizer and water regularly. Watch the tulips grow during the winter and spring. Put some narcissus and hyacinth bulbs in an indoor pot or a glass of water and watch them grow.

## • *TERRARIUM*

Make a terrarium from an old aquarium or large jar. Put in a thin layer of small stones. Cover those with aquarium charcoal and then a layer of soil. Place a variety of small plants in the soil. Water sparingly. Cover with plastic and poke air holes in the top. Use your terrarium as a temporary home to observe small animals and insects.

## • *MEASURING TEMPERATURE USING A THERMOMETER*

Show students how to read a thermometer. Put a thermometer outside and have volunteers check the temperature at the same time each morning and/or afternoon. Record the measurements on a table. Use the data to make a line graph. Ask a variety of questions about the graph.

## • *TELEPHONE*

1. Have students use a play phone to learn their home telephone numbers. Invite them to sign the telephone pattern (page 100) when they know their telephone numbers.

2. Teach students how to dial 911 in case of an emergency. Emphasize that this number is to be used only if there is a fire, if someone is very sick or injured and needs an ambulance, or if they need the police. Role-play various emergency situations.

## • *TIE SHOES*

Demonstrate how to tie a shoe. Have students practice regularly. When they have learned how to tie their shoes, invite them to sign the sneaker pattern (page 99).

## • *TERRIBLE TODAY AND TERRIFIC TUESDAY*

1. On Monday, read aloud *Alexander and the Terrible, Horrible, No Good Very Bad Day* by Judith Viorst (Atheneum, 1972). Ask: *What is a good (bad) day? Have you ever had a good (bad) day? What happened? Do you think Alexander will never have another bad day if he moves to Australia? Why or why not? How do you deal with bad days?*

2. Have a Terrific Tuesday Tea Time. Together, share some decaffeinated tea and toast triangles, buttered and sprinkled with cinnamon sugar or covered with jam.

# Bibliography

**Books**

Anderson, Hans Christian. *Thumbelina.* Troll, 1979.

Berenstain, Stan and Jan. *The Berenstain Bears and the Prize Pumpkin.* Random House, 1990.

Berenstain, Stan and Jan. *The Berenstain Bears and Too Much TV.* Random House, 1984.

Carle, Eric. *The Tiny Seed.* Picture Book Studio, 1990.

Curran, Eileen. *Life in the Forest.* Troll, 1985.

Curran, Eileen. *Look at a Tree.* Troll, 1985.

Cutts, David. *Tom Thumb.* Troll, 1988.

Ehlert, Lois. *Red Leaf, Yellow Leaf.* HBJ, 1991.

Fowler, Allan. *It Could Still Be a Tree.* Childrens Press, 1990.

Fowler, Allan. *Tasting Things.* Childrens Press, 1991.

Grimm, Brothers. *Twelve Dancing Princesses.* Troll, 1979.

Grossman, Virginia and Sylvia Long. *Ten Little Rabbits.* Chronicle, 1991.

Hayward, Linda. *The First Thanksgiving.* Random House, 1990.

Kroll, Steven. *Oh, What a Thanksgiving.* Scholastic, 1988.

Kroll, Steven. *One Tough Turkey.* Weekly Reader Books, 1987.

Miller, Edna. *Mousekin's Thanksgiving.* Simon and Schuster, 1985.

Parker, Ed, illustrator. *The Three Billy Goats Gruff.* Troll, 1979.

Poulin, Stephane. *Travels for Two.* Firefly Books, 1991.

Romanova, Natalia. *Once There Was a Tree.* Dial, 1985.

Scarry, Richard. *Things That Go.* Western, 1987.

Siebert, Diane. *Train Song.* HarperCollins, 1990.

Siebert, Diane. *Truck Song.* HarperCollins, 1984.

Silverstein, Shel. *The Giving Tree.* Harper & Row, 1964.

Smith, Kathie B. *Tasting.* Troll, 1987.

Waters, Kate. *Samuel Eaton's Day: A Day in the Life of a Pilgrim Boy.* Scholastic, 1993.

Waters, Kate. *Sarah Morton's Day: A Day in the Life of a Pilgrim Girl.* Scholastic, 1989.

Whitehead, Pat. *Best Thanksgiving Book.* Troll, 1985.

**Technology**

*Tiger's Tales.* (Software for reading and social skills); CD-ROM for MAC; Sunburst, P.O. Box 100, Pleasantville, NY 10570; 1-800-321-7511.

*Trains.* (Video); 14 min. Coronet/MTI Film and Video, P.O. Box 2649, Columbus, OH 43216; 1-800-321-3106.

*Trees.* (Video); 8 min. Troll Associates, Catalog Sales Dept., 100 Corporate Dr., Mahwah, NJ 07498; 1-800-929-8765.

*Turtles.* (Video); 8 min. Troll Associates, Catalog Sales Dept., 100 Corporate Dr., Mahwah, NJ 07498; 1-800-929-8765.

*What's It Like to Be a Teacher?* (Cassette); Troll Associates, Catalog Sales Dept., 100 Corporate Dr., Mahwah, NJ 07498; 1-800-929-8765.

# The Tasty Tom Turkey

Enlarge the following key picture by creating an overhead transparency of this page. Project and trace it on white poster board. Paint the turkey's body brown; its beak and feet yellow; its wattle red; and its tail feathers red, brown, orange, and yellow. Cut out the turkey. Allow the glue to dry. Then laminate the turkey. Refer to the key picture each day, especially when you discuss the calendar (page 9). At the end of the week, tape the turkey to a wall as part of an alphabet line-up.

# The Mayflower

**Directions:** Color the picture.

The name of this boat is the *Mayflower*.

In 1620, the Pilgrims came to America on the *Mayflower*.

# Pilgrims and Native Americans

Color the picture for the Thanksgiving mural as described on page 79. Display it on the Class Tree/Calendar bulletin board (page 9).

Pilgrims

Native Americans

# The First Thanksgiving

**Directions:** Color the picture. Write a story to tell about the first Thanksgiving.

_____

_____

# The T Turkey

**Directions:** Say the name of each picture shown in the boxes at the bottom of the page.  If the name of the picture begins with the letter **t**, glue it onto the turkey's tail feathers.

# Teaching Turkey

Enlarge for use with the whole class, or reproduce as is for use with small groups.

# Letter Matching

Reproduce the feathers shown below. On each feather write an uppercase or lowercase letter. Cut out and laminate the feathers. Ask students to identify the letter names or match the uppercase and lowercase letters before placing them on the Teaching Turkey (page 94).

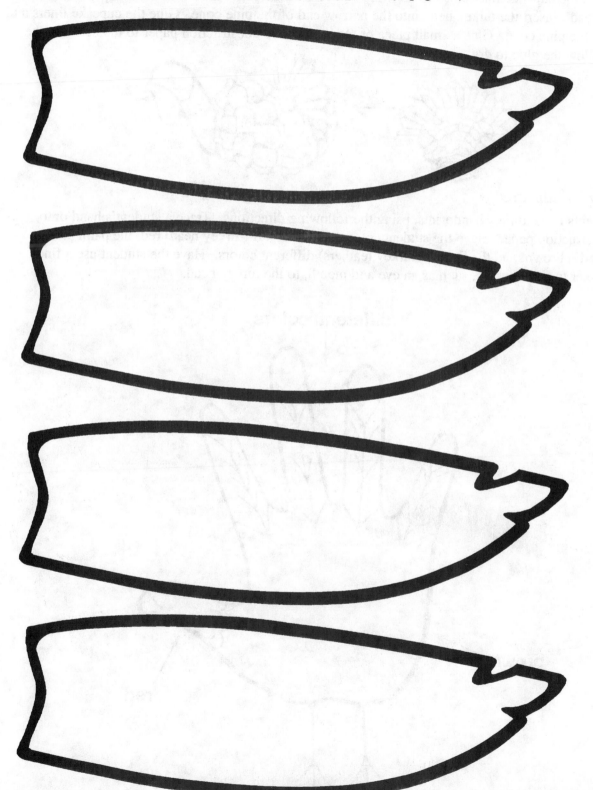

# Turkey Art

### • *Pine Cone Turkeys*

Help students make pine cone turkeys, using the following directions. Fold several cupcake liners in half. Insert the cupcake liner close to the wide end of the pine cone. Use construction paper to cut out a turkey head. Insert the turkey head into the narrow end of the pine cone. Glue the cupcake liners and head onto the pine cone. Glue a small piece of red yarn or red construction paper to the beak for the wattle. Allow the glue to dry.

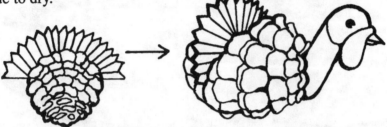

### • *Turkey Handprints*

Help students make turkey handprints, using the following directions. Trace a student's hand onto white construction paper. Have the student color the thumb part (turkey head) red, the palm part (turkey body) brown, and the fingers (turkey feathers) different colors. Have the student use a fine black marker to add features, such as an eye and mouth, to the turkey head.

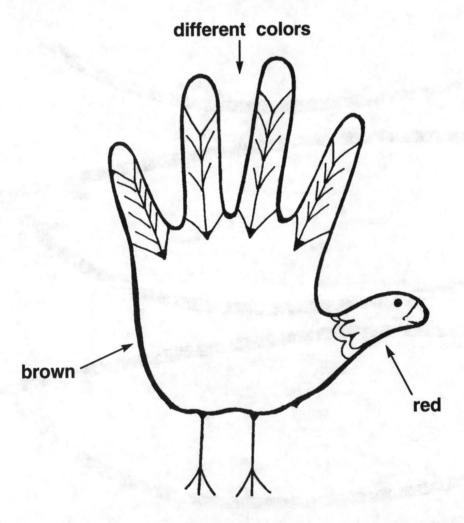

**different colors**

**brown**

**red**

# Pilgrim Boy's Hat

Reproduce the following pattern on white construction paper. Have students use gold to color the buckle and black to color the hat. Help them cut out the pattern. Make a tagboard headband for each student. Staple each hat to a headband. Adjust each headband to fit a student's head. Staple the ends.

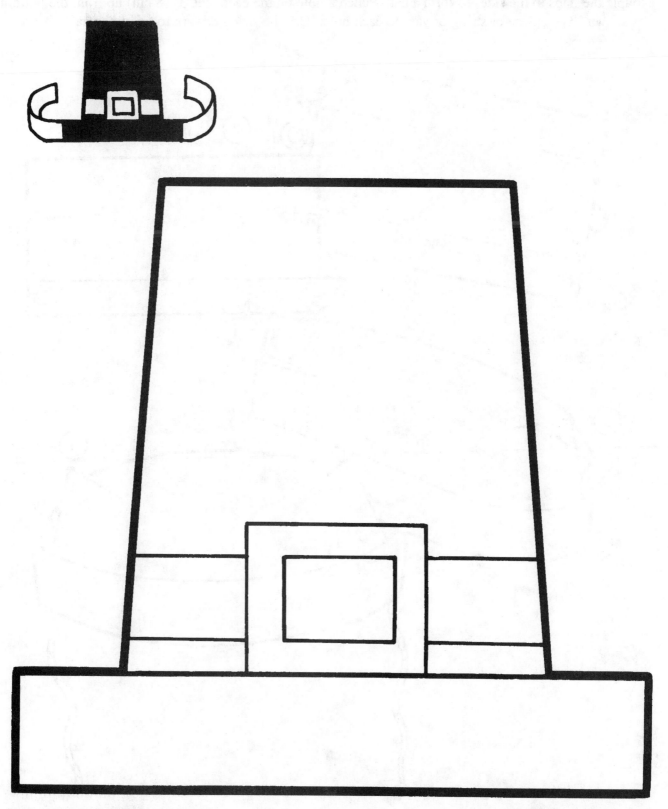

# Pilgrim Girl's Hat

Use the following directions to make each Pilgrim girl's hat.  Use a 12" x 18" (30 cm x 46 cm) piece of white construction paper.  Cut 6" (15 cm) slits on the sides 3" (8 cm) down from the top as shown. Fold up the front along a line that is 3" (8 cm) from the bottom.  Pull back on the top flaps that you cut. Staple the flaps to the sides to form a hat.  Punch a hole on the each side 3" (8 cm) up from the bottom as shown.  Tie a piece of string or yarn to each hole.  Use the string or yarn to tie on the hat.

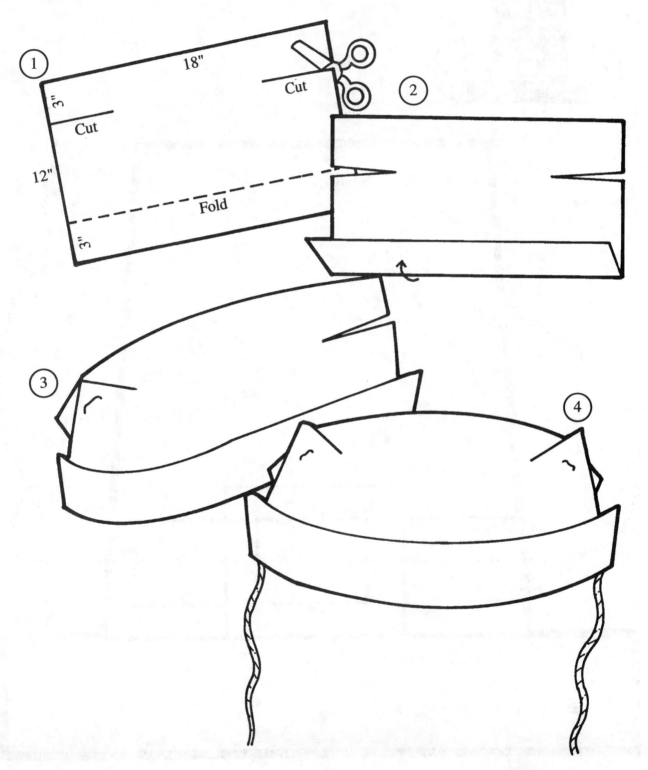

# Tying Shoes

Enlarge the following pattern by creating an overhead transparency of this page, then projecting and tracing it on poster board. Color the poster board shoe, and write "I can tie my shoes!" in large letters on the shoe as shown. Laminate the picture. Allow students to sign the shoe with water-based markers when they have learned how to tie their shoes.

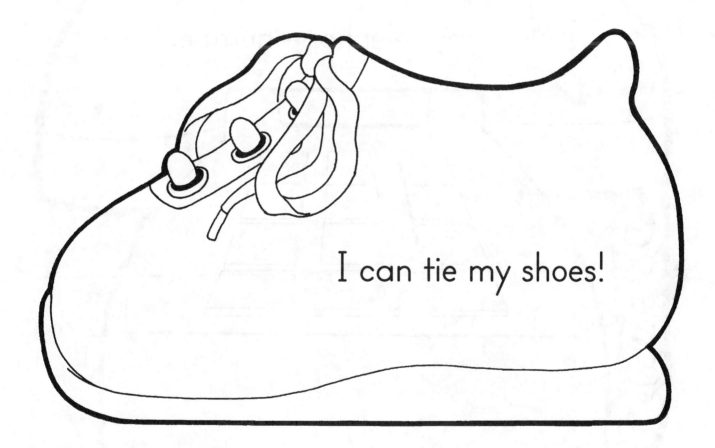

I can tie my shoes!

# My Telephone Number

Enlarge the following pattern by creating an overhead transparency of this page, then projecting and tracing it on poster board. Color the poster board telephone, and write "I know my telephone number!" in large letters on the telephone as shown. Laminate the picture. Allow students to sign the telephone with water-based markers when they have learned their telephone numbers.

# The Letter N

• *LETTER OF THE WEEK*

Display the key picture of A Nice Nurse Holding a Newspaper (page 107). Refer to it each day. During the week, have students make the letter **N** using a variety of materials such as noodles, crushed nutshells, torn pieces of newspaper, etc.

• *NATIVE AMERICANS*

1. Talk about Native Americans this week as an introduction to Thanksgiving. Point out that Christopher Columbus named the people he found already living here Indians because he thought he had traveled to India. Explain that there were many different tribes, or groups, living all over the Americas. Today we call these peoples Native Americans. Explain that you will be learning about how Native Americans lived in the 1600s—about 400 years ago—and that they do not live that way today. Read aloud one or more books with Native American tales to set the background. See the bibliography (page 106) for suggestions.

2. Remind students that there were no grocery stores or malls to shop at 400 years ago. Ask where they think the Native Americans might have gotten their food. Explain that they hunted deer, bear, buffalo, rabbits, squirrels, and other animals with bows and arrows that they made from sticks and sharpened rocks. They fished with spears that they made using sticks and rocks. Some Native Americans grew crops, such as beans, pumpkins, squash, and corn that they fertilized with fish heads and bones. They gathered nuts, berries, and fruits in the forest. Ask how the native peoples cooked their food. Lead students to conclude that they cooked outside over a fire. Explain that meat was turned on a stick over the fire. Vegetables were cooked in clay pots, which they made by hand. The women ground corn and made flat cakes which they cooked on a flat rock in the fire.

3. Show students pictures of Native American clothing. Ask: *Where did the Native Americans get their clothes?* Explain that they made their clothes from animal skins. Needles were made from small bones. The clothes were sewn together with thin strips of skin.

4. Talk about how the Native Americans traveled from place to place. Point out that they used canoes, which are boats made by burning and hollowing out trees.

5. Discuss some of the different kinds of traditional homes that Native Americans used. Tell students that Native Americans living in the plains had homes called tepees. These were made by tying tall poles together at the top and covering them with animal skins. They could take these houses with them as they roamed the plains, looking for buffalo to hunt. Native Americans living in the East had homes called wigwams or longhouses. Wigwams were rounded houses made of poles tied together and covered with bark or reed mats. Longhouses were made very much the same way. They were round on top but longer. The Native Americans that the Pilgrims met probably lived in longhouses. They were the Woodland Native Americans. Reproduce the Tepee (page 109) and the Longhouse (page 108) for students. Work together to compare/contrast these types of homes with the kinds of homes students live in today. Then allow them to color the pictures.

# The Letter N *(cont.)*

• *NATIVE AMERICANS (cont.)*

6. Let students make tepees from cone-shaped cups, coffee filters, or small paper plates. To use a paper plate cut it from the rim to the center. Shape the filter or plate into a cone to look like a tepee. Then staple the sides together. Have students decorate their tepees with Native American symbols. As an alternative, cut triangles from brown paper grocery bags. Have students make the bags look like deer skin by crumpling then smoothing them. Remind students to be sure to cut a door for each tepee. Then they can draw some Native American symbols on their tepees.

7. Show the class pictures of wigwams and longhouses. Have students make these structures with torn tan or gray construction paper. You may prefer to have students gather sticks or reeds and tie them together to make longhouses. Use the wigwams and longhouses to make a Native American village in a sandbox. Create the scenery, such as the woods near these homes, by using twigs, rocks, etc. Reproduce the Native Americans (page 91). Allow students to color the figures, tape them to craft sticks, and place them in the sandbox.

8. You may want to create a tepee for the class. Tie several long sticks together at the top and spread them out in a circle at the bottom. Cover the sticks with a sheet or burlap painted with Native American designs.

9. Some Native Americans used shells or beads for money. They called it *wampum.* Have students string beads or circular colored cereal onto yarn in a pattern to make wampum necklaces.

10. Help students make Native American vests from decorated brown paper grocery bags (page 110). You may wish to have them make headbands, as well.

11. Ask parents if their children have any food allergies or dietary restrictions. Then serve some popcorn—a gift from the Native Americans.

12. Practice making and reading symbols from a Native American sign language. Cut brown paper bags to look like animal skins. Crumple then smooth out the "skins." Model how to tell a story using picture symbols. Then encourage students to write their own stories by drawing picture symbols on the "skins."

13. After reading aloud *The Mud Pony* by Caron Lee Cohen (Scholastic, 1988), students may want to make their own ponies from dough. Add two parts flour to one part salt. Mix well. Add enough water to make the mixture into a dough. After the ponies are completed, allow the dough to dry. Students may paint their ponies if desired. Work together to write and illustrate stories about pony adventures. Combine the stories into a class book.

14. Read *Rainbow Crow* by Nancy van Laan (Alfred A. Knopf, 1989). Reproduce the Rainbow Crow (page 111). Have students use crayons or paints to decorate the crows in beautiful rainbow colors. Add the rainbow crows to your Thanksgiving mural (page 79).

15. Read aloud some books that describe different tribes of Native Americans. See the bibliography (page 106) for suggestions. Have students compare/contrast the lifestyles of some different tribes.

16. Share parts of Susan Jeffers' beautifully illustrated version of *Hiawatha* by Henry Wadsworth Longfellow (Dial, 1983). Ask: *Which animals would you choose for your brothers and sisters?*

# The Letter N *(cont.)*

## • *NATIVE AMERICANS (cont.)*

17. Obtain a copy of *Brother Eagle, Sister Sky,* a speech given by Chief Seattle during the 1850s and illustrated exquisitely by Susan Jeffers (Dial, 1991). First show the pictures and ask students what they think is happening or what they see in each. Then slowly read the book. Ask students what they think Chief Seattle was saying. Reread each page and talk about it. Ask who is responsible for taking care of the earth. *Ask:* If all the trees were cut down, what would happen to us? Lead students to conclude that we would die because trees give us oxygen. Point out that trees are also an important source of food for people and animals and wood for houses and furniture. If the flowers are our sisters and the animals are our brothers, we are to love and care for them just like we do our own families. We are to keep our rivers, streams, and oceans clear and clean because they are our life stream—without them we would die. When we do cut down trees to use, we should plant new ones. It takes a very long time for a tree to grow large enough for us to use. Point out that when we destroy the earth, we are destroying ourselves. When we love and preserve the earth, we are ensuring our continued existence.

18. Have students name some ways we can help preserve the earth. Ask: *What can we recycle or reuse at home and at school? How can we save trees by not wasting paper at school?* Talk about local recycling efforts. Begin a recycling program at your school if you do not already have one. Emphasize throughout the school year the need to care for our planet.

19. Read also Paul Goble's *I Sing for the Animals* (Bradbury, 1991). Compare the reverence for nature expressed in Goble's and Jeffers' books.

20. After reading aloud *The Legend of the Bluebonnet* and *The Legend of the Indian Paintbrush,* both by Tomie de Paola (Putnam, 1988), take the class for a walk outside and collect wild flowers and fall leaves. Help students learn the names of the flowers and leaves by finding them in field books. Give each student a magazine. Have students put the flowers or leaves between the pages. Stack the magazines and put heavy books on top to press, leaving them there to dry for about ten days. When they are dry, arrange them between two pieces of wax paper.  Put newspaper on top and press briefly with a warm iron. **Warning:** Students should never be allowed near a warm iron. Ask students to write legends about their favorite flowers.

## • *NAME*

Invite students to practice writing their names in a variety of ways. For example, they can sprinkle noodles or gelatin over glue. Display the names.

## • *NUMBERS*

Have students practice writing and identifying numbers 1–10. Have them write with crayons, markers, and chalk, as well as with pencils. You may also wish to have them practice writing in sand, salt, and pudding on small paper plates. Students can make numbers with clay, cookie and pretzel dough, and peanut butter clay (equal parts of peanut butter, honey, and powdered milk). Have them make "Noodle Numbers" by covering the outline of large numbers with glue and placing noodles on top. Encourage students to find numbers in newspapers, books, on calendars, cereal boxes, and all around the classroom.

# The Letter N *(cont.)*

### • *NUTS*

(**Note:** If students are to eat the nuts, check for any allergies. Make sure the nuts are in small pieces.)

1. Buy assorted edible nuts to use with various activities this week. Ask: *Where do nuts come from? What types of animals eat nuts?* Show students how to sort them and talk about the different kinds. Provide bowls in the discovery center for students to practice sorting nuts.

2. Give each student half of a clean egg carton with the numerals 1–6 written inside the cups. Have students use the egg cartons to practice making groups of nuts. Have them place one nut in the cup marked with a 1, two nuts in the cup marked 2, etc. Then have them do some simple addition and subtraction problems with the nuts. Example: Two pecans and three almonds make five nuts. You may also wish to make patterns using the nuts for students to duplicate.

3. Ask students to bring nutcrackers from home if possible. Discuss the different ways to crack nuts. Give students the opportunity to use their nutcrackers to shell and taste different kinds of nuts. **Warning:** Be sure to closely supervise students while they use the nutcrackers. Ask students which type of nut was their favorite and which they liked least. Have them brainstorm a list of foods, such as brownies or cookies, in which nuts are often included.

4. Add a collection of metal and plastic nuts, bolts, and washers to the discovery center. Students can develop fine-motor coordination by matching them up and screwing them together.

5. Read *The Nutcracker Ballet* by Carol Thompson (Scholastic, 1994) or *The Nutcracker* by Pat Whitehead (Troll, 1988). If possible, listen to a recording of the music from the ballet or watch the video. Let students move to "The Dance of the Sugarplum Fairy" and "The Waltz of the Flowers." If available, display an ornamental nutcracker soldier.

### • *NOODLE NECKLACE*

Use red, blue, yellow, and green dye to color wheel-shaped and large round macaroni. The dyes can be made by putting about one tablespoon (15 mL) of rubbing alcohol and twelve or more drops of food coloring in a reclosable plastic bag. Add the macaroni, seal the bag, and shake it until the desired color is reached. Spread the dyed macaroni on wax paper and allow it to dry overnight. Cut lengths of yarn to fit around students' necks. Students can choose two or three colors of macaroni and make a pattern if desired. Have them string the macaroni on the pieces of yarn. Tie each student's necklace in the back. Students may wish to wear their "Noodle Necklaces" with their Native American vests and headbands (page 110).

### • *NEWSPAPER*

Provide each student with a page from the newspaper. Have students circle uppercase and lowercase N's. Invite students to examine whole newspapers to determine what is inside of them. Discuss the different sections of the newspaper. Then ask students what the paper is made from and how to recycle newspapers.

### • *NEIGHBORHOOD*

Take students on a walk around the neighborhood where the school is located. Publish a Neighborhood Newspaper and distribute it to other classes in the school. Work together to draw a map of the neighborhood.

# The Letter N *(cont.)*

- ### *NIGHT*

  1. Read aloud a book that tells a story about the night. See the bibliography (page 106) for suggestions. Have students draw pictures of what some animals do at night. Then tell them to paint over the picture with a thin black wash. After the paint is dry, have them put foil stars in the sky. Ask each student to dictate a sentence about his or her picture. Write the sentence on the back of the picture. Combine the pictures into a book with black construction paper covers. Use white paint to write the title, "Nighttime," making the letters look fluffy.

  2. After reading *Dark Night, Sleepy Night* by Harriet Ziefert and Andrea Baruffi (Viking, 1994), you may wish to have students make a mural illustrating the book. Use black butcher paper for the background sky. Put sparkly stars cut from aluminum foil and a moon in the sky. Students may paint or color sleeping people in houses or animals with Z Z Z's coming up from the mural. They can draw pictures of where they sleep for the mural.

- ### *NURSE*

Invite your school nurse to visit your class to tell about his or her job. Have the nurse tell what things she or he likes about the job, why she or he decided to become a nurse, how she or he got to be a nurse, if she or he has been a nurse somewhere else, how his or her job is different from other nurses. If possible have the nurse bring and demonstrate the tools that nurses use. Have the nurse discuss ways to keep healthy: eating proper food, getting enough rest, keeping clean, and saying "no" to drugs and alcohol. The nurse may want to take this opportunity to send information home to parents. Write a class thank-you note and take students to the nurse's office to deliver it. After these positive experiences, students will feel more comfortable about visiting the nurse in times of illness or injury.

- ### *NEST*

Take the class on a fall walk to look for abandoned bird nests to take back to the classroom to observe. Caution students that nests should never be disturbed in the spring or summer when eggs or baby birds could be harmed.

- ### *NUTTY NOODLES AT NOON*

Make a toy clock show noon. Ask: *What do we do at noon?* Have students watch for noon on a real clock. Before noon, melt together chocolate chips and butterscotch chips, a 6-ounce (150 g) package of each. Mix in a bag or can of Chinese noodles and a small can of peanuts. Drop by tablespoons (15 mL) onto wax paper. Allow the noodle nests to cool before eating them at noon.

- ### *NICKEL*

Show students that a nickel is the same amount of money as five pennies. Provide them with nickels to make nickel rubbings of both sides. Have them practice identifying a nickel by itself and among other coins.

# Bibliography

**Books**

Baylor, Byrd. *I'm in Charge of Celebrations.* Scribner, 1986.

Begay, Shonto. *Ma'ii and Cousin Horned Toad: A Traditional Navajo Story.* Scholastic, 1992.

Caduto, Michael J. and Joseph Bruchac. *Keepers of the Animals: Native American Stories and Wildlife Activities.* Fulcrum, 1991.

Caduto, Michael J. and Joseph Bruchac. *Keepers of the Earth: Native American Stories and Environmental Activities for Children.* Fulcrum, 1989.

Carey, Valerie Scho. *Quail Song.* Putnam, 1990.

Cleaver, Elizabeth. *The Enchanted Caribou.* Atheneum, 1985.

Cohen, Caron Lee. *The Mud Pony.* Scholastic, 1988.

DeArmond, Dale. *Berry Woman's Children.* Greenwillow, 1985.

de Paola, Tomie. *The Legend of the Indian Paintbrush.* Putnam, 1988.

Duvall, Jill D. *A New True Book: The Tuscarora.* Childrens Press, 1991.

Esbensen, Barbara Juster. *Ladder to the Sky.* Little, Brown and Company, 1989.

Esbensen, Barbara Juster. *The Star Maiden.* Little, Brown and Company, 1988.

Goble, Paul. *Beyond the Ridge.* Bradbury, 1989.

Goble, Paul. *Buffalo Woman.* Bradbury, 1984.

Goble, Paul. *Death of the Iron Horse.* Bradbury, 1986.

Goble, Paul. *Dream Wolf.* Bradbury, 1990.

Goble, Paul. *The Great Race of the Birds and Animals.* Bradbury, 1985.

Goble, Paul. *Her Seven Brothers.* Bradbury, 1988.

Goble, Paul. *Iktomi and the Berries: A Plains Indian Story.* Orchard, 1989.

Goble, Paul. *Iktomi and the Boulder: A Plains Indian Story.* Orchard, 1988.

Goble, Paul. *Iktomi and the Buffalo Skull: A Plains Indian Story.* Orchard, 1991.

Goble, Paul. *Iktomi and the Ducks: A Plains Indian Story.* Orchard, 1990.

Goble, Paul. *I Sing for the Animals.* Bradbury, 1991.

Hayward, Linda, et. al. *People in My Neighborhood.* Children's Television Workshop, 1989.

Lepthien, Emilie U. *A New True Book: The Cherokee.* Childrens Press, 1985.

Longfellow, Henry Wadsworth; illustrated by Susan Jeffers. *Hiawatha.* Scholastic, 1992.

Lundell, Margo. *The Wee Mouse Who Was Afraid of the Dark.* Platt & Munk, 1990.

Murray, Patrick. *Ten Little Indians.* Kensington, 1988.

Osinski, Alice. *A New True Book: The Navajo.* Childrens Press, 1987.

Osinski, Alice. *A New True Book: The Sioux.* Childrens Press, 1984.

Potter, Eloise F. and John B. Funderburg. *Native Americans: The People and How They Lived.* North Carolina State Museum of Natural Sciences, 1986.

Roth, Susan L. *Kanahena, a Cherokee Story.* St. Martin's Press, 1988.

Shemie, Bonnie. *Houses of Bark.* Tundra, 1990.

Sneve, Virginia Driving Hawk. *Dancing Tepees: Poems of American Indian Youth.* Holiday House, 1989.

Steptoe, John. *The Story of Jumping Mouse.* Lothrop, Lee, & Shepherd, 1984.

Van Laan, Nancy. *Rainbow Crow.* Knopf, 1989.

Whitehead, Pat. *The Nutcracker.* Troll, 1988.

Ziefert, Harriet. *Dark Night, Sleepy Night.* Scholastic, 1989.

Zitkala-Sa. *Old Indian Legends.* University of Nebraska Press, 1985.

# A Nice Nurse Holding a Newspaper

Trace the following key picture on poster board to make a nurse. Then laminate the nurse. Refer to the key picture each day, especially when you discuss the calendar. At the end of the week, tape the nurse to a wall as part of an alphabet line-up.

# Longhouse

**Directions:** Color the picture.

When the Pilgrims came to America they met Native Americans who lived in longhouses. These homes were made from small trees covered with bark or reed mats.

# Tepee

**Directions:** Color the picture.

The tepee was a type of home used by Native Americans who lived on the plains.

# Native American Vest

Make a Native American vest for each student using the following directions. Open a large paper bag. Draw circles where the neck and arms will go. Draw a line up the center of bag for the opening in the front of the vest. Cut the center line from the bottom of the bag to the neck circle. Reinforce each side of the cut line with cellophane tape. Cut out the neck and arm circles. Cut some fringe along the bottom. Carefully cut small holes at equal distances along each side of the opening in the front of the vest. Cut pieces of yarn to tie each set of holes. Then allow the student to decorate the vest with pictures and designs using crayons, paints, or markers. You may also wish to have students make and decorate headbands to go with their vests.

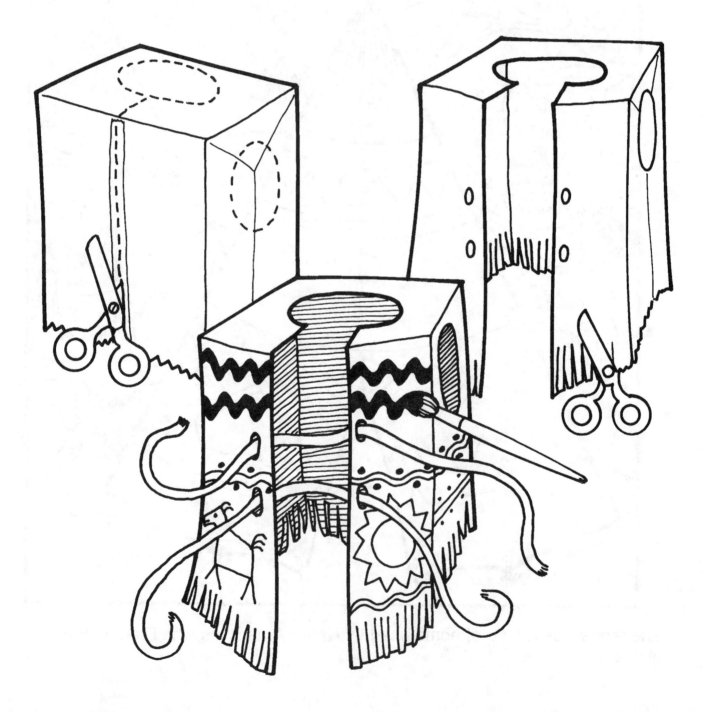

# Rainbow Crow

**Directions:** Use rainbow colors for the crow.  Add the crow to the Thanksgiving mural.

# The Letter C

## • DECEMBER

Reproduce A Colorful Christmas Candle (page 121).  Have them cut out and color the candles.  Then place their candles on the Class Tree (page 9).  Students may also enjoy adding other Christmas ornaments that begin with the letter **C** such as candy canes and cranberries.

## • LETTER OF THE WEEK

Display the key picture of the Colorful Christmas Candle (page 121).  Refer to it each day.  During the week, have students make the letter **C** using a variety of materials such as cotton (preferably recycled from medicine bottles), corn, coffee, cocoa, candy, etc.

## • CHRISTMAS GAME CENTER

1.  Create a Christmas Game Center.  Use a piece of green tagboard to draw and cut out a large Christmas tree.  Write the numerals 1–10 in random order, scattering them on the tree before laminating it.  Stick Velcro® under each numeral.  Make ornaments with 1–10 stickers or stars on them.  Place the other part of the Velcro® on the back of the ornaments.  Have students count the stickers or stars on the ornaments and put them on the tree under the proper numeral.

2.  Make additional games to teach desired skills using pages from holiday notepads.  For example, write uppercase letters on Santa's beard and lowercase letters on smaller gift or tree-shaped note pads.  Glue the notepad pages on tagboard and laminate them.  Ask students to match uppercase and lowercase letters and/or sequence the letters in alphabetical order.  In math you can write numerals on Christmas notepad pages or tagboard shapes for students to arrange in sequence.  Provide small wrapped candies, cotton balls, pom poms, dyed Christmas tree-shaped macaroni, etc. for counting practice.

3.  Cut out tagboard Christmas candles and flames using the pattern on page 122.  Write lowercase letters on the flames and uppercase letters on the candles.  As an alternative you can write numerals on the flames and put a corresponding number of dots or small Christmas stickers on the candles.  Students should match the correct flames to the candles.

4.  Make puzzles using large Christmas notepad pages or tagboard shapes.  For each piece of construction paper, write a letter on the top half, glue pictures beginning with that letter on the bottom half, cut in the middle to make into a puzzle.  Have students match letters and pictures by putting puzzles together.

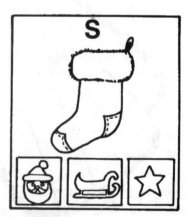

5.  Store the games in boxes with the tops and bottoms wrapped like Christmas gifts.

6.  Use individual Christmas tree patterns to keep track of who has completed each game.  Write each student's name on a page from a Christmas notepad or a construction paper tree.  Put numbers on the trees that correspond to the numbers for specific games that are used to practice particular skills (i.e., learning telephone numbers or home addresses).  Check a student's answers to a game.  If the skill is mastered, put a star or sticker over that number on his or her tree.  This will make it easy for you to know who needs to complete each game.  Students will enjoy taking their decorated trees home after all of the numbers are covered.

7.  A vast selection of seasonal notepads, large and small, may be used for practicing a variety of skills throughout the year.

# The Letter C *(cont.)*

## • *"C" ORNAMENTS FOR A CHRISTMAS TREE*

1. Collect evergreen cones if available. In a well ventilated area, use gold spray paint or adhesive to lightly cover the cones. If you prefer, the cones can be dipped in red tempera paint. While they are wet, have students sprinkle glitter on them. Use yarn to hang them on the tree. If cones are not available, have students carefully string cranberries and stale popcorn for the tree.

2. Make cornstarch clay using the following directions. Mix 2 cups (500 mL) of salt with ⅔ cup (170 mL) of water and boil in a microwave or on the stove. Mix 1 cup (250 mL) of cornstarch and ⅔ cup (170 mL) of cold water. Add the salt mixture and thoroughly combine. Gradually stir in additional dry cornstarch until the dough is stiff enough to roll out. Sprinkle the table and rolling pin with cornstarch. Have students help you roll out the dough and cut it with Christmas cookie cutters. Bells and stars work well. Poke a hole in the top of each ornament and hang it with a large paper clip. Allow the ornaments to dry for two days, turning them on the second day. Have students decorate them using tempera paint on the third day. Sprinkle the ornaments with glitter, confetti, or sequins while they are still wet. When they are dry, tie a strand of gold thread or cord to each, and hang the ornaments on the tree.

3. Provide red and white pipe cleaners. Demonstrate how to twist one red and one white pipe cleaner and curve one end to make an ornament that looks like a candy cane. Allow students to make pipe cleaner candy canes. Hang the candy cane ornaments on the tree.

4. Use tagboard to trace, color, and cut out gingerbread boys and girls (page 123). Spread glue over one side of each ornament and sprinkle with a mixture of cinnamon, cloves, nutmeg, and ginger. Allow the ornaments to dry. Then do the other sides. If you prefer, mix a large box of cinnamon with applesauce to make dough. Roll it out and cut with small cookie cutters. When dry, cut a hole in the top of each ornament and hang it with gold cord.

5. Mix 2 cups (500 mL) flour, 1 cup (250 mL) salt, 2 tablespoons (30 mL) cinnamon, 1 tablespoon (15 mL) cloves, 2 tablespoons (30 mL) ginger, 1 tablespoon (15 mL) nutmeg, and approximately 1 cup (250 mL) water. Roll out the dough and have students cut an ornament using a small gingerbread boy or girl cookie cutter. Punch a hole in the top of each ornament using a straw. Allow students to glue candies onto their ornaments. Wait until the glues thoroughly dried. Use pieces of ribbon to hang the ornaments.

6. Have students stuff gingerbread boy or girl cutouts with cotton balls dipped in a reclosable plastic bag of ginger, cinnamon, cloves, and nutmeg.

## • *CABOOSE AND CHRISTMAS DREAMS*

Read aloud *The Polar Express* by Chris Van Allsburg (Houghton Mifflin, 1985). Ask students what they might see if they were to sneak a ride on the Polar Express headed for the North Pole. On caboose-shaped paper (page 124), have students draw what they think Santa's home might look like and dictate a sentence about a gift they would ask for. Use the pages to make a "Christmas Caboose" class book with caboose-shaped covers. Then reproduce the smoke puffs (page 125). Have students cut pictures from catalogs of things they want for Christmas and glue them onto the smoke puffs. Cover a bulletin board with white paper for snow. Scatter the smoke puffs on the bulletin board above a Christmas train.

# The Letter C *(cont.)*

### • *COCOA, CANDY, AND COOKIES*

Ask parents if their children have any food allergies or dietary restrictions. Invite students to enjoy a warm cup of cocoa and Christmas nougat candy or Christmas cookies while you read aloud a Christmas story. See the bibliography (page 120) for suggestions.

### • *CALENDAR COUNT*

1. Use a calendar to count the number of days until Christmas, the number of days you come to school before Christmas, the number of days until winter, the number of days until the end of the year. Cut up old calendar pages to create number flash cards. Students may practice identifying, matching, and sequencing numbers, as well as counting Christmas candies.

2. Have each student make a red and green construction paper chain, and write the numerals 1–25 on the links. Students should remove one link each day, use it for a bracelet, and count the number of days remaining until Christmas. You may prefer to write the numerals 1–25 in circles on Mr. Claus's beard. Ask a volunteer to glue a piece of cotton onto a circle each day. Have the class count the remaining circles.

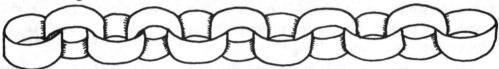

3. As you talk about the weather each day, ask if it is cloudy or clear, cold or cool.

### • *COUNTING*

1. Ask students to count out sets of 1–5 small objects (crayons, cookies, candies, etc.). If any are unable to do this, practice with them until they feel confident. Students who are ready to go on can practice making sets of 6–10.

2. Write the numbers 1–10 on construction paper Christmas trees (page 126). Students may glue on the appropriate number of pieces of Christmas-colored cereal. Counting and number identification skills may be reinforced in the Christmas Game Center (page 112).

### • *CHRISTMAS CANDLES*

Have students color Christmas candles (page 127) and tape them to a window facing outward. Cut out large yellow letters to spell *Peace* and tape them above the candles so that the word can be read from outside your classroom.

### • *CHRISTMAS CARDS*

1. Recycle old Christmas cards to create gifts for parents. Have students fold red or green construction paper in half. Then have them cut and glue pictures from the old cards onto the front of the construction paper cards. Take a class picture, make copies, and glue inside the cards. Let students write or dictate a holiday greeting and sign their names with love. Make coupons (page 133) good for chores around the house. Students can color, sign, and attach these to their cards.

2. Cut out pictures from old Christmas cards and have students sort them into different groups—Santas, trees, stockings, etc.

# The Letter C *(cont.)*

## • *CHRISTMAS ALPHABET*

Read *A Christmas Alphabet* by Carolyn Wells (Putnam, 1989). Make a class ABC book using pictures cut from Christmas cards. Obtain red and green construction paper. Write a letter on each piece of paper, alternating between red and green. Cooperatively decide on which page each picture belongs and glue them onto the construction paper. Laminate the pages for durability and bind the book using red and green yarn. Some picture suggestions follow for each letter:

**A** is for angels and animals.

**B** is for birds, bells, bears, and babies.

**C** is for candles, cats, candy canes, children, churches, carriages, and camels.

**D** is for dove, door, donkey, drummer boy, dreams, dogs, deer, and dolls.

**E** is for evergreens and elves.

**F** is for furry creatures, flowers, fire in the fireplace, and father.

**G** is for geese, greetings, gifts, and gingerbread.

**H** is for holly, horses, houses, and hearts.

**I** is for ice skates on ice and icicles.

**J** is for jingle bells and jolly.

**K** is for kindness, kings, and kisses.

**L** is for lights, list, lambs, and lamp.

**M** is for mouse, mailbox, manger, man, and mother.

**N** is for night, Noel, noise, and nutcracker.

**O** is for owl and ornaments.

**P** is for poinsettias, pajamas, pine cones, presents, puppies, partridges, and pear trees.

**Q** is for quiet quail and a quiet sleep under a quilt.

**R** is for rabbits, ribbons, and reindeer.

**S** is for Santa in his sleigh on a starry sky, singing songs as he fills stockings.

**T** is for teddy bears, trimming the tree, a train under the tree, and a tasty turkey on a table.

**U** is for the decorations that are up on the tree, Santa going up the chimney, and the presents under the tree.

**V** is for violins and voices in the village.

**W** is for wreaths and windows.

**X** is for X-mas trees.

**Y** is for yule logs and yellow starlight.

**Z** is for zestful celebrations and Santa's ZZZZ's after his long night!

# The Letter C *(cont.)*

### • *THE GINGERBREAD MAN*

1. Read several versions of *The Gingerbread Man,* including one in which he gets eaten and one in which he gets away. Make a gingerbread man-shaped Big Book using the pattern on page 128. Enlarge the pattern by making it into an overhead transparency and projecting it onto brown tagboard. Trace and cut out two copies of the pattern for the covers of the book. Decorate the front cover with holiday stickers, and write the title "The Gingerbread Man." Laminate both the front and back covers. Use large white paper to trace and cut out the gingerbread man pattern for each student. You may wish to have parent volunteers or older students help you do this. Give students the patterns and ask them to draw and dictate what they think chased the gingerbread man. Write the sentences under their drawings. As a class, vote on whether they think the gingerbread man got away or was eaten. Invite a volunteer to draw the last page and write a sentence that shows how the class wanted the story to end. Place students' pages between the tagboard covers. Punch holes in the left hands and the left feet and bind the book with metal rings. Hang the book on the stick-on plastic hooks on your classroom door or in the library center.

2. Help students use the following recipe to make and decorate some gingerbread people. After they have cooled, the class can enjoy eating them.

## Gingerbread People

### *Ingredients:*

| | |
|---|---|
| $2/3$ cup (170 mL) shortening | 1 egg |
| 1 tsp. (5 mL) baking powder | 1 tsp. (5 mL) cloves |
| $1/2$ cup (125 mL) sugar | 3 cups (750 mL) sifted flour |
| 1 tsp. (5 mL) soda | 1 tsp. (5 mL) ginger |
| $1/2$ cup (125 mL) molasses | $1/2$ tsp. (2.5 mL) salt |
| 1 tsp. (5 mL) cinnamon | $1/2$ tsp. (2.5 mL) nutmeg |

### *Directions:*

In a bowl, cream the shortening, sugar, and molasses. Add the egg and mix well. In a separate bowl, sift together the dry ingredients and then blend them into the creamed mixture. Chill the dough for a few hours or overnight. Roll the dough on a lightly floured cutting board until it is $1/4$"(0.6 cm) thick. Cut the dough with a 5–6" (13–15 cm) cookie cutter for gingerbread people. Carefully place the cookies on a greased baking sheet. Decorate the cookies with raisins or candies. Bake at 350° F (175° C) for 8–10 minutes. Makes about 30 cookies.

### • *COLORFUL CRISPIES*

Mix and melt together one box of fruit cereal with $1/4$ cup (63 mL) margarine and a bag of miniature marshmallows. Give each student about $1/3$ cup (83 mL) of the mixture to create a colorful Christmas tree or wreath. Have students decorate their colorful crispies by sticking on small candy decorations with some tube frosting.

# The Letter C *(cont.)*

## • *CHRISTMAS CONCENTRATION*

Glue duplicate Christmas card pictures onto 3" x 5" (8 cm x 13 cm) cards. Laminate the cards. Show students how to play Concentration by mixing up the cards and placing them face down. It is best to start with 12 cards (4 rows x 3 columns). Demonstrate how to turn two cards over so that the pictures can be seen. Explain that the purpose of the game is to try to match identical pictures. If the pictures match, tell students that they get to keep the cards. If the pictures do not match, tell them to turn the cards back over. Allow students to play the game with partners until all of the pictures are matched. Increase the number of cards as students become more skillful at "concentrating."

## • *COLORS*

Cut paper in the shape of Christmas ornaments. Place the ornament cutouts, paints, paintbrushes, and glitter in the art center. Allow students to go to the center to experiment with mixing colors on the ornament-shaped paper. Tell them to sprinkle glitter on the paint while it is still wet. These ornaments can be hung from the ceiling using yarn or string.

## • *CHRISTMAS CALICO CAT*

1. Make a stuffed cat for your library center. Cut out two cat-shaped pieces of Christmas calico print material, using the pattern on page 130. (Calico is a tiny print material usually made from cotton.) Sew the pattern together most of the way and stuff with fiberfill. Then finish sewing the pattern together. Add button eyes and a stuffed tail. If you prefer, the tail can be made from red and/or green braided yarn.

2. Ask students to imagine what Calico Cat likes to do at Christmas. Have them write a story about "Calico Cat's Country Christmas Cottage" and make a house-shaped book. For the covers make two copies of the cottage pattern (page 129). Color the cottages, mount them on tagboard, and laminate them. Give each student a house-shaped piece of white paper. Let students draw Calico Cat inside its cottage which is decorated for Christmas. Have them dictate a sentence about what the cat likes to do at Christmas as you write it below their pictures.

3. Reproduce the Christmas Cottage (page 131). Write a student's address on each cottage. If they are able, allow students to write their own addresses on their cottages. Have them color their cottages and use the picture to help them learn their home addresses. Add the cottages to "The Polar Express" bulletin board described under the heading *Caboose and Christmas Dreams* (page 113).

## • *CARTON COTTAGES*

Have students make carton cottages according to either set of directions provided on page 132. Allow them to take their cottages home as gifts for family members. If you prefer, have students place their cottages in the block center to make a "Christmas City." You may wish to add other features, such as miniature trees, a toy train, toy cars, and small plastic figures, to the city.

# The Letter C *(cont.)*

- **CARE PACKAGES**

1. Read aloud *Claude the Dog: A Christmas Story* by Dick Gackenbach (Scholastic, 1974). Ask: *What did Claude do with his Christmas gifts? What is Christmas all about? What is important to remember at Christmas?* Try to elicit the response from students that Christmas is not about what you can get—but about what you can give. Christmas is about caring—for those you love as well as for those less fortunate than you are. Have your class organize a Christmas drive to collect canned goods, clothes, and toys. Take these items to a local social services agency for distribution.

2. Have students make "Care Packages" by putting cookies and candies in plastic sandwich bags, tying them with red and/or green yarn, and decorating them with holiday stickers. Have them deliver these packages to some special helpers in your building such as the art, music, and gym teachers; the principal and assistant principal; the secretaries and/or clerks; the librarian; the nurse; the custodians; etc.

- **COUPONS**

Collect coupons from newspapers and magazines, and place them in the housekeeping center. Students may use them when they role-play buying groceries. They may like to choose their favorites to add to their Christmas cards for their parents (page 114). You may wish to send a note home requesting parents to send extra coupons that can be donated with the canned food collections.

- **COCONUT CLOUDS**

Ask parents if their children have any food allergies or dietary restrictions. Show a whole coconut to the class. Point out that this is the largest seed in the world. Coconuts come from palm trees in tropical places, like Hawaii, that are always warm. Find the coconut's "eyes" (three spots). Make holes in these with a nail and pour out the coconut milk. Allow students to taste some. Use a hammer to crack open the coconut. Pry out the white meat, peel, and have students taste this, as well. Shred the meat of the coconut in a food processor. In a large bowl, combine the shredded coconut with a can of pineapple tidbits, sliced oranges (a can of mandarin oranges can be substituted), bananas, grapes, and a bag of miniature marshmallows. Moisten with vanilla yogurt and refrigerate a few hours or overnight. Then allow students to eat the Coconut Clouds.

- **CALL**

1. Invite students to practice making phone calls on a play telephone. Role-play what to say if someone calls their homes. Stress that they should never to say they are home alone. Tell students to always say that "Mom (or Dad) cannot come to the phone now." Model how to take a message. Allow them to practice taking messages.

2. Review with students how to dial 911 in case of an emergency. Emphasize that this number is to be used only if there is a fire, if someone is very sick or injured and needs an ambulance, or if they need the police. Role-play various emergency situations.

# The Letter C *(cont.)*

## • *CLOCKS*

Make clocks by writing numbers around small paper plates. Cut out poster board clock hands, and attach them to the center of the plates with brads. Demonstrate how to tell time by the hour. Have students use their paper plate clocks to practice telling time. Talk about what students do at various times during the day and night.

## • *CRUSTACEANS*

Show pictures of crustaceans
(page 173). Have students role-play
being crustaceans.

## • *CLOTHES*

Look on the calendar to find out when winter begins. Discuss what kinds of clothes are necessary for cold weather. Allow students to cut pictures out of catalogs to make a "Winter Clothes Collage." Add scraps of corduroy to the collage, explaining that this fabric is popular for winter clothing. Have students touch the corduroy and talk about how it feels. Read aloud *Corduroy* by Don Freeman (Viking, 1968). Ask: *What toy would you like to rescue from a toy store?*

## • *CORNSTARCH*

Mix cornstarch with water, keeping the mixture thick. Put it in a plastic container. As students play with it, they will discover it turns from a solid to a liquid as they move it through their hands.

## • *CRYSTALS*

Obtain reference books about crystals. See the bibliography (page 120) for suggestions. If possible, have students observe different kinds of crystals (salt, sugar, snow) on black construction paper with magnifying glasses. Use the following recipes to create several crystals for your class to observe.

1. Salt crystals: Pour ¹/₂ cup (125 mL) boiling water in an aluminum foil pie pan. Add salt, stirring to dissolve it. Continue adding salt, until no more can be dissolved in the water. Allow the solution to cool. Place in a location where it will not be disturbed. Large salt crystals will form on the sides and bottom of the pan.
2. Epsom Salts® crystals: In a small jar, mix 1 tablespoon (15 mL) of Epsom Salts® with 1 tablespoon (15 mL) of water. Add ¹/₄ teaspoon (1.2 mL) of food coloring. Have students watch with magnifying glasses as the water evaporates and the crystals appear.
3. Coal or charcoal crystals: Put several pieces of coal or charcoal on a disposable plate. Mix 3 tablespoons (45 mL) of each: salt, water, and laundry bluing. Add 1 tablespoon (15 mL) of ammonia. Mix and slowly spoon over the charcoal. Crystals should form in about 24 hours.

## • *COMPUTER*

Set up a classroom computer center if possible. Provide a variety of software to reinforce skills that students are learning this year. Examples include the alphabet, numbers, counting, adding, subtracting, and writing stories. The computer provides excellent motivation for students to practice these skills. There are also several children's books available on CD-ROM.

# Bibliography

**Books**

Anno, Mitsumasa. *Anno's Counting Book.* Harper & Row, 1977.

Beall, Pamela Conn and Susan Hagen Nipp. *Wee Sing for Christmas.* Price, Stern, Sloan, 1986.

Bemelman, Ludwig. *Madeline's Christmas.* Viking Penguin, 1985.

Berenstain, Stan and Jan. *The Berenstain Bears Meet Santa Bear.* Random House, 1984.

Brett, Jan. *Wild Christmas Reindeer.* Putnam, 1990.

Bright, Robert. *Georgie's Christmas Carol.* Weekly Reader, 1975.

Bullis, Douglas. *Crystals: The Science, Mysteries, and Lore.* Crescent Books, 1990.

Carle, Eric. *Have You Seen My Cat?* Putnam, 1987.

Cosgrove, Stephen. *Jingle Bear.* Price, Stern, Sloan, 1985.

Curran, Eileen. *Little Christmas Elf.* Troll, 1985.

Darling, Peter. *Crystal Identification.* Mallard Press, 1991.

Fleming, Denise. *Count!* Scholastic, 1992.

Kahn, Peggy. *The Care Bears Help Santa.* Random House, 1984.

Mercer, Ian F. *Crystals.* Harvard University Press, 1990.

Paris, Pat. *Christmas Around the World.* Troll, 1990.

Rosenburg, Amye. *The Biggest, Most Beautiful Christmas Tree.* Western, 1985.

Seuss, Dr. *How the Grinch Stole Christmas!* Random House, 1985.

Thaler, Jane. *Gus Was a Christmas Ghost.* Weekly Reader, 1970.

Van Allsburg, Chris. *The Polar Express.* Houghton Mifflin, 1985.

Wells, Carolyn. *A Christmas Alphabet.* Putnam, 1989.

Whitehead, Pat. *The Nutcracker.* Troll, 1988.

**Technology**

*Champ on Ice!* (Video about Champ the bear); 8 min. Troll Associates, Catalog Sales Dept., 100 Corporate Dr., Mahwah, NJ 07498; 1-800-929-8765.

*Clouds.* (Video); 8 min. Troll Associates, Catalog Sales Dept., 100 Corporate Dr., Mahwah, NJ 07498; 1-800-929-8765.

*Copycat Dog.* (Video about a dog who acts like other farm animals); 9 min. Troll Associates, Catalog Sales Dept., 100 Corporate Dr., Mahwah, NJ 07498; 1-800-929-8765.

*Hi, Cat!* (Videotape/Videodisc includes *Pet Show* and *Goggles*); 35 min. Coronet/MTI Film and Video, P.O. Box 2649, Columbus, OH 43216; 1-800-321-3106.

*Little Christmas Elf.* (Cassette); Troll Associates, Catalog Sales Dept., 100 Corporate Dr., Mahwah, NJ 07498; 1-800-929-8765.

*Three Little Chicks.* (Video about three chicks hatching and playing); 8 min. Troll Associates, Catalog Sales Dept., 100 Corporate Dr., Mahwah, NJ 07498; 1-800-929-8765.

# A Colorful Christmas Candle

Enlarge the following key picture by creating an overhead transparency of this page and projecting it onto poster board. Then trace each part to make a red candle, green candlestick holder, and yellow flame. Cut out the poster board pieces and glue them together. Allow the glue to dry and laminate the candle. Refer to the key picture each day, especially when you discuss the calendar (page 9). At the end of the week, tape the candle to a wall as part of an alphabet line-up.

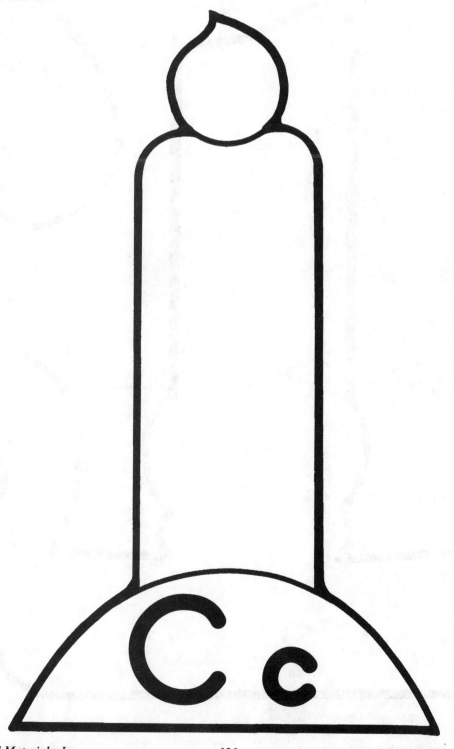

# Candle Game

Use the pattern below to make green and/or red tagboard candles and yellow tagboard flames. Write uppercase letters on the candles and lowercase letters on the flames. Have students sequence letters and/or pair uppercase and lowercase letters by correctly matching the flames with the candles.

# Ornament Patterns

Use the large patterns to have students make ornaments from gingerbread boys and girls. Use the small patterns to have them make cinnamon ornaments.

# Caboose

**Directions:** Draw a picture on the caboose to show what Santa's home looks like.

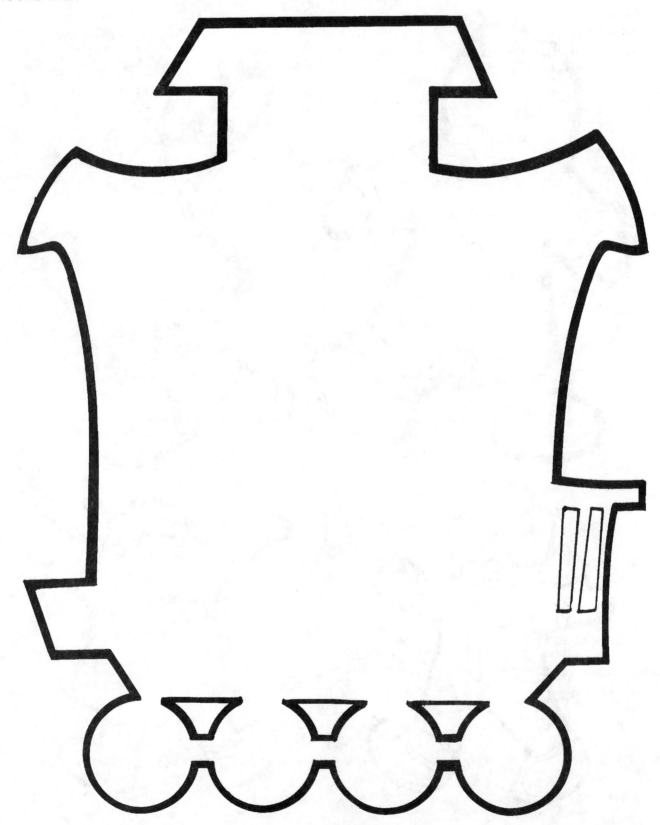

# Christmas Dreams on the Polar Express

Reproduce the smoke puffs for students. Have students cut out pictures from catalogs of things they want for Christmas. Ask them to glue the pictures onto their smoke puffs. Place the smoke puffs above the Christmas train bulletin board (page 113).

# Christmas Counting

Write numerals in the stars on the tree patterns shown below. Reproduce the patterns on green construction paper. Have students count out the correct number using pieces of cereal and place them on the trees according to the numerals shown in the stars.

# Candle Decoration

**Directions:** Color for the Class Tree and to decorate your windows.

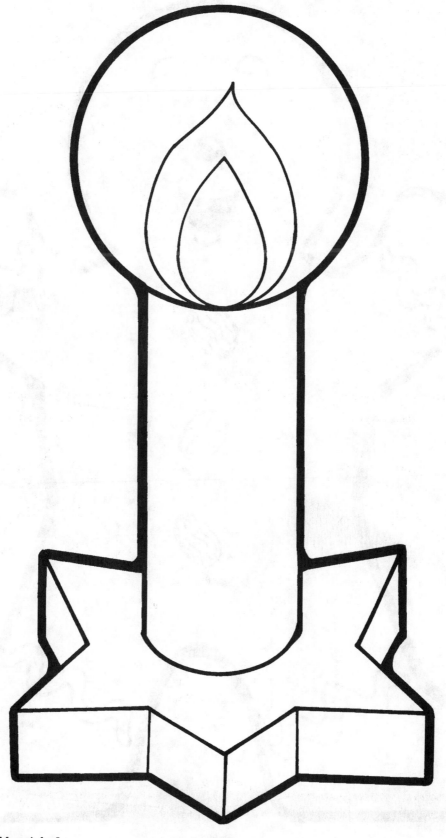

# Gingerbread Man Big Book

Create a Big Book, using the directions on page 116 and the pattern shown below.

# Calico Cat Christmas Cottage

# Calico Cat

Use the pattern shown below and the directions on page 117 to make a stuffed cat for your library center.

Cat Body Front
Cut 1

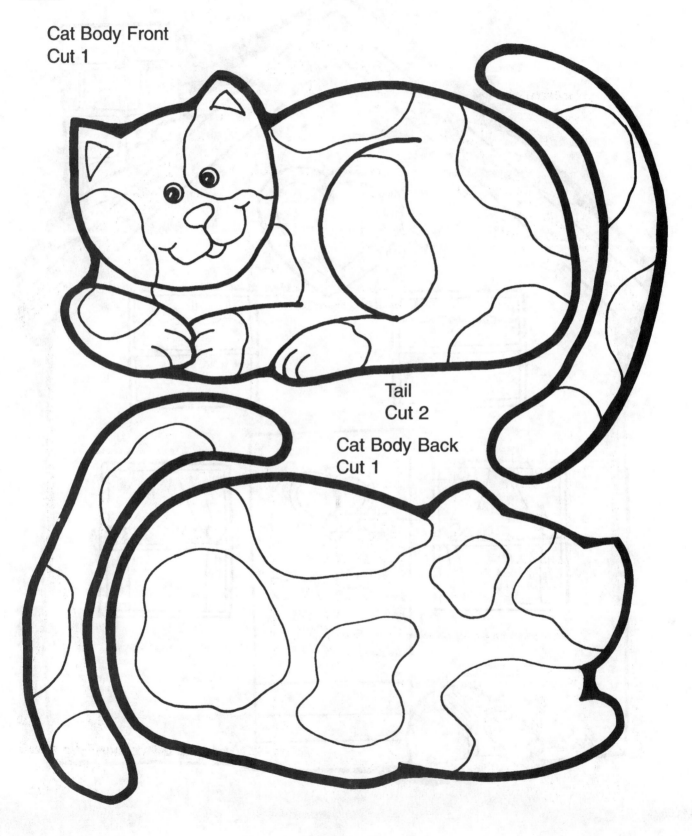

Tail
Cut 2

Cat Body Back
Cut 1

# My Christmas Cottage

**Directions:** Color the cottage.  Use the picture to learn your home address.

# Carton Cottage

Ask students to save small empty milk cartons. Thoroughly wash and dry the milk cartons. Help students cover the cartons with wrapping paper. Tell them to use construction paper and scissors to add features, such as doors, windows, chimneys, and wreaths to the carton cottages. Have them glue cotton to the top of the chimney for smoke. Students may wish to make small artificial gifts to place inside their cottages.

As an alternative activity, have students use their cartons to make small gingerbread houses. For each house, break graham crackers so that there are four pieces that are large enough to cover the sides of the milk carton and two pieces that are large enough to cover the top surfaces. Have students frost the front and back of the graham cracker "walls," and place those pieces on the sides of the carton. Then have them frost the front and back of the graham cracker "roof," and place those pieces on the top surfaces of the carton. Show them how to fill the cracks between the graham crackers with frosting. Help students use colored icing in a tube to draw a door and some windows. Allow students to decorate their gingerbread houses with candies. Use these houses for decorative purposes only.

# Christmas Coupons

**Directions:** Fill in the coupons.  Cut them apart.  Then give them away as gifts.

## Valuable Coupon
Good for one room cleaning.

To: _____

From: _____

## Valuable Coupon
Good for one room cleaning.

To: _____

From: _____

## Valuable Coupon
Good for one kitchen duty.

To: _____

From: _____

## Valuable Coupon
Good for one kitchen duty.

To: _____

From: _____

## Valuable Coupon
Good for one trash take out.

To: _____

From: _____

## Valuable Coupon
Good for one trash take out.

To: _____

From: _____

## Valuable Coupon
I will do one job for you.

To: _____

From: _____

## Valuable Coupon
I will do one job for you.

To: _____

From: _____

# The Letter S

## • *JANUARY*

Reproduce the Cardinal pattern (page 140) and Blue Jay pattern (page 141) for students. Have them cut out and color these snowbirds. Then place their snowbirds on the Class Tree (page 9).

## • *LETTER OF THE WEEK*

Display the key picture of A Smiling Snowman (page 139). Refer to it each day. During the week, have students make the letter **S** using a variety of materials such as salt, sugar, sand, star stickers, seeds, sequins, sponge paint, stripes, etc.

## • *SNOW*

1. Read aloud *The Snowy Day* by Ezra Jack Keats (Viking, 1962). If possible, do the following activity on a Friday so it can dry over the weekend. Make some "soap snow" by mixing equal parts of detergent flakes and water with an electric mixer on high. Cut white bulletin board paper to fit the length of a bulletin board. Place it on a table or on the floor. Allow students to spread the soap snow all over the paper. They may want to make tracks with their fingers or try to make snowballs. Ask: *Will this snow melt? Why or why not?* Provide them with evergreen tree cutouts. The pattern on page 126 can be utilized for this purpose. Have students dab "soap snow" on the trees. Put blue butcher paper on the top part of the bulletin board to represent the sky and the "soap snow" white paper at the bottom to represent the ground. Scatter the evergreens around in the "snow."

2. Ask students to draw small pictures of themselves wearing snowsuits, mittens, and snowboots. Add these to the snow scene bulletin board described above.

3. Reproduce the snowman (page 139) for students. Have them color the scarf, hat, facial features, and buttons. Prepare a mixture made from equal parts of Epsom salts and warm water. Allow students to paint their snowmen with the mixture. Allow the pictures to dry so sparkly crystals will form. Add the snowmen to the snow scene bulletin board described above.

## • *SNOWPEOPLE*

1. Provide toothpicks and various sizes of Styrofoam® balls in the art center for students to build snowpeople. As an alternative to Styrofoam® balls, silver glitter can be added to white dough made from a mixture of 2 cups (500 mL) flour, 1 cup (250 mL) salt, and water. Allow students to use fabric scraps, construction paper, buttons, pom poms, etc. to decorate their snowpeople.

2. Have students draw snow pictures on gray, blue, or black construction paper using white chalk, crayon, or paint applied with cotton swabs. Have them add cotton ball snowpeople.

## • *SHARKS, SAND DOLLAR, AND GIANT SQUID*

Show pictures of sea animals whose names start with the letter **S**. You may wish to use the pictures in this book—sharks (page 169), a sand dollar (page 170), and a giant squid (page 171). Divide the class into cooperative learning groups. Have students paint on butcher paper to show a sea scene with their favorite sea creatures.

# The Letter S *(cont.)*

## • *SHAVING CREAM*

1. Invite students to create a snow village by molding shaving cream on a table top.

2. Read aloud *Frosty the Snowman* by Annie North Bedford (Western, 1950). If possible, have students listen to and learn the song. Watch the video *Frosty's Winter Wonderland and the Leprechauns' Gold* (Live Home Video, 1991). Make a snowman-shaped Big Book. On individual snowman-shaped pages, students should complete the sentence, "When I put the magic hat on my snowman's head, he. . . ." or "When some magic snow fell last night, I built a snowman and he . . . ." Ask students to draw pictures to illustrate their stories.

## • *SOFT MITTENS*

1. Read *The Mitten* by Jan Brett (Putnam, 1989). Reproduce the mitten pattern (page 142) on various colors of construction paper. Allow each student to choose a construction paper mitten. Ask them to draw pictures of the animals that live in their mittens (page 143) and complete the sentence to tell what their animals are. Glue their pictures inside the construction paper mittens. Staple the backs of the mittens around the snow scene bulletin board (page 134). Be sure you do not staple the mittens closed. Students should still be able to open and read them.

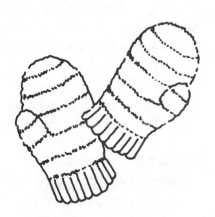

2. Teach students to recite *The Three Little Kittens* by Paul Galdone (Clarion, 1986).

## • *MITTEN GAMES*

1. Cut ten mitten shapes from each of two different colors of tagboard, using the pattern on page 144. Write the numerals 1–10 on one set and corresponding number words on the other set. Have students sequence numbers and match pairs. Then, if capable, they can count out the correct number of white pom pon or cotton ball "snowballs" onto the mittens.

2. Cut two more sets of 26 mittens from two more colors of tagboard. Write uppercase letters on one set and lowercase letters on the other set for students to sequence and match.

3. You may wish to make a third set of mittens for students to match rhyming words or the beginning sounds of picture names.

## • *SIX AND SEVEN*

Ask: *How many ways can you make 6 and 7?* Make groups of 6 and 7 out of blocks, interlocking cubes, bear counters, toothpicks, star stickers, and other classroom materials. Have students write 6 and 7 with glue and sprinkle with sand, salt, or sugar.

## • *SENSES*

1. Review the five senses. Point out that we use our eyes to see and our noses to smell. Set up a smell center. Include things such as herbs, spices, coffee, cocoa, orange peel, onion, evergreen tree needles, perfume, vinegar, vanilla, mint, and lemon extract, etc. Place each sample in a reclosable plastic bag. Liquids may be put on cotton balls and then enclosed in bags.

2. Challenge students to try to identify the scent from stickers that smell without seeing what they are.

# The Letter S *(cont.)*

## • *SANDPAPER*

Cut out letters and numbers from sandpaper. Students may identify them using their sense of touch instead of sight. Discuss how the sandpaper feels. Provide objects for sorting and boxes labeled *Rough, Smooth, Hard,* and *Soft.*

## • *SOUND*

Make a string telephone for each pair of students. Thoroughly wash two empty cans with one end cut out of each. Hammer down any rough edges to avoid injuries. Punch a hole in the center of the remaining end of each can. Insert the end of a 6-foot (1.8 cm) piece of string in each hole. Then tie a large knot in each end so it will remain in the can. Have students stretch the string and talk into the cans. Explain that sound travels from one can to the other, through the string.

## • *STRANGERS*

Read aloud *The Berenstain Bears Learn About Strangers* by Stan and Jan Berenstain (Random House, 1985). Talk about who strangers are and why students should never talk to them.

## • *STAMPS*

1. Obtain postage stamps. Have students examine and sort the stamps into categories of their choosing. Then allow students to make a stamp collage.

2. Give each child ¼ of a piece of construction paper that has been cut with pinking shears on each side like a stamp. Ask them to design their own personal postage stamp.

## • *DR. SEUSS*

Enjoy as many Dr. Seuss books as possible this week.

## • *SUPERMARKET*

Set up a supermarket in the housekeeping center. Collect empty and cleaned cans and boxes from home to stock the store. Ask those who are saving the cans to open them upside down so they will look unopened when the children are playing with them. Allow students to use coupons when role-playing in the supermarket.

## • *SEEDS*

Add a variety of seeds to your chart (page 10).

## • *STRAWBERRY SNOWBALL SUNDAE AND S'MORES*

Ask parents if their children have any food allergies or dietary restrictions.

1. Add sweetened strawberries to scoops of vanilla ice cream and top with whipped topping. (For easier prepation, use frozen strawberries that have been thawed.)
2. Have students layer a graham cracker square, a square of milk chocolate candy (equivalent in size to the graham cracker square), and a marshmallow. Microwave on high for 10–15 seconds, until the marshmallow begins to melt. Add another graham cracker square on top and allow students to eat them when they have cooled.

# The Letter S *(cont.)*

## • *SKY SEARCHERS, SUN, AND SPARKLING STARS*

1. Have students pretend that a sand table is the moon. Put up black butcher paper behind it for the sky. Cut a large circle of yellow butcher paper for the sun. Let students smear red and orange chalk on the sun. Scatter Sparkling Stars (page 145) around the sun. Explain that if students were standing on the moon, they would see the earth in the sky, just as we see the moon in the sky while standing on the earth. Cut out a small blue circle for the earth. Lightly rub with glue and have volunteers dab cotton clouds all over it. Put it in your sky. Tell students that, since there is no air on the moon, the sky looks black there instead of blue. Point out that nothing grows on the moon because there is no water. There are sand and rocks everywhere. Several astronauts, or space explorers, traveled to the moon in the 1960s and brought back some rocks. However, no one has been there in several years. Ask parents to take their children outside for several nights and observe the changes in the shape of the moon. As it gets larger, it becomes a round full moon. As it gets smaller, it disappears, and we call it a new moon. It reappears as a small crescent, then it gets larger again.

2. Provide simple basic facts about the sun and the stars. See the bibliography (page 138) for suggested books. The sun is a huge hot ball of burning gases. Hold up a beach ball and a grain of sand. Explain that if the sun were the size of a beach ball, the earth, where we live, would be the size of a grain of sand. Tell students that the sun looks small because it is far away. Have students observe playground equipment from afar and notice how it looks as they walk closer.

3. Tell students that the sun is actually a small star. However, the stars at night appear so much smaller than our sun because they are farther away. Ask: *Where do the stars go during the daytime?* Lead students to conclude that it is too light to see the stars because the sun is so bright. Shine a penlight in the room with the lights on and with the lights off so students can see that it is much more visible with the lights off.

4. Explain that we get heat and light from the sun. Plants need the sun to grow. Put a plant in a dark closet for a few days and have students observe what happens to it. Cut a snowflake from paper and put it on top of a piece of black paper in the sunlight. Remove the snowflake and ask: *What do you see?* Show students how water changes its state of matter from solid (ice) to liquid (water) to gas (clouds). Discuss the water cycle and its importance.

## • *SPACESHIP*

Have students help decorate an appliance box to look like a spaceship. Make space helmets out of paper bags or recycled large plastic milk jugs. Make the face area by cutting off the tops and handles of the jugs. Allow students to decorate them.

## • *SPARKLING SUGAR STARS*

Invite students to help you make cookies. Slice refrigerated sugar cookie dough and cut with a star-shaped cookie cutter. Sprinkle the top with sugar mixed with a few drops of food coloring before baking according to directions. Allow students to eat the cookies as they pretend to journey to the moon in their spaceship.

# Bibliography

## Books

Aliki. *My Five Senses.* HarperCollins, 1989.

Asch, Frank. *Skyfire.* Prentice Hall, 1984.

Barasch, Lynne. *A Winter Walk.* Ticknor and Fields, 1993.

Barkan, Joanne. *A Very Merry Snowman Story.* Scholastic, 1992.

Bedford, Annie North. *Frosty the Snowman.* Western, 1950.

Berenstain, Stan and Jan. *The Berenstain Bears Learn About Strangers.* Random House, 1985.

Branley, Franklyn M. *Snow Is Falling.* Crowell, 1986.

Brett, Jan. *The Mitten.* Putnam, 1989.

Carle, Eric. *Draw Me a Star.* Scholastic, 1990.

Cole, Joanna. *The Magic School Bus® Lost in the Solar System.* Scholastic, 1990.

Drexler, Carol Joan, retold by. *Sleeping Beauty.* Troll, 1970.

Flanagan, Terry. *Charlie Brown Is Lost.* Random House, 1984.

Fowler, Allan. *Seeing Things.* Childrens Press, 1991.

Fowler, Allan. *Smelling Things.* Childrens Press, 1991.

Fowler, Allan. *The Sun Is Always Shining Somewhere.* Childrens Press, 1991.

Fowler, Allan. *The Sun's Family of Planets.* Childrens Press, 1992.

Gibbons, Gail. *Sun Up, Sun Down.* HBJ, 1987.

Hammond, Lucille. *Glow in the Dark Trip to the Planets.* Western, 1990.

Harrison, David. *Wake Up, Sun.* Random House, 1986.

Hines, Anna Grosnickle. *Sky All Around.* Clarion, 1989.

Hoban, Tana. *Dots, Spots, Speckles, and Stripes.* Greenwillow, 1987.

Keats, Ezra Jack. *The Snowy Day.* Viking, 1962.

Loretan, Sylvia and Jan Lenica. *Bob the Snowman.* Scholastic, 1988.

Moche, Dinah L. *If You Were an Astronaut.* Western, 1985.

Pearson, Susan. *My Favorite Time of Year.* Scholastic, 1988.

Peters, Lisa W. *The Sun, the Wind, and the Rain.* Holt, 1988.

Pluckrose, Henry. *Smelling.* Watts, 1986.

Smith, Kathie B. *Rand McNally Question Books: The Senses.* Macmillan, 1986.

Smith, Kathie B. *Seeing.* Troll, 1988.

Smith, Kathie B. *Smelling.* Troll, 1988.

Smith, Kathie B. *Thinking.* Troll, 1987.

Smith, Kathie B. *Touching.* Troll, 1987.

Tibo, Gilles. *Simon and the Snowflakes.* Tundra, 1988.

Wandelmaier, Roy. *Now I Know Stars.* Troll, 1985.

Wandelmaier, Roy. *Stars.* Troll, 1985.

## Technology

*Sammy's Science House.* (Software about plants, animals, seasons, weather); CD-ROM for MAC, WIN, and DOS; National School Products, 101 East Broadway, Maryville, TN 37804; 1-800-251-9124.

*Stars.* (Video); 8 min. Troll Associates, Catalog Sales Dept., 100 Corporate Dr., Mahwah, NJ 07498; 1-800-929-8765.

# A Smiling Snowman

Enlarge the following key picture by creating an overhead transparency of this page and projecting it onto poster board. Then trace the following key picture on poster board to make a white snowman with a red hat. Cut out the poster board pieces and glue them together. Allow the glue to dry. Paint the snowman with equal parts of Epsom salts and warm water. Allow the mixture to dry so sparkling crystals will form. Refer to the key picture each day, especially when you discuss the calendar (page 9). At the end of the week, tape the snowman to a wall as part of an alphabet line-up.

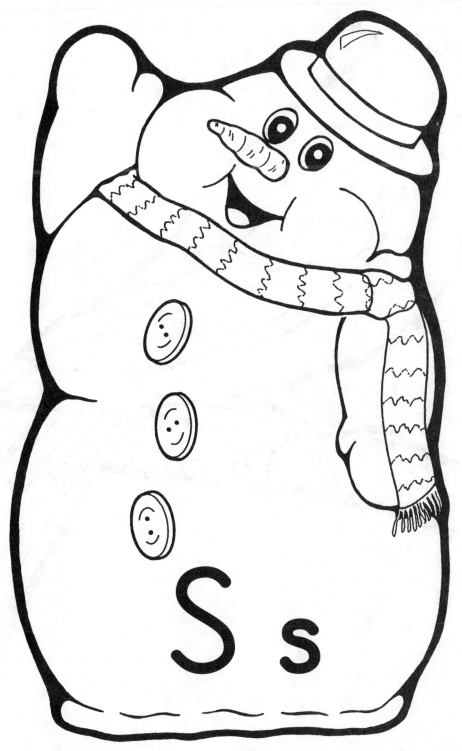

# Cardinal

**Directions:** Color and cut out the cardinal. Add it to the Class Tree.

# Blue Jay

**Directions:** Color and cut out the blue jay. Add it to the Class Tree.

# Mittens

Cut out the mitten pattern. Select construction paper that is a variety of colors. Fold the pieces of construction paper in half. Place the pattern along the fold of one piece of paper. Trace and cut out the pattern from the paper. Continue tracing and cutting from the other pieces of construction paper. Ask each student to select a construction paper mitten. Have students glue their drawings (page 143) inside the construction paper mittens.

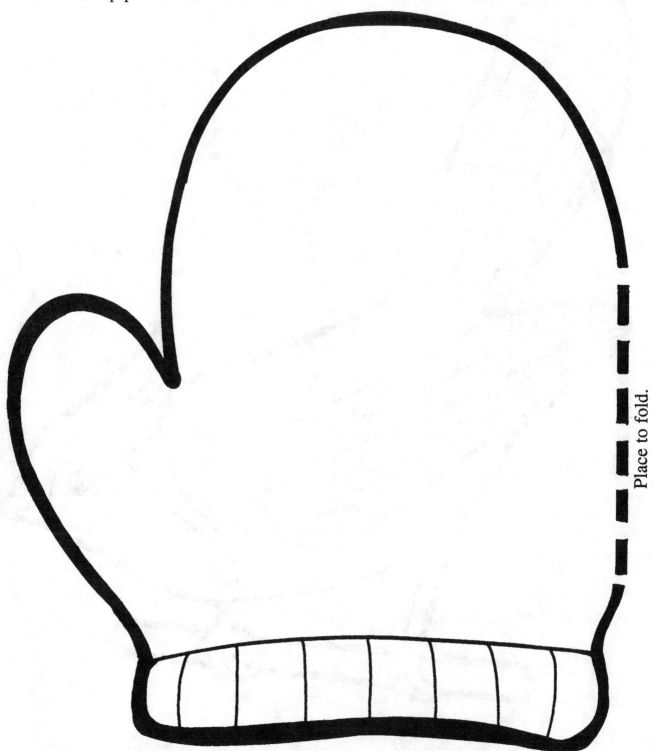

Place to fold.

# Mittens *(cont.)*

**Directions:** Draw what was in your mitten. Complete the sentence. Cut out and glue this mitten inside a construction paper mitten.

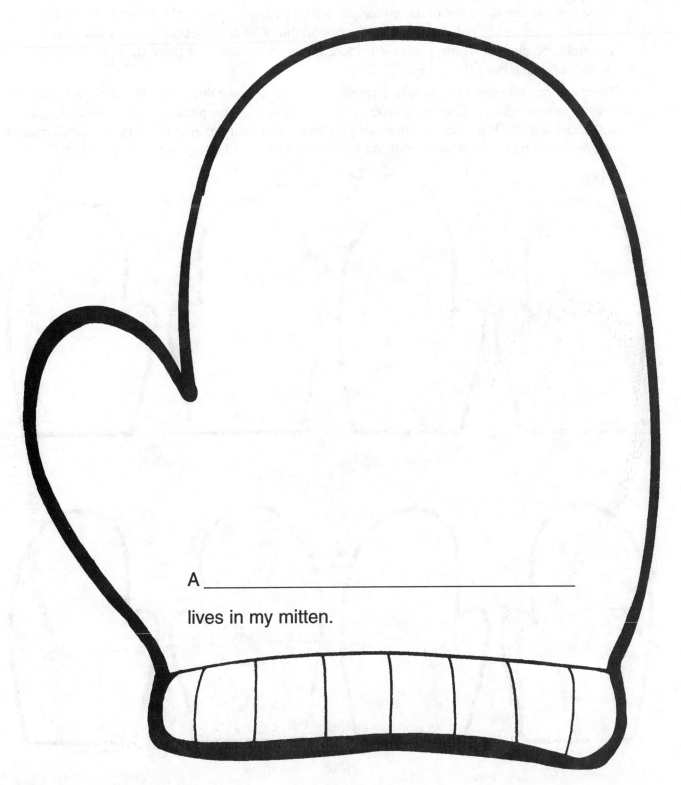

A _____

lives in my mitten.

# Mittens Games

Create the following games using the mitten pattern shown on this page.

1. Trace and cut out 26 copies of the mitten pattern on two colors of tagboard. Write uppercase letters on one color and lowercase letters on the other color. Have students match uppercase and lowercase letters, or have them place the letters in alphabetical order.

2. Trace and cut out 10 copies of the mitten pattern on two more colors of tagboard. Write the numerals 1–10 on one color and number words on the other color. Have students match the numerals and number words, place the mittens in numerical order, or place the appropriate number of counters on the mittens.

3. Trace and cut out copies of the mitten pattern on two different colors of tagboard. Use one set of mittens to write the letters of the alphabet. On the other set, glue pictures whose names begin with those letters. Have students match the pictures with their beginning letters. As an alternative you can write pairs of rhyming words on the two sets of mittens and have students match them.

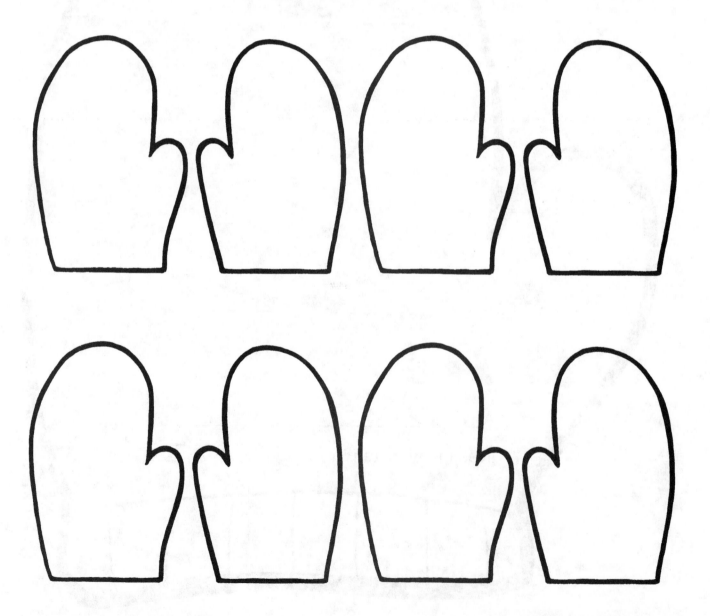

# Sparkling Star

Use the star pattern shown below for the Solar System bulletin board (page 137). Reproduce the pattern on yellow construction paper. Spread a thin layer of glue on one side. Sprinkle glitter over the glue. Place the stars on the bulletin board, scattering them around the sun.

# The Letter B

• *LETTER OF THE WEEK*

Display the key picture, A Brown Blinking Ballerina Bear Wearing Blue and Black (page 150). Refer to it each day. During the week, have students make the letter **B** using a variety of materials such as beans; buttons; blue, black, or brown paint; etc.

• *BEARS*

1. Celebrate A.A. Milne's birthday on January 18 with a week of Winnie the Pooh and other bear activities. Read aloud as many Winnie the Pooh books during the week as possible. See the bibliography (page 149) for suggestions. There are several good videos available, as well.

2. Read aloud the Jan Brett's version of *Goldilocks and the Three Bears* (TCM550) or Jan Brett's (Putnam, 1987). Allow students to enjoy the illustrations. Make or purchase flannel board figures and character masks for students to use when they practice retelling the story in the correct sequence. You may wish to put the figures and masks in the library center for further practice and fun. Reproduce the sequencing activity (page 151). Ask students to order small, medium, and large bears, bowls, chairs, and beds. Then have them sequence the events of the story (page 152).

3. Read *My Teddy Bear Loves* by Katherine Wilson (Antioch, 1988). Give students bear cutouts (using the pattern provided on page 154) or pages from bear-shaped notepads. Have them draw what their bear loves and dictate sentences. These can be made into a class book, put on the wall as a Teddy Bear Parade, or worn as a necklace.

4. To teach alphabet and number skills, make games using bear-shaped note paper glued onto tagboard and laminated. On large bears, write uppercase letters for sequencing. On small bears write lowercase letters to match with the uppercase letters. On another set of bears, put the numerals 0–10 and the appropriate number of bee stickers on honey jars (page 154). Make other sets to match up rhyming picture names, beginning sounds, colors and color words, or other skills you are teaching at this time.

• *BITTY BEAR BOOK*

Have the class dictate a story about a Bitty Bear. Allow them to illustrate the story, leaving a space in each picture to add a sponge-printed bear. Mix equal parts of soap flakes and water in a jar. Shake until the mixture is thick. Add brown tempera paint, and shake again. Make a small bear-shaped sponge. Ask students to dip the sponge in the paint mixture and press it onto their pictures, making a print where the bear should be. After the paint has dried, they may add features if they wish.

• *BEAR T-SHIRT*

Trace the bear and balloon pattern (page 153) onto tracing paper with an embroidery pencil (available at craft stores). Iron the transfer onto students' T-shirts. Invite students to paint the design with non-toxic fabric paint. When the paint is dry, trace around the pictures with a black fabric pen. Students will wear their creations proudly. Enlist parent volunteers to help with the tracing and ironing.

# The Letter B *(cont.)*

## • *BEAR MATH*

1. Give each child a reclosable plastic bag containing a random mixture of about 20 honey and chocolate bear-shaped crackers. Ask how they are different. The obvious way to sort them is according to flavor. Ask if there is another way they are different. They can then sort each flavor with hands up and hands down. Count the number in each of the four groups. Ask: *Which group has the most? Which group had the least?* Ask them to design a pattern with the bears.

2. Make a "Best Bear" graph. Ask students to eat one bear of each flavor to decide which they like best. Provide students with bear cutouts (page 154). Have students color their bears light brown if they liked the honey flavor best or black if they liked the chocolate best. One at a time, invite students to glue their bears onto a tagboard graph. You may wish to have students write their names beside their choices. Ask questions about the graph.

3. On another day, give each student a reclosable plastic bag with 10 gummy candy bears of any color. Have students count out groups of 8 and 9. Then have them sort the bears according to colors and make a graph. Tell them to count each color. Ask which color they had the most of and which they had the least of. You may wish to introduce addition. Say: *Joe has 3 red and 2 green bears. How many bears does he have?* Allow the class to respond. Practice in this manner, adding the different colors that students have. Write the equations on the chalkboard if desired. On another day, practice subtraction. Ask: *If Nancy has 3 red bears and she eats 1 red bear, how many red bears does she have left?* Have the class respond. Later, you can allow students to make up the problems as you write the equations on the chalkboard. Include the concept of zero. Ask: *Are there any blue bears?* Lead students to conclude that there are zero blue bears. Ask: *If I have 2 red bears and 0 blue bears, how many bears do I have? If I have 0 blue bears, can I eat 2 blue bears?* For each equation, allow the class or volunteers to respond.

4. Provide balance scales and have students weigh Three Bear Family Counters. Have them compare the weights of the bears to each other and to objects in the classroom.

## • *BIG BEAR'S BIRTHDAY BASH*

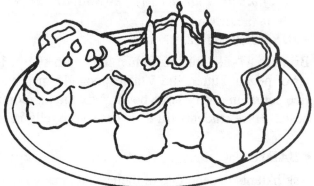

Send home the invitation (page 155) to have students bring their teddy bears for a Big Bear's Birthday Bash on Friday. Serve a brown (chocolate) bear-shaped cake. This can be done using a store-bought pan or by using a 10-inch (25 cm) round pan for the body, an 8-inch (20 cm) round pan for the head, two cupcakes for the ears, and four cupcakes for the paws. Frost the entire cake and add features with blue candies or blue tube icing. Place blue candles on the cake and ask a volunteer to blow them out. **Warning:** Check with your school's fire safety code before lighting the candles. Serve the cake with Berry Blue Bubbly Juice (made with blue juice and club soda). Allow students to: blow soap bubbles, use plastic soda bottles for indoor bowling, bounce balls, and bat balloons into the air with their hands.

## • *BIRTHDAY*

As students learn their birthdays, allow them to sign the enlarged cake pattern (page 52).

# The Letter B *(cont.)*

## • BEAUTIFUL

Give students their favorite color of paper. Ask them to cut out things they think are beautiful and make individual collages. Allow time for students to share their collages with the class.

## • BUTTON BOX

Ask students to bring buttons to add to a Button Box. Invite them to think of ways to use buttons. Make button patterns and designs. Use the buttons to sort, count, add, and subtract.

## • BIRDS

1. Allow time for students to observe the birds that come to your window feeder. Have them keep a journal, drawing pictures of the birds that they see. Identify the birds using a field guide. Ask students to identify different colors on the birds.

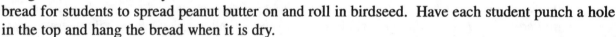

2. Make some special food for the birds. Help students string apple and orange slices, popcorn, O-shaped cereal, and cranberries on 10-inch (25 cm) pieces of wire, bend the wires to make wreaths, and hang them on a nearby tree. Have students stuff pine cones with peanut butter and roll them in birdseed. Hang them in a tree with yarn. Provide toasted stale bread for students to spread peanut butter on and roll in birdseed. Have each student punch a hole in the top and hang the bread when it is dry.

3. Celebrate Dr. Martin Luther King's birthday (January 15) by making doves of peace (page 156). Read aloud the "I Have a Dream" speech from Jim Haskins' *I Have a Dream: The Life and Words of Martin Luther King, Jr.* (Millbrook Press, 1992). Discuss Dr. King's contributions.

## • BIRDS' NESTS

Bring to a boil 1 cup (250 mL) light corn syrup, 1 ½ cups (375 mL) brown sugar, one 18-ounce (500 g) jar of peanut butter, and 1 tablespoon (15 mL) vanilla. Pour the mixture over 9 cups (2.25 L) crispy rice cereal in a very large bowl. Mix the ingredients together and cool slightly. Quickly shape into nests. Have students fill their nests with jelly beans or egg-shaped candies.

## • BABY

Ask parents to send one of their child's baby pictures or a color copy of a photo for an art project. Have students work together to make a class collage. Ask them to try to guess who each baby is.

## • DAFFODIL AND HYACINTH BULBS

Have students grow flowers inside by putting the bulbs in a shallow dish of pebbles and water. Place in a sunny window until they bloom. Transplant them outside after they bloom.

## • BANANA BREAD

Enjoy baking some banana bread with your students. Use your favorite recipe or a prepared mix.

# Bibliography

## Books

Berenstain, Stan and Jan. *The Berenstain Bears series.* Random House.

Bond, Michael and David McKee. *Paddington at the Fair.* Putnam, 1985.

Brett, Jan. *Goldilocks and the Three Bears.* Putnam, 1987.

Carlstrom, Nancy White. *It's About Time, Jesse Bear, and Other Rhymes.* Scholastic, 1990.

Curran, Eileen. *Birds' Nests.* Troll, 1985.

Dawe, Neil and Karen. *The Bird Book.* Workman, 1988.

DuBois, William Pene. *Bear Party.* Puffin, 1987.

Fowler, Allan. *It Could Still Be a Bird.* Childrens Press, 1990.

Fowler, Allan. *Please Don't Feed the Bears.* Childrens Press, 1991.

Gretz, Suzanna. *Teddy Bears 1 to 10.* Macmillan, 1986.

Hague, Kathleen. *Alphabears: An ABC Book.* Holt, Rinehart, and Winston, 1984.

Hoban, Lillian. *Arthur's Honey Bear.* Harper & Row, 1974.

Holabird, Katherine. *Angelina Ballerina.* Crown, 1988.

Kahn, Peggy. *The Care Bears: "Try, Try Again!"* Random House, 1985.

Katz, Bobbie. *Month By Month: A Care Bear Book of Poems.* Random House, 1984.

Leach, Michael. *Bears.* Mallard, 1990.

Leonard, Marcia. *Bear's Busy Year: A Book About Seasons.* Troll, 1990.

Milne, A.A. *Winnie the Pooh and Eeyore's Birthday.* Western, 1978.

Milne, A.A. *Winnie the Pooh and the Fire Alarm.* Disney, 1978.

Milne, A.A. *Winnie the Pooh and the Honey Patch.* Western, 1980.

Milne, A.A. *Winnie the Pooh and the House at Pooh Corner.* Dell, 1970.

Milne, A.A. *Winnie the Pooh and Tigger.* Western, 1968.

Milne, A.A. *Winnie the Pooh: A Tight Squeeze.* Western, 1965.

Nentl, Jerolyn. *The Grizzly.* Crestwood, 1984.

Rosen, Michael. *We're Going on a Bear Hunt.* Macmillan, 1989.

Schubert, Ingride Dieter. *The Magic Bubble Trip.* Kane Miller, 1985.

Slier, Avery. *The Day Teddy Bear Got Lost.* Random House, 1986.

Ward, Lynd. *The Biggest Bear.* Houghton Mifflin, 1992.

Wilson, Katherine. *My Teddy Bear Loves.* Antioch, 1988.

## Technology

*Bears.* (Video); 8 min. Troll Associates, Catalog Sales Dept., 100 Corporate Dr., Mahwah, NJ 07498; 1-800-929-8765.

*Beauty and the Beast.* (Software with interactive narrative, illustrations, graphics, and sound); CD-ROM for MPC and MAC; Troll Associates, Catalog Sales Dept., 100 Corporate Dr., Mahwah, NJ 07498; 1-800-929-8765.

*Birds.* (Video); 8 min. Troll Associates, Catalog Sales Dept., 100 Corporate Dr., Mahwah, NJ 07498; 1-800-929-8765.

*Birthday Buddies.* (Video about a bear's special birthday present for his grandfather); 8 min. Troll Associates, Catalog Sales Dept., 100 Corporate Dr., Mahwah, NJ 07498; 1-800-929-8765.

# A Brown Blinking Ballerina Bear Wearing Blue and Black

Enlarge the following key picture by creating an overhead transparency of this page and projecting it onto poster board. Then trace each part to make a brown bear, a blue tutu, and pink ballet slippers. Cut out the poster board pieces and glue them together. Allow the glue to dry. Then laminate the bear. To make the skirt of the tutu, gather and tape blue netting onto waist of the bear. Wrap pink ribbons around the bear's ankles and glue them in place for the ballet slipper laces. Refer to the key picture each day, especially when you discuss the calendar (page 9). At the end of the week, tape the bear to a wall as part of an alphabet line-up.

# Sequencing

**Directions:** Cut out the bears, bowls, chairs, and beds. Glue the pictures on a piece of construction paper in order—small, medium, and large.

# The Three Bears

**Directions:** Cut out the pictures. Place the pictures in the correct order to show what happened in the story.

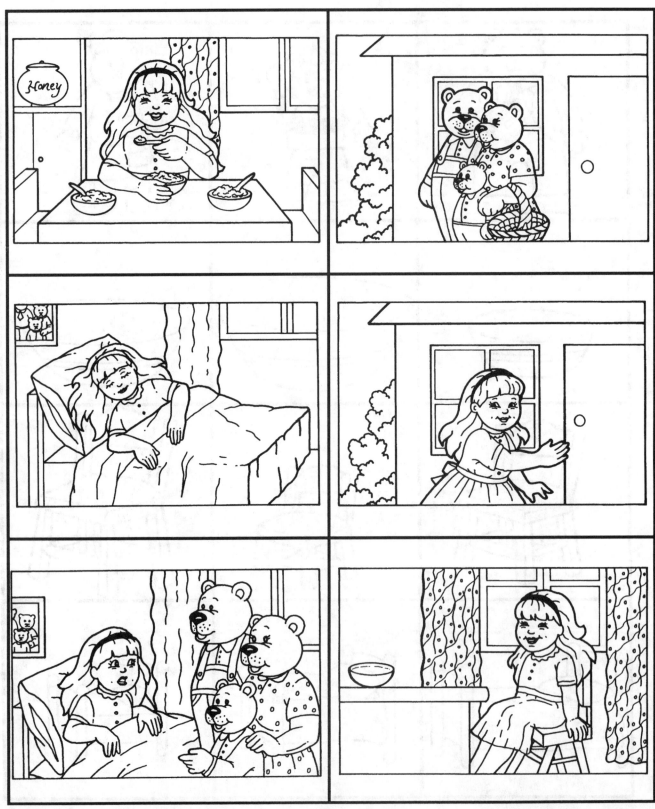

# A Bear with Balloons

# A Bear with a Honey Pot

Use the bear and honey pot patterns shown below to make games that will give students the opportunity to practice matching uppercase and lowercase letters, numerals and dots or numerals and number words, etc.

# Birthday Invitation

You're invited to
Bear's Birthday Bash
to complete **B** Week.
Please bring your
favorite Teddy Bear
to school with you
tomorrow for a day of
fun **B** things!

# Dove of Peace

On January 15, celebrate Dr. Martin Luther King's birthday. Reproduce the white dove shown below. Cut out the doves. Use safety pins to attach them to students' shirts or staple them to tagboard bands for students to wear as hats.

# The Letter O

## • *LETTER OF THE WEEK*

Display the key picture of the Orange Octopus in the Ocean (page 160). Refer to it each day. During the week, have students make the letter **O** using a variety of materials such as dry oatmeal, O-shaped cereal, orange prints, etc.

## • *ORANGE OCTOPUS IN THE OCEAN*

1. Obtain books with colorful pictures of ocean animals. Read aloud some interesting facts from them. Then display the books in the discovery center along with any seashells you have. Make an ocean mural by covering a large bulletin board with green paper and painting it with thin blue tempera. Paint swirls of red and green seaweed at the bottom of your ocean. You may wish to glue sand and dyed seashell macaroni on your ocean floor, as well.

2. Have students cut Orange Octopuses (page 161) from construction paper. Together, count their eight arms. Tell students that octopuses have suckers on the underside of their arms to hold onto rocks as they glide along the bottom of the ocean. Have them stick notebook paper hole reinforcers along their octopuses' arms for suckers. Put the octopuses on the ocean mural.

## • *OCEAN ANIMALS*

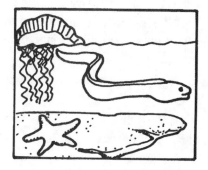

1. Read about other ocean animals such as starfish, sea horses, jellyfish, eels, whales, dolphins, sharks, sea otters, shellfish, and other brightly colored fish such as angelfish. Provide art materials so students can create additional ocean animals (pages 163–175) for the mural.

2. Share the beautiful book *The Rainbow Fish* by Marcus Pfister (Scholastic, 1992). Give students a copy of the Rainbow Fish (page 175) to decorate and add to the mural.

3. Talk about the food that we get from the ocean. Allow students to taste dried seaweed, available from Japanese markets or the oriental section of your local supermarket.

4. In ocean animal-shaped books, write stories that students dictate. For example, an octopus-shaped book could be entitled "Ollie the Octopus." If you prefer, students can draw ocean animals that they have learned about and put them in a book entitled "My Ocean Book." Then have them dictate a sentence about each animal.

5. Make a set of 25 colorful tagboard fish. Write the numerals 1–25 on one side of each fish. On the other side of each fish, glue a small picture whose name begins with each letter of the alphabet (excluding **X**) and that can be rhymed with another word. Examples include ant, boat, cake, duck, egg, fox, goat, horn, ink, jam, kite, leg, mail, nest, ox, pink, quail, rake, snake, truck, up (an arrow pointing up), vest, white, yellow, zipper. Laminate the fish and put a paper clip in each one's mouth. Make a fishing pole by tying one end of a string to a stick and the other end to a magnet. Seat students in a circle. Tell them to imagine the area in the middle is the ocean. Place the fish in the center, and allow students to catch them with the magnet. After all of the students have had a turn, have one student at a time return the fish to the "ocean" in numerical order. Then give each student a turn to catch another fish, name the picture, and tell what letter its name begins with. Have students work together to name as many rhyming words as they can.

6. Allow students to count out and place the appropriate number of fish-shaped crackers onto each laminated fish (page 158) and practice adding and subtracting with the crackers.

# The Letter O *(cont.)*

## • *OCEAN ANIMALS (cont.)*

7. Ask students to bring seashells if they have any. Tell students to examine the shells with magnifying glasses. Have them sort the shells according to shape and kind. Point out how the same kind of shell comes in different sizes. Learn about the animals that lived in each shell.

8. Have "A Day at the Ocean" to culminate your two weeks of study. Ask students to wear comfortable clothing and bring beach toys. Allow them to make sand castles and hunt for seashells in the sandbox, toss a beach ball, float boats in pans of water, and picnic on beach towels in the classroom. Together, watch the video *The Little Mermaid* (Disney Home Video, 1989).

## • *OCEAN ANIMAL COOKIES*

Prepare or buy sugar cookie dough. Give each student about ¹/₄ cup (63 mL) of dough. Add food coloring if desired. They may roll out the dough, cut with ocean animal cookie cutters, and decorate as desired. Bake the cookies according to the directions.

## • *OWL*

Read aloud *The Owl and the Pussycat* by Edward Lear and illustrated by Jan Brett (Putnam, 1991). Identify the ocean animals in the borders and tell what is going on there. Give students pieces of pea-green paper to make boats. Have them try to memorize parts of the poem. Add them to the ocean mural.

## • *OFFICE*

Visit the school office. Ask the secretary to tell about his or her job. Point out the tools the secretary uses. Invite parents to tell about their offices. Allow students to role-play office work.

## • *OPPOSITES*

1. Read aloud one or more books about opposites. See the bibliography (page 159) for suggestions. Discuss the meaning of opposites. Encourage students to brainstorm a list of opposites as you write them on the chalkboard.

2. Students can cut out magazine pictures of opposites and make a group poster.

## • *O-SHAPED CEREAL*

Together, count out ten O-shaped pieces of cereal onto paper plates. Ask students to determine how many ways they can arrange the pieces of cereal. Tell them to glue the cereal onto construction paper in their favorite pattern.

## • *OATMEAL*

Ask parents if their children have any food allergies or dietary restrictions. Together, make oatmeal cookies following the recipe on the box. Then allow students to eat them.

## • *OVAL OLIVES AND OTHER OBJECTS*

Have students draw ovals, while tasting oval olives. Ask them to name oval-shaped objects. (Remember to check for food allergies beforehand.)

# Bibliography

**Books**

Abbott, R. Tucker, Ph.D. *Seashells of the World*. Golden. 1991.

Carle, Eric. *A House for Hermit Crab*. Picture Book Studio, 1987.

Cole, Joanna. *The Magic School Bus® on the Ocean Floor*. Scholastic, 1992.

Cosgrove, Stephen. *Maui-Maui*. Price Stern Sloan, 1984.

Curran, Eileen. *Life in the Sea*. Troll, 1985.

Gordon, Sharon. *Dolphins and Porpoises*. Troll, 1985.

Heller, Ruth. *How to Hide an Octopus*. Putnam, 1985.

Hoban, Tana. *Over, Under, and Through*. Macmillan, 1972.

Hoban, Tana. *Push, Pull, Empty, Full: A Book of Opposites*. Macmillan, 1972.

Ingoglia, Gina. *Strange Sea Creatures*. Western, 1991.

Jablonsky, Alice. *Discover Ocean Life*. Publications International, 1991.

Kipling, Rudyard. *Crab That Played with the Sea: A Just So Story*. Bedrick, 1983.

Koch, Michelle. *By the Sea*. Greenwillow, 1991.

Lear, Edward. *The Owl and the Pussycat*. Putnam, 1991.

Lewis, Jean. *Glow in the Dark Under the Sea*. Western, 1991.

Low, Donald. *Sea Shells*. Price Stern Sloan, 1987.

Matthias, Catherine. *Over-Under*. Childrens Press, 1984.

McBarnet, Gill. *The Whale Who Wanted to Be Small*. Ruwanga Tradition, 1986.

McCarthy, Patricia. *Ocean Parade*. Dial, 1990.

McDonald, Megan. *Is This a House for Hermit Crab?* Orchard, 1990.

O'Connor, Karen. *Let's Take a Walk on the Beach*. Childrens Press, 1986.

Oppenheim, Joanne. *Follow That Fish*. Bantam, 1990.

Pallotta, Jerry. *The Ocean Alphabet Book*. Charlesbridge, 1986.

Pfister, Marcus. *The Rainbow Fish*. Scholastic, 1992.

Rockwell, Anne F. *At the Beach*. Macmillan, 1987.

Selberg, Ingrid. *Secrets of the Deep*. Dial, 1990.

**Technology**

*The Kitten Twins: A Book About Opposites*. (Cassette); Troll Associates, Catalog Sales Dept., 100 Corporate Dr., Mahwah, NJ 07498; 1-800-929-8765.

*Opposites Attract*. (Software with Sesame Street characters about opposites); PC; National School Products, 101 East Broadway, Maryville, TN 37804; 1-800-251-9124.

*Reading Adventures in Oz*. (Software for reading skills); PC, National School Products, 101 East Broadway, Maryville, TN 37804; 1-800-251-9124.

*What's Under the Ocean?* (Video); 8 min. Troll Associates, Catalog Sales Dept., 100 Corporate Dr., Mahwah, NJ 07498; 1-800-929-8765.

# Orange Octopus in the Ocean

Enlarge the following key picture by creating an overhead transparency of this page and projecting it onto poster board. Then trace each part to make an orange octopus. Glue him onto a blue backround to create an ocean. Allow the glue to dry and laminate. Refer to the key picture each day, especially when you discuss the calendar (page 9). At the end of the week, tape the octopus to a wall as part of an alphabet line-up.

# Orange Octopus

Reproduce the octopus pattern on orange construction paper. Give students notebook hole reinforcers to stick to the arms for suckers.

# Fish Tales

Create a Big Book, using the directions on page 157 and the pattern shown below.

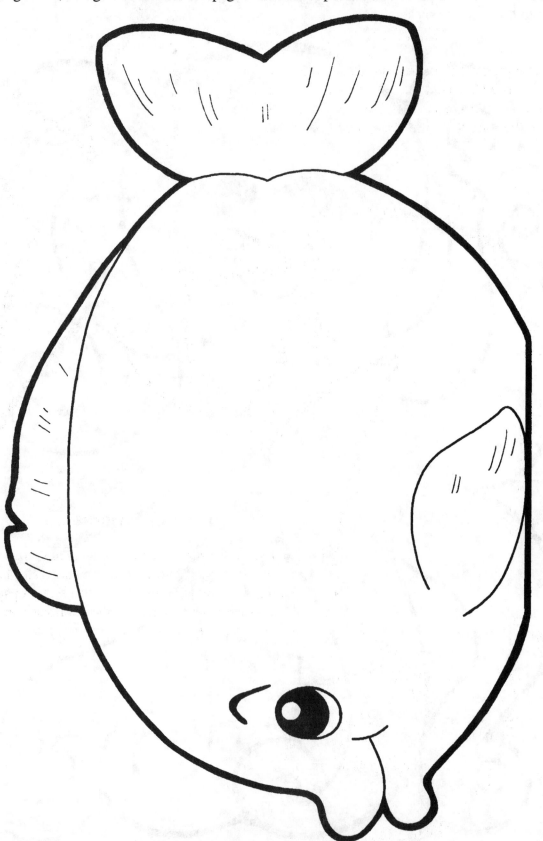

# Ocean Animals

## Starfish

Reproduce the starfish pattern on green construction paper. Have students cut out the starfish, spread glue on them, and dip them in sand. Allow the glue to dry. Then put the starfish on the ocean mural (page 157).

## Sea Horse

Reproduce the sea horse pattern on green construction paper. Help students cut out the sea horses. Then have them glue on bits of torn brown construction paper or paper grocery bags. Then put the sea horses on the ocean mural (page 157).

# Ocean Animals (cont.)

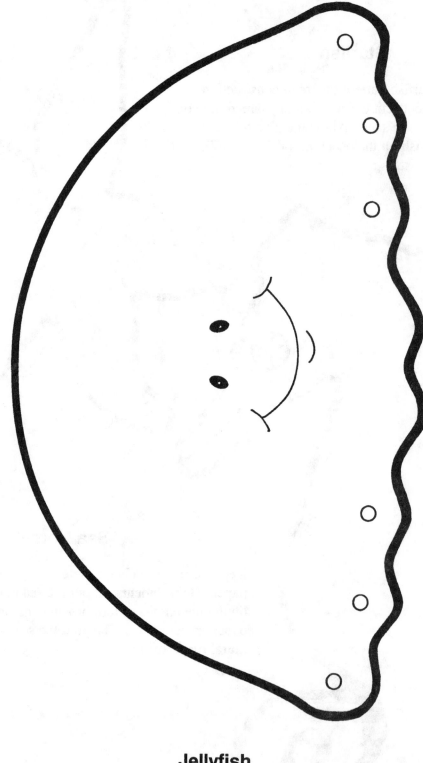

## Jellyfish

Reproduce the jellyfish pattern on purple construction paper. Have students cut out the jellyfish. Punch holes where indicated. Then help students tie on strands of lavender curling ribbon or yarn to hang as tentacles. You may wish to use one blade of a pair of scissors to make the pieces of ribbon make tighter curls. Then put the jellyfish on the ocean mural (page 157).

# Ocean Animals *(cont.)*

### Moray Eel

Reproduce the moray eel pattern on white
construction paper.  Allow students to cut out the
eels and color them gray.  Then put the moray eels
on the ocean mural (page 157).

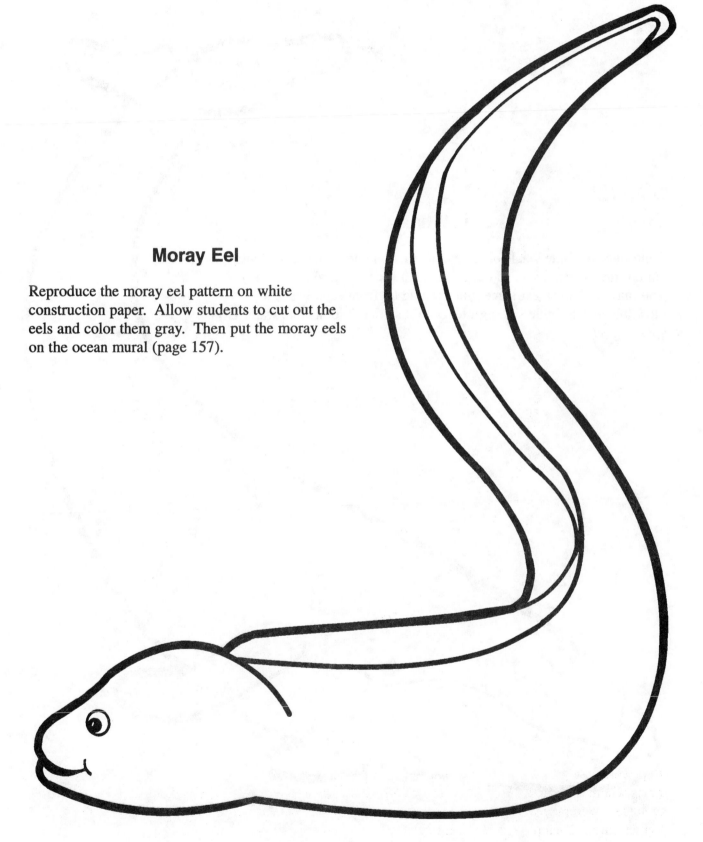

# Ocean Animals *(cont.)*

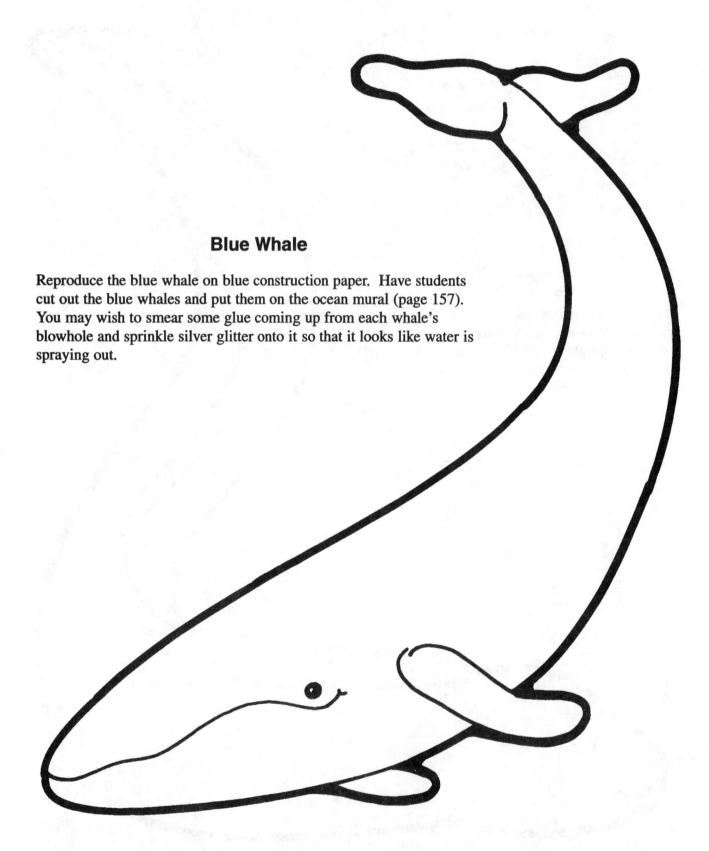

### Blue Whale

Reproduce the blue whale on blue construction paper. Have students
cut out the blue whales and put them on the ocean mural (page 157).
You may wish to smear some glue coming up from each whale's
blowhole and sprinkle silver glitter onto it so that it looks like water is
spraying out.

# Ocean Animals *(cont.)*

## Orca

Reproduce the orca pattern on white construction paper. Point out to students that orca are black with a white underside. Have students cut out the white construction paper whales. Allow them to use white chalk to trace the outline of the whales on black fabric. Tell them to cut out the black fabric orca. Then have them cut off the stomach areas from the white construction paper and glue those onto their black fabric whales. Then put the orca on the ocean mural (page 157).

# Ocean Animals *(cont.)*

**Dolphin**

Reproduce the dolphin pattern on gray construction paper. Have students cut out the dolphins. Ask them to decide if their dolphins are jumping into the air, swimming along the surface, catching a fish, or diving. Have them position their dolphins accordingly on the ocean mural (page 157).

# Ocean Animals *(cont.)*

**Sharks**

Reproduce the shark patterns on white construction paper. Have students cut them out and put them on the ocean mural (page 157).

# Ocean Animals (cont.)

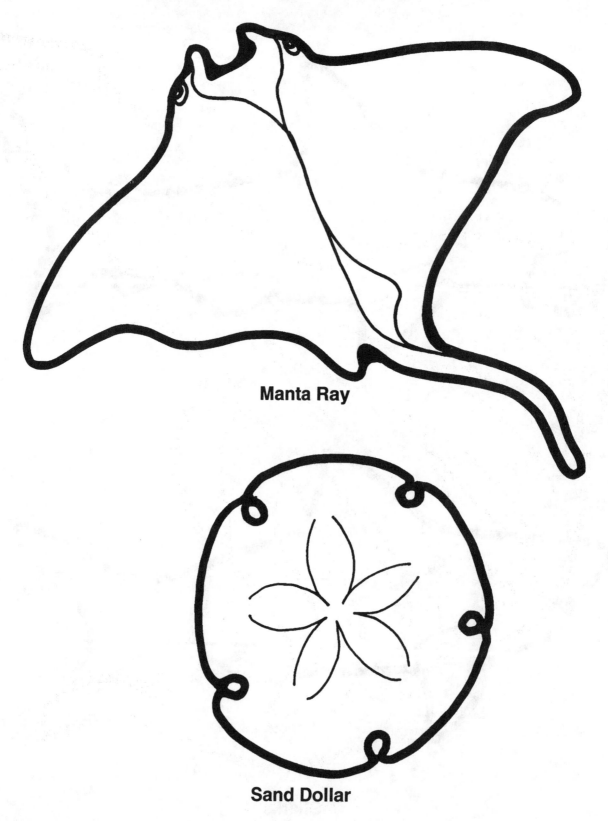

**Manta Ray**

**Sand Dollar**

Reproduce the manta ray and sand dollar patterns on poster board. Have students place the poster board patterns on sand paper and trace them. Then have them cut out the sand paper manta rays and sand dollars and put them on the ocean mural (page 157).

# Ocean Animals *(cont.)*

**Giant Squid**

Reproduce the giant squid on green construction paper. Ask students to cut out the squid and glue green yarn along the tentacles. Then put the giant squid on the ocean mural (page 157).

# Ocean Animals *(cont.)*

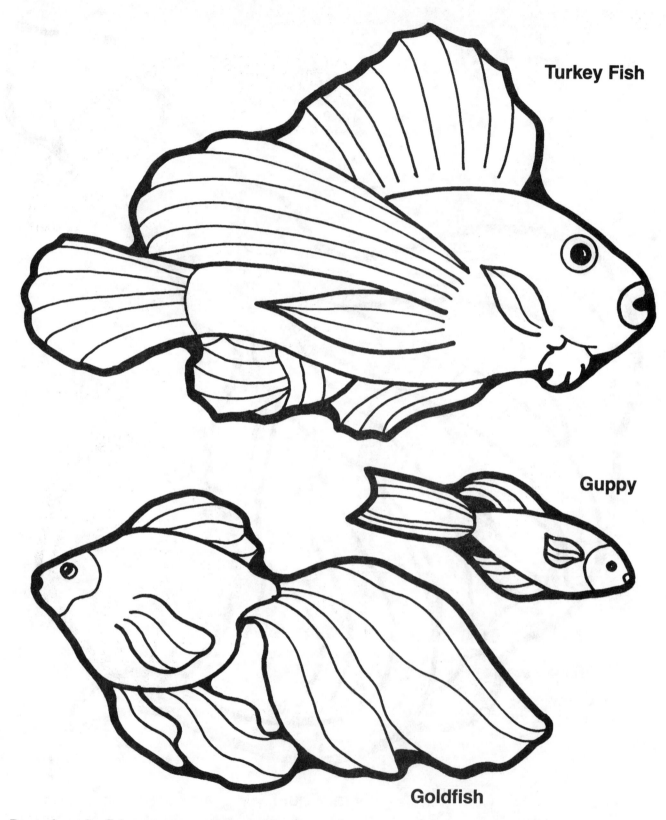

**Turkey Fish**

**Guppy**

**Goldfish**

Reproduce the fish patterns on white construction paper. Ask students to paint the fish and cut them out. Then put the fish on the ocean mural (page 157).

# Ocean Animals *(cont.)*

**Crustaceans**

**Hermit Crab**

**Lobster**

**Shrimp**

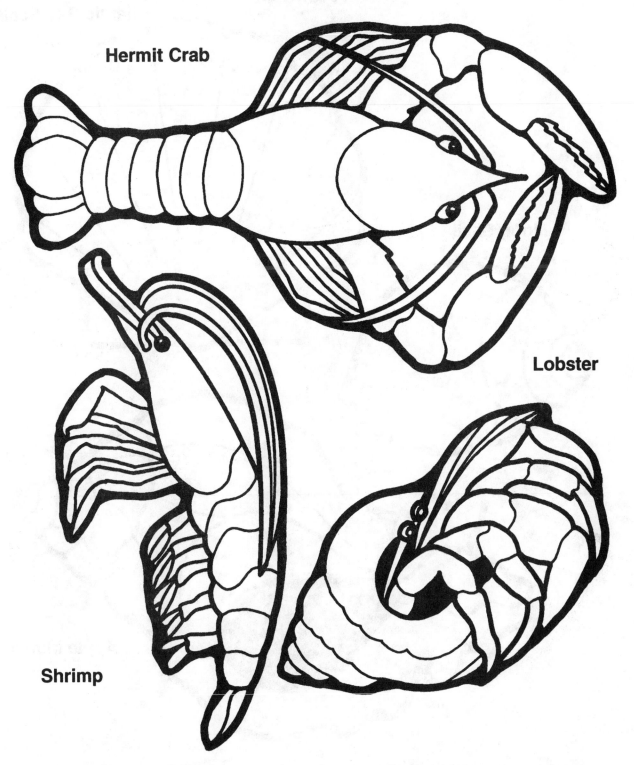

Reproduce the crustacean patterns on pink construction paper. Invite students to cut out these sea animals. Allow them to glue pink pipe cleaners onto the antennae and sequins for the eyes. Then put the crustaceans on the ocean mural (page 157).

# Ocean Animals *(cont.)*
## Mollusks

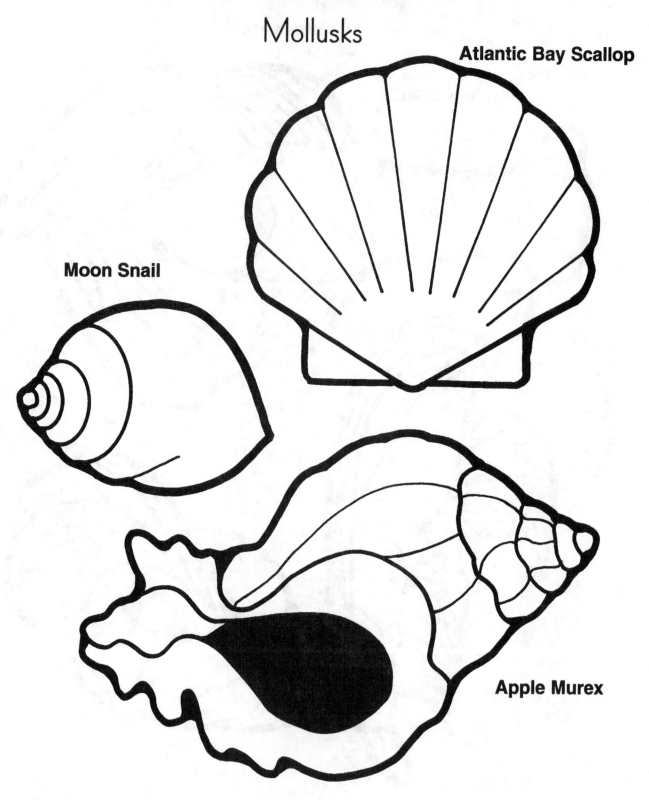

**Atlantic Bay Scallop**

**Moon Snail**

**Apple Murex**

Reproduce the mollusk patterns on white construction paper. Tell students to paint the mollusks by dipping sponge squares in paint and then on their papers. After the paint has dried, ask students to cut out their mollusks and put them on the ocean mural (page 157).

# Ocean Animals *(cont.)*

**Rainbow Fish**

Reproduce the rainbow fish pattern on yellow construction paper. Ask students to decorate their rainbow fish with crayons, glitter, and sequins. Then put the rainbow fish on the ocean mural (page 157).

# The Letter H

### • *FEBRUARY*

Reproduce the heart creature patterns (pages 181–186) for students. Have them cut out and color the creatures. Then place their creatures on the Class Tree (page 9).

### • *LETTER OF THE WEEK*

Display the key picture of the Happy Heart House (page 180). Refer to it each day. During the week, have students make the letter **H** using a variety of materials such as hearts cut out of wrapping paper, wallpaper, construction paper, doilies, stickers, handprints, etc.

### • *HEARTS*

Provide students with the patterns (pages 181–186). Give students a variety of sizes of red, white, violet, and pink construction paper; doilies; sticker hearts; scrap paper and lace bits. Allow them to create heart people, butterflies, fish, dogs, caterpillars, mice, or other animals. Display the heart creatures on the Class Tree bulletin board (page 9) with heart flowers.

### • *HEART HOUSE*

1. Have students make mail bags for a classroom exchange of Valentines. Tell them to color a heart pattern onto paper lunch bags. They can add stickers or other scraps if desired.

2. Teach the class the poem entitled "The Queen of Hearts" (*The Real Mother Goose,* Rand McNally, 1944). Have students make tarts by spreading strawberry jam on heart-shaped cookies.

3. Make several heart-shaped games to reinforce skills that you have already taught. Cut tagboard hearts in half different ways to be matched like puzzles. On one part of each heart, write an uppercase letter; on the matching parts of the hearts write the lowercase letters. Do the same for students to practice initial consonants and pictures, rhyming words, opposites, numerals and sets of heart stickers or numerals and number words. If students have a hard time manipulating the heart puzzles, you can have students match small hearts with large hearts to practice the same skills. For example, write uppercase letters on large hearts and lowercase letters on small hearts. Students should match the small and large hearts by placing the correct lowercase letters with the uppercase letters. The game for each skill could have different colored hearts or have a hearts with different stickers or gift wrap on the back. Number each game. Give each student a construction paper heart with his or her name and the numbers of the games written on it in any order. As the student successfully completes each game, put a heart sticker over that number. This will make it easy for you to see who needs to complete the games.

### • *HABITAT*

Discuss what a habitat is. Ask students what kind of habitats people live in. Have them compare and contrast human habitats with those of different animals.

# The Letter H (cont.)

- **HOLIDAYS**
  1. Talk about the February holiday symbols such as hearts for Valentines Day, top hats for Lincoln's birthday, and hatchets for Washington's birthday. Have students practice making patterns of first two then three of these symbols.
  2. Have students practice identifying and matching symbols with different holidays and months throughout the year.

- **HUNDRED**
  1. Celebrate the hundredth day of school, which should occur about now. Together, count and color 100 hearts and attach them to a bulletin board in 10 x 10 rows. Ask: *Is 100 a lot? Does it look like more or less than you thought it would?* Allow students to count 100 cents. Pin together 10 groups of 10 safety pins or paper clips. Help students learn how to count by 10's to 100. Ask them to bring a collection of 100 small things to school to share on the 100th day. Have them draw pictures and dictate sentences in response to one of the following questions: *What would you do with $100? What will you be doing when you are 100 years old?*
  2. Make a Hundred Snack. Provide 10 snacks such as cereal, raisins, pretzel sticks, sunflower seeds, nuts, mini marshmallows, candy-coated chocolates, crackers, cookies, or candies. Give each child a reclosable plastic bag and allow them to count out 10 of each snack to make 100. Make this a Hug Day and encourage students to hug each other at least once.

- **HOUSE**
  1. Read aloud *The Little House* by Virginia Lee Burton (Houghton Mifflin, 1942). Students can color or design their own "Heart House." Copy students' home addresses on their houses for them to learn. They may sign a large laminated house (page 51) after they learn their addresses. Cut out houses and glue them to a larger piece of paper. Students should draw where they would like for their houses to be—in the country or in the city. Ask: *What things surround your house?* Make a country and city mural or a Class Book.
  2. Students may choose to make a Heart House mural. Divide a length of green butcher paper into two sections, one for the city and the other for the country. If students wish to live in the city, have them place their houses in straight rows, close together, along streets. If students wish to live in the country, have them place their houses further apart. Students may use markers to fill in landscape features. Ask: *What materials can be used to build a house?*
  3. Read aloud *A House for a Hermit Crab* by Eric Carle (Picture Book Studio, 1987). Design a wonderful house for a hermit crab or another ocean animal (page 187).

- **HATS**
  1. Invite students to make a hat collage by cutting out pictures from magazines and gluing them to a huge hat or to an **H** shape drawn on paper.
  2. Identify the occupations represented by different hats.

# The Letter H *(cont.)*

## • *HEARING*

1. Review the five senses.  Read aloud *Polar Bear, Polar Bear, What Did You Hear?* by Bill Martin, Jr. (Scholastic, 1991).

2. Set up a "Hearing Center" in your classroom.  Include a string telephone, xylophone, bells, megaphone, a large conch shell, glasses or bottles with different amounts of water to play gently with a spoon, blocks of wood to play with a spoon and to strike together, two wooden blocks covered with sandpaper to rub together, and other rhythm instruments that are available to you.  Put various things, such as beans, rice, coffee, sand, cotton, paper clips, etc. in clean medicine bottles.  Tightly tape the lids onto the bottles.  Have students try to guess what is in each bottle by shaking it.

3. Make sounds by bouncing a ball, dropping a tin pie pan, ringing a bell, dropping a ping pong ball, crumpling up paper, etc. where students can hear you but they cannot see you.  Let them guess what made the sound and how many times the object bounced on the ground.

4. Invite students to make drums by covering and decorating oatmeal boxes.  They may also wish to make shakers by stapling together two decorated paper plates with beans inside.

## • *HAIR COLORS*

Have students sign their names, color in a square, or draw a picture of themselves on a graph labeled blonde, black, brown, red hair.  Ask questions about the graph.

## • *HANDPRINTS*

Provide smocks.  Allow students to create pictures by placing their hands in plates of finger-paints and pressing them onto finger-paint paper.  Tell them to name their creations.  Write the titles on the paintings.  Encourage students to take the art work home to share with their families.

## • *HELP*

Discuss what students should do in emergency situations.  Review how to dial 911.  Continue to stress that this number is to be used only if there is a fire, if someone is very sick or injured and needs an ambulance, or if they need the police.  Allow them to role-play scenarios that you create.

## • *HOSPITAL*

Read *A Visit to the Sesame Street Hospital* by Deborah Hantzig (Random House, 1985).  Set up a hospital in your housekeeping center.  Include a stethoscope, play thermometers and shots, bandages, and dolls in beds.  A local hospital or doctor's office may donate supplies.

## • *HIDE AND HOP*

Teach students how to play Hide-and-Seek and Hopscotch and how to dance the Hokey Pokey and the Bunny Hop.

# Bibliography

## Books

Alborough, Jez. *Hide-and-Seek.* Candlewick Press, 1994.

Allington, Richard L. and Kathleen Krull. *Hearing.* Raintree, 1985.

Barton, Byron. *Building a House.* Greenwillow, 1981.

Blos, Joan W. *Martin's Hats.* William Morrow, 1984.

Brown, Marc. *Hand Rhymes.* Viking, 1992.

Fowler, Allan. *Hearing Things.* Childrens Press, 1991.

Frandsen, Karen G. *Michael's New Haircut.* Childrens Press, 1986.

Hantzig, Deborah. *A Visit to the Sesame Street Hospital.* Random House, 1985.

Hayward, Linda. *Hello, House!* Random House, 1988.

Johnson, Crockett. *Harold and the Purple Crayon.* Weston Woods, 1955.

Kroll, Virginia. *Hats Off to Hair!* Charlesbridge Publishing, 1995.

Marshall, James. *Hansel and Gretel.* Viking, 1990.

Martin, Bill. *Happy Hippopotami.* HBJ Big Book, 1991.

Martin, Bill. *Polar Bear, Polar Bear, What Do You Hear?* Scholastic, 1991.

Morris, Ann. *Hats, Hats, Hats.* William Morrow, 1993.

O'Neill, Mary. *Hailstones and Halibut Bones.* Doubleday, 1961.

Peppe, Rodney. *The House That Jack Built.* Delacorte, 1985.

Ryan-Lush, G. *Hairs on Bears.* Firefly, 1994.

Scott, Ann Herbert. *Hi.* Putnam, 1994.

Smith, Lane. *Happy Hocky Family.* Viking, 1993.

Sonnenschein, Harriet. *Harold's Hideaway Thumb.* Simon & Schuster, 1993.

Watanabe, Shigeo. *I Can Build a House.* Putnam, 1985.

Ziefert, Harriet. *A Clean House for Mole and Mouse.* Scholastic, 1989.

## Technology

*ABC with Hickory and Me.* (Software for practicing letters and sounds); MAC and WIN; Troll Associates, Catalog Sales Dept., 100 Corporate Dr., Mahwah, NJ 07498; 1-800-929-8765.

*The Hare and the Tortoise.* (Video); 6 min. Troll Associates, Catalog Sales Dept., 100 Corporate Dr., Mahwah, NJ 07498; 1-800-929-8765.

*Henny Penny.* (Video); 6 min. Troll Associates, Catalog Sales Dept., 100 Corporate Dr., Mahwah, NJ 07498; 1-800-929-8765.

*Horses.* (Video); 8 min. Troll Associates, Catalog Sales Dept., 100 Corporate Dr., Mahwah, NJ 07498; 1-800-929-8765.

*The House that Jack Built.* (Video); 4 min. Troll Associates, Catalog Sales Dept., 100 Corporate Dr., Mahwah, NJ 07498; 1-800-929-8765.

# Happy Heart House

Enlarge the following key picture by creating an overhead transparency of this page. Project and trace it onto poster board. Cut out the house and color it. Then laminate the house. You may wish to add heart stickers to the house. Refer to the key picture each day, especially when you discuss the calendar (page 9). At the end of the week, tape the house to a wall as part of an alphabet line-up.

# Heart Person

**Directions:** Use the pattern to make a heart person.

# Heart Butterfly

**Directions:** Use the pattern to make a heart butterfly. Make the body pink and the wings red. Glue thin red scraps onto the antennae.

# Heart Fish

**Directions:** Use the pattern to make a heart fish.

# Heart Dog

**Directions:** Use the pattern to make a heart dog.

# Heart Caterpillar

**Directions:** Use the pattern to make a heart caterpillar.

# Heart Mouse

**Directions:** Use the pattern to make a heart mouse. Cut a large heart for the mouse. Fold it in half. Cut a small heart for the ears. Fold it in half over the head. Add a string tail with a heart on the end as shown.

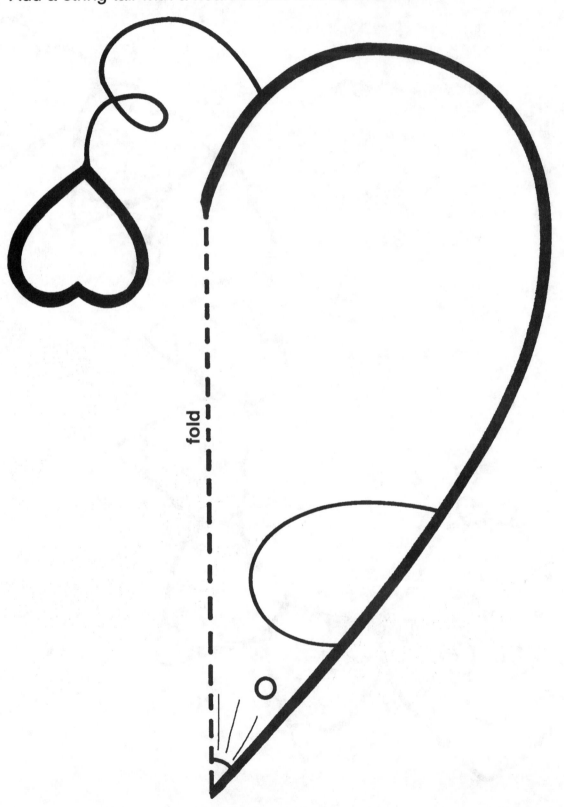

fold

# Hermit Crab House

**Directions:** Draw a wonderful new house for a hermit crab or another ocean animal.

# The Letter V

• *LETTER OF THE WEEK*

Display the key picture, A Very Violet Velvety Valentine (page 192).  Refer to it each day.  During the week, have students make the letter **V** using a variety of materials such as old Valentines, violet-colored pictures, pictures of vegetables, pressed violets, violet-colored paint or markers, plastic vines, etc.

• *VALENTINES*

1. Read aloud a Valentine's story.  See the bibliography (page 191) for suggestions.

2. Provide heart cutouts, doilies, wrapping paper, lace, rick-rack, and other interesting scraps for students to make Valentines for their parents and each other.

3. Compose a verse together.  Reproduce the verse and allow students to glue the poems into their Valentines.

4. On the chalkboard write, "I love you." Have students practice writing this sentence.  Ask students to brainstorm a list of ways to show love to someone.  Students suggestions might include cleaning up a room, helping to set the table, taking out the trash, visiting someone who is sick and taking that person some flowers, giving someone a hug and saying "I love you." Encourage students to go home and practice some of these ways.

5. Have students practice using lacing cards.  Then draw a Valentine heart on a small piece of burlap for each student.  Students can sew around the heart with violet yarn.  Then have them use black marker to write, "I love you," and sign their names inside the heart.  Allow students to give their burlap Valentines as gifts to family members.

6. Be sure to ask parents if their children have any food allergies or dietary restrictions.  Make a violet vanilla Valentine's cake for Valentine's Day.  Use cake mix and bake in an 8" (20 cm) or 9" (23 cm) round pan and an 8" (20 cm) or 9" (23 cm) square pan.  Ask if anyone can figure out how to make a Valentine from these shapes.  Give a hint by asking: *Where can we get the point and where can we get the two curved pieces?* After the cake is baked and cooled, show how to cut the circle in half and match to the sides of the square to form a heart.  Mix blue and red food coloring into some vanilla frosting to make it violet.  Ask students to take turns spreading the violet frosting on the cake.  Top with sprinkles and enjoy with vanilla ice cream.  You may wish to invite parents and other volunteers to come to the Valentine's celebration.  Present them with thank-you Valentines made by the class.

• *HEART-CREATURE VALENTINES*

Students can use the patterns on pages 181–186 to make as Valentine's cards and/or gifts for family members and friends.

• *VIOLET VELVET*

Collect scraps of velvet (especially violet) for students to touch.  Talk about how it feels.  Compare the velvet with other material or clothing, especially corduroy.  Allow students to cut strips of violet velvet ribbon and glue them onto white construction paper in a **V** shape.

# The Letter V *(cont.)*

• *VEGETABLES AND VITAMINS*

1. Read aloud *Stone Soup* retold and illustrated by Marcia Brown (Atheneum, 1947). Ask each parent to send a specific vegetable with his or her child. Taste some raw—plain and with dip. Ask: *Which vegetable is your favorite? Which vegetable do you like the least?* Make a vegetable soup by cooking vegetables in a chicken broth until they are tender.

2. Ask: *Why is it important to eat vegetables?* Point out that vegetables contain vitamins which help keep our bodies well. Explain that when people do get sick, vitamins may help them get better sooner.

3. Provide magazines and blunt scissors. Allow students to cut out pictures to make a vegetable collage on a V-shaped cutout. Talk about a healthful diet using a Food Pyramid: breads and cereals, fruits and vegetables, meats, and dairy products. Larger quantities of breads and cereals should be eaten, then fruits and vegetables. Smaller quantities of meats and dairy products should be chosen. Very limited amounts of fats and sugar should be eaten. Students can cut out pictures of food from each group and glue their healthful lunches on paper plates.

4. During Dental Health Week, talk about the importance of choosing snacks without sugar. Have students brainstorm a list of healthful snacks. Point out that it is important for them to brush their teeth at least twice a day, rinse with fluoride, and brush or rinse after they eat something with sugar. Explain that these dental habits will help them prevent plaque buildup and cavities as well as promote good checkups when they visit the dentist.

• *VALENTINE VILLAGE*

Visit a nearby village if possible. Ask: *How is a village different from a city or the country?* Have students work cooperatively to build a "Valentine Village" in the block center. Make houses and shops by covering milk cartons or other boxes. (A Toy Village may be ordered from Creative Publications, 5040 W. 111th St., Oak Lawn, IL 60453. Houses, shops, vehicles, and people are included.) You may wish to have students use a tape recorder to dictate stories about the people who live in the village. Language skills are developed as students set up and play with the village. Counting and sorting skills may also be practiced.

• *VOWELS*

Make a vowel banner on a long piece of butcher paper divided in half lengthwise and into five equal sections widthwise. Write a short vowel in each section at the top and a long vowel in each section at the bottom. Ask students to cut out pictures whose names contain each vowel sound and glue them on the appropriate sections of the banner. Have them dictate the word to be written under each picture.

• *VESTS*

Have students celebrate "Vest Day" by wearing vests to school. Encourage them to wear violet and/or velvet ones if they have any. If you prefer, use the directions on page 110 and have students make and decorate violet vests from large paper bags. Ask: *How is a vest different from a shirt or sweater?*

# The Letter V *(cont.)*

- ## *VIOLETS IN A VASE*

  1. If you live in an area where violets grow wild, display some in a vase.  Grow an African Violet.  If possible, take a trip to a local greenhouse to see different kinds of violets.

  2. Have students draw a vase on a violet piece of construction paper.  Tell them to decorate their vases with leftover Valentines or velvet scraps.  Cut small squares of violet tissue paper.  Show students how to wrap one around the eraser end of a pencil, dip it in glue, and stick it onto the paper to create flowers.  If students prefer, they can glue balls of tissue paper onto the paper to make the flowers.  Tell them to draw green stems and green heart-shaped leaves.  Encourage students to visit someone special and share their gifts of violets.

- ## *VALENTINE MATH*

Have students count out Valentine candy onto construction paper hearts, make a graph to show their favorite kind of candy, and match the number of candies to numerals (1–10).

- ## *VANILLA, VINEGAR, VIOLETS*

Pour some vanilla and vinegar on cotton balls.  Then place the cotton balls in reclosable plastic bags.  In addition, place some violet petals in a reclosable plastic bag.  Invite students to smell these three **V** scents.  Ask: *Which smells do you like?  Which smells do you dislike?*

- ## *VISORS*

Reproduce the visor pattern (page 193) on tagboard or white construction paper.  Cut out the visors, let students color them, then laminate them.  Allow students to decorate their visors with sequins, glitter, beads, etc.  Punch holes on the ends of each visor and tie in the back with a string.  You may prefer to buy visors from a craft store and allow students to decorate and wear those.

- ## *VIOLIN*

Listen to a recording of violin music.  If possible, invite a musician to demonstrate the violin in your classroom.  Allow students to examine the violin.

- ## *VETERINARIAN*

Ask a veterinarian to visit your classroom and tell about his or her job.  Ask the veterinarian to discuss how to care for a pet.

- ## *VOLLEYBALL*

Ask a P.E. teacher to practice playing volleyball with your class.  If the P.E. teacher is not available, have students practice volleying the ball over a rope or against a wall.

- ## *VISIT*

Take students to visit a retirement or nursing home in your community if there is one nearby.  Before going, have students make Valentines.  Then ask them to present their Valentines to the people they visit.

# Bibliography

## Books

Berenstain, Stan and Jan. *The Bears' Vacation.* Beginner Books, 1968.

Branley, Franklyn M. *Volcanoes.* Childrens Press, 1986.

Brook, Ruth. *Sweet Hearts for Dolly.* Troll, 1988.

Brown, Marc. *Arthur's Valentine.* Little, Brown, 1980.

Florian, D. *Vegetable Garden.* HBJ, 1991.

Gibbons, Gail. *Valentine's Day.* Holiday House, 1986.

Grauer, Rita. *Vasalisa and Her Magic Doll.* Philomel, 1994.

King, C. *Vegetables Go to Bed.* Crown, 1994.

Mullins, P. *V is for Vanishing: An Alphabet of Endangered Animals.* Harper & Row, 1994.

Murphey, Shirley. *A Valentine for Dragon.* Atheneum, 1984.

Pallotta, Jerry. *Victory Garden Alphabet Book.* Charlesbridge Publishing, 1992.

Watson, Clyde. *Valentine Foxes.* Franklin Watts, 1993.

Watson, Wendy. *Valentine for You.* Houghton Mifflin, 1993.

Williams, Margery. *The Velveteen Rabbit.* Avon, 1975.

Yoaker, Harry. *View.* Dial, 1991.

Ziefert, Harriet and Martha Gradisher. *Valentine for Ms. Vanilla.* Viking, 1994.

## Technology

*Little Mouse's Big Valentine.* (Video); 10 min. SRA, P.O. Box 543, Blacklick, OH 43004; 1-800-843-8855.

*Valentine's Day Grump.* (Video); 8 min. Troll Associates, Catalog Sales Dept., 100 Corporate Dr., Mahwah, NJ 07498; 1-800-929-8765.

*Valentine's Day Mess.* (Cassette and four paperbacks); Troll Associates, Catalog Sales Dept., 100 Corporate Dr., Mahwah, NJ 07498; 1-800-929-8765.

*The Velveteen Rabbit.* (Cassette and four paperbacks); Troll Associates, Catalog Sales Dept., 100 Corporate Dr., Mahwah, NJ 07498; 1-800-929-8765.

*Video Vowels Series.* (Videos for teaching vowel sounds); Each video-25 min. National School Products, 101 East Broadway, Maryville, TN 37804; 1-800-251-9124.

*What's It Like to Be a Veterinarian?* (Cassette and four paperbacks); Troll Associates, Catalog Sales Dept., 100 Corporate Dr., Mahwah, NJ 07498; 1-800-929-8765.

# A Very Violet Velvety Valentine

Enlarge the following key picture by creating an overhead transparency of this page. Project and trace it onto white poster board. Leave the background white. Use a variety of purples to color the hearts, ribbons, and flowers. Then laminate the Valentine. (See the alternatives shown below.) Refer to the key picture each day, especially when you discuss the calendar (page 9). At the end of the week, tape the Valentine to a wall as part of an alphabet line-up.

**Alternative 1:** Use purple poster board for the background and glue the picture from a store-bought Valentine onto it. Allow the glue to dry. Then laminate the Valentine.

**Alternative 2:** Cut a heart-shape from a doily and glue it onto purple poster board. Then place and glue ribbon and small flowers in a heart shape on the doily. (Doilies, ribbon, and small flowers can be purchased at craft stores.)

Especially for You

# Visor

# The Letter Q

### • *LETTER OF THE WEEK*

Display the key picture of The Quiet Queen's Quilt (page 197). Refer to it each day. During the week, have students make the letter **Q** using a variety of materials such as quarter rubbings, feather quills, fabric glued into a quilt pattern, quick-cooking (uncooked) oat cereal, etc.

### • *QUEEN'S QUILT*

1. Read *Patchwork Quilt* by Valerie Flourney (Dial, 1985). Show pictures of quilts and quilt designs. Allow students to examine some real quilts if possible. Talk about how people make quilts by sewing together leftover scraps of fabric. Explain that the pieces are quilted together with cotton in the center for warmth.

2. Ask the class to make a quilt fit only for a queen. Give each student half of a 9" x 12" (23 cm x 30 cm) piece of yellow construction paper to design a quilt square using crayons or markers. Put your quilt together on a piece of 36" (91 cm) wide red butcher paper. Cut 2 ½" (6.3 cm) blue squares of construction paper. On the red paper, glue students' yellow construction paper quilt squares turned lengthwise—three across, separated by blue squares. Display the quilt with a picture of a queen at the top holding it.

3. Students may wish to make a quilt for the housekeeping center. They may bring a piece of material that means something to them and share their stories. The pieces of material may then be stitched together. If desired, cut another piece of material the size of the completed quilt. Sew the two together with some cotton batting in the center.

### • *QUIET Q*

Read aloud a book about someone or something being quiet. See the bibliography (page 196) for suggestions. Talk about times and places that people have to be quiet. Examples include movie theaters, hospitals, libraries, when a baby is sleeping, when someone is talking or reading a story, and when someone is on the phone. Give each student half a piece of white construction paper. Ask them to quietly cut out pictures of quiet things. Attach them to a bulletin board in the shape of a "**Q**," and label it "Quiet Things."

# The Letter Q *(cont.)*

## • *QUIET GAME*

Have students play the Quiet Game. This is an especially good game to play when the class is waiting in line to go somewhere. To play, select one quiet student to be "it." Then that student stands out from the line and watches the other students to see who is the quietest. The student who is the quietest is then selected to be "it" next. Play continues in this manner for the amount of time that you designate.

## • *QUARTER*

1. Look at a quarter. Identify it from a group of coins containing a penny, nickel, and a dime. Ask: *How much is a quarter worth? How many other ways can you make 25 cents? What will a quarter buy?* Tell students whose pictures are on quarters, pennies, nickels, dimes, and dollar bills.

2. Set up a store in the dramatic play center. Put 1-cent, 5-cent, 10-cent, and 25-cent price tags on crayons, erasers, pencils, scissors, etc. Give each student a play-money quarter and help him or her decide how to spend it. Help students discover that they can buy 25 1-cent crayons for the same quarter that can be used to buy one 25-cent pair of scissors.

## • *QUESTION GAME*

Ask a question. The person who answers it correctly may ask the next question and choose someone to answer it. Continue in this manner until each student has had the opportunity to ask a question.

## • *QUILL*

Explain that long ago people wrote with ink and feathers called quills. Purchase some large feathers from a craft or hobby store. Have students practice writing by dipping the feathers into ink or paint. You might wish to have them practice writing their names, addresses, the alphabet, or numerals (1–10).

## • *QUIVER*

Write the word *quiver* on the chalkboard. Say it aloud and ask students what it means. Point out that they are going to learn a new word using dictionaries. Provide a picture dictionary for each pair of students. Encourage them to work together to look up the word in the dictionary. After they have located *quiver,* read the definition to them. Then have each student make an illustration of a quiver. Frequently ask students to learn new words using the dictionary.

## • *QUICK SNACK*

Ask parents if their children have any food allergies or dietary restrictions. Invite students to help you make instant pudding or quick bread from a mix. Then allow them to enjoy their quick snack.

# Bibliography

## Books

Bond, Michael. *Paddington Meets the Queen.* HarperCollins, 1993.

Brown, Margaret Wise. *The Quiet Noisy Book.* HarperCollins, 1993.

Carey, Valerie. *Quail Song: A Pueblo Indian Folktale.* Putnam, 1990.

Carle, Eric. *The Very Quiet Cricket.* Philomel, 1990.

Casey, Patricia. *Quack, Quack.* Lothrop, Lee and Shepherd, 1988.

Coerr, Eleanor. *The Josefina Story Quilt.* Harper & Row, 1986.

de Paola, Tomie. *The Quicksand Book.* Holiday, 1977.

Flourney, Valerie. *Patchwork Quilt.* Dial, 1985.

Fowler, Allan. *Quack and Honk.* Childrens Press, 1993.

Gravois, Jeanne. *Quickly Quigley.* William Morris, 1994.

Hoban, Julia. *Quick Chick.* Viking, 1995.

Hopkins, Lee, ed. *Questions.* Harper & Row, 1994.

Hurd, Thacher. *Quiet Evening.* Greenwillow, 1992.

Johnston, Tony and Tomie de Paola. *The Quilt Story.* Putnam, 1985.

Jonas, Ann. *The Quilt.* Greenwillow, 1985.

Langton, Jane. *The Queen's Necklace: A Swedish Folktale.* Walt Disney Press, 1994.

Low, Alice. *The Quilted Elephant and the Green Velvet Dragon.* Simon and Schuster, 1991.

Mahy, Margaret. *The Queen's Goat.* Dial, 1991.

McDonnell, Janet. *The Quarterback's Adventure in Alphabet Town.* Childrens Press, 1992.

Merriam, Eve. *Quiet, Please.* Simon and Schuster, 1993.

Moncure, Jane B. *Question Books* (Series). Childrens Press, 1984.

Murphy, Jill. *Quiet Night In.* Candlewick Press, 1994.

Murphy, Joelie. *Quick, Go Peek!* HarperCollins, 1995.

Polacco, Patricia. *The Keeping Quilt.* Simon and Schuster, 1988.

Prelutsky, Jack. *Queen of Eene.* Greenwillow, 1978.

Smith, Kathie B. *Rand McNally Question Books: The Senses.* Macmillan, 1986.

Stevenson, James. *Quick! Turn the Page.* Greenwillow, 1990.

Wild, Margaret. *The Queen's Holiday.* Orchard, 1992.

Wood, D. *Quick As a Cricket.* Child's Play, 1990.

Zolotow, Charlotte. *The Quarreling Book.* Harper & Row, 1963.

## Technology

*The Keeping Quilt.* (Video); 11 min. Pied Piper/AIMS Multimedia, 9710 De Soto Ave., Chatsworth, CA 91311; 1-800-367-2567.

*The Quarreling Book.* (Video); 16 min. Coronet/MTI Film and Video, P.O. Box 2649, Columbus, OH 43216; 1-800-321-3106.

# The Quiet Queen's Quilt

Enlarge the following key picture by creating an overhead transparency of this page. Project and trace it onto white poster board. Then color the quilt. Then laminate the quilt. Refer to the key picture each day, especially when you discuss the calendar (page 9). At the end of the week, tape the quilt to a wall as part of an alphabet line-up.

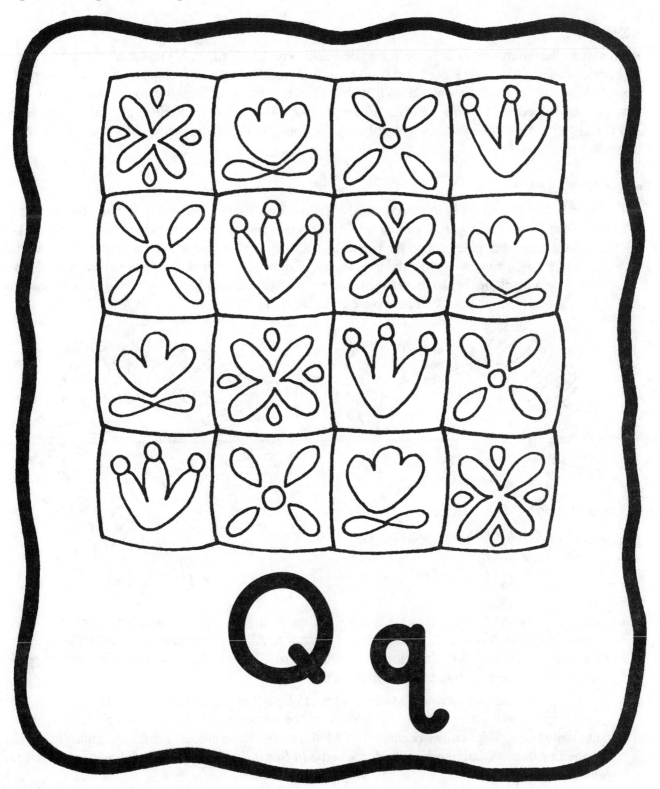

# The Letter Y

• *LETTER OF THE WEEK*

Display the key picture of the Yellow Yarn Yo-Yo (page 202). Refer to it each day. During the week, have students make the letter **Y** using a variety of materials such as yellow yarn, raw yam prints, yogurt, etc.

• *YARN*

Read aloud *Charlie Needs a Cloak* by Tomie de Paola (Prentice Hall, 1973) and *A New Coat for Anna* by Harriet Ziefert (Alfred A. Knopf, 1986). Try to find in a students' encyclopedia how wool comes from a sheep to being yarn in a sweater. If it is available, read the information to students. Or if possible obtain a copy of *Spring Fleece: A Day of Sheepshearing* by Catherine Paladino (Little, Bown and Co., 1990.) Although this book is text heavy for young children the black and white photos will prove helpful.

• *YELLOW YARN*

1. On or before March 1st help students make Yellow Yarn Lions. Use the following directions to make each lion: Wind yellow yarn around two fingers and cut on each end so that it is about 2–3" (5–8 cm) long. Put glue around the rim of a small paper plate and attach the yellow yarn so that it looks like a lion's mane. Allow the glue to dry. Color the center of the plate yellow for the lion's face. Use a black marker to draw facial features. After students have completed their Yellow Yarn Lions, place them on your Calendar bulletin board (page 9).

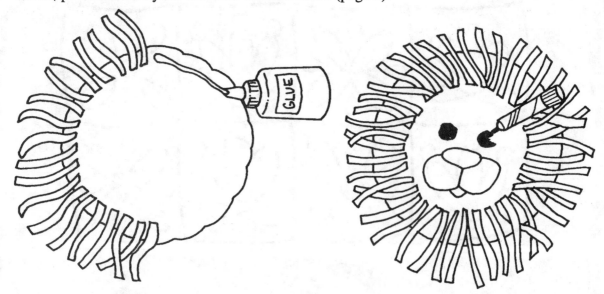

2. Review the following shapes: circle, square, rectangle, and triangle. Model how to make these shapes by gluing yellow yarn onto pieces of tagboard. Allow students to copy your shapes with glue and yellow yarn. Ask them to make Yellow Yarn **Y**'s, as well. Students may want to create pictures with glue and strands of colorful yarn.

3. Have students learn the saying, "March comes in like a lion and goes out like a lamb." Ask: *Do you think this saying is true?* Discuss how "lion" or winter weather occurs when March begins and "lamb" or spring weather occurs when March ends. Have students name examples of each. On the first day of March, ask: *Did March come in like a lion? Do you think it will go out like a lamb?*

# The Letter Y *(cont.)*

## • *YELLOW YARN BALL*

Spin a "yarn" with a yellow yarn ball. Wind yellow yarn into a ball. Have students tell a story as they toss the yarn ball, allowing it to unwind as it goes around the room. As each person catches the yarn ball he or she must add a line to the story before throwing it to someone else. On another day, allow students to name yellow things as they toss the yarn ball and let it unwind.

## • *YELLOW DAFFODILS*

1. The daffodil bulbs that you planted (page 148) should be blooming by now. Have students recall the growth sequence: bulb, sprout, leaf and bud, flower. Fold pieces of white construction paper into fourths and cut them apart. Provide four parts to each student. Students should draw the growth sequence from memory on the four pieces of construction paper and number them 1–4. After students have completed their drawings, ask them to put them in order. Staple each set of four pages together to make a booklet. Make a cover for each booklet by folding half of a piece of yellow construction paper over the picture pages. Staple the covers in place. Have students use orange to color the center of yellow cupcake papers. Tell them to glue the cupcake paper daffodil on the front of their covers. After the glue is dry, have them draw green stems. Write "Yellow Daffodil" as the title for each booklet.

2. Have students make yellow daffodils for your spring bulletin board. For each daffodil, use the following directions: Cut two pieces of yellow crepe paper or tissue paper using the pattern on page 203. Cross the two pieces in the center. In the middle, hold a small gold or white candy liner paper with a 1" (2.5 cm) bottom. Poke a green chenille stem up through the center of the two crepe or tissue paper pieces and the candy liner. Bend the end of the chenille stem to secure it. Fold up the other end to make a leaf. Staple the flowers under the Class Tree (page 9).

3. Start a backwards countdown to spring. On sentence strips or adding machine tape, write the numbers backwards to count the days until spring. Have students mark off a number each day and count backwards to zero as you talk about the calendar (page 9).

## • *YARD*

1. Take the class on a walk around the school yard. Have students smell pansies or other flowers that might be blooming. Ask: *Can you find any daffodils or other yellow flowers? How have the bulbs that you planted last fall changed? Are they blooming yet? What season is coming next? Can you find signs of its arrival?*

2. Talk about what you see in the school yard. Take paper bags and encourage students to make a "yard collection" of litter. Have students make posters showing themselves collecting the litter. Display the posters on a bulletin board entitled "Keep Our School Yard Clean!"

## • *YO-YOS*

Have a Yo-Yo Day when students may bring yo-yos to school and practice their spins. Have extras for those who do not have one. You may wish to provide an inexpensive yo-yo for each child as a treat.

# The Letter Y *(cont.)*

- *YANKEE DOODLE*

  1. Have students make Yankee Doodle Hats (page 204) using pages from the newspaper. Provide real or paper feathers for them to stick in their hats.

  2. Have a patriotic parade on George Washington's birthday (February 22). Let students wear the hats, carry a flag, sing "Yankee Doodle," and enjoy some frozen cherry yogurt.

- *YEAR*

Help students count and name the months in the year. Ask: *Which holidays are in each month? What are the four seasons? Which months are in each season?* Read several books about the months and seasons of the year.

- *YES OR NO*

Have students play Twenty Questions. In this game the person who is "it" thinks of an object. The rest of the class asks twenty "yes" or "no" questions and tries to determine what the object is. The student who correctly guesses the answer is "it." If no one guesses correctly, the person who is "it" can select the next player.

- *YESTERDAY*

When you discuss the calendar (page 9) each day, include the following statements: "Yesterday was
_____. Today is _____. Tomorrow will be
_____. Have the class fill in the blanks. Ask students to draw a picture of what they did yesterday.

- *YOGA*

Teach the class how to do some easy yoga stretches.

- *YUMMY YELLOW YOGURT*

Mix 2 cups (500 mL) of lemon yogurt, several drops of yellow food coloring, and 8 ounces (225 g) of whipped topping. For each student, put a lemon wafer in the bottom of a plastic cup and top it with the yogurt mixture. You may want to try lemon or peach frozen yogurt. Allow students to taste several different flavors of yogurt and make a graph showing each student's favorite flavor.

- *YAM YUM YUM*

In a large casserole dish, combine 2 cans of drained yams and 2 cans of sliced apples or apple pie filling. Sprinkle the mixture with brown sugar and cinnamon. Dot with some margarine. Bake at 350° F (175° C) until bubbly (about 20–30 minutes). If desired, you can place miniature marshmallows on top and return the dish to the oven until they are melted.

- *"Y" LITERATURE*

Read aloud a book that has the letter **Y** as part of its theme. See the bibliography (page 201) for suggestions.

# Bibliography

## Books

Abrams, Judith Z. *Yom Kippur—A Family Service.* Kar-Ben Copies, 1990.

Ahlberg, Janet and Allan. *Yum Yum.* Viking Kestrel, 1984.

Bang, Molly. *The Yellow Ball.* Houghton Mifflin, 1986.

Blocksma, Mary. *Yoo Hoo, Moon!* Bantam Books, 1992.

Curtis, Jamie Lee. *When I Was Little: A Four-Year-Old's Memoir of Her Youth.* HarperCollins, 1993.

Dolgin, Phyllis. *Yin's Special Thanksgiving.* January Productions, 1985.

Ehlert, Lois. *Red Leaf, Yellow Leaf.* HBJ, 1991.

Giff, Patricia. *Yankee Doodle Drumsticks.* Yearling, Dell, 1992.

Greenburg, Dan. *Young Santa.* Viking, 1991.

Greenfield, Karen Radler. *Sister Yessa's Story.* HarperCollins, 1992.

Hefter, Richard. *Yakety Yak Yak.* Holt, Rinehart and Winston, 1977.

Johnston, Tony. *Yonder.* Dial, 1988.

Jones, Diana Wynne. *Yes, Dear.* Greenwillow, 1992.

Leonard, Marcia. *Bear's Busy Year: A Book About Seasons.* Troll, 1990.

Lobel, Arnold. *Frog and Toad All Year.* Harper & Row, 1976.

Locker, Thomas. *Young Artist.* Viking, 1993.

Marshall, James. *Yummers, Too.* Houghton Mifflin, 1986.

McPhail, David. *Yesterday I Lost a Sneaker.* Silver Burdett, 1995.

Munsch, Robert N. *Purple, Green, and Yellow.* Annick, 1992.

Pallotta, Jerry. *The Yucky Reptile Alphabet Book.* Charlesbridge, 1989.

Pearson, Susan. *My Favorite Time of Year.* Scholastic, 1988.

Raschka, Chris. *Yo! Yes?* Orchard Books, 1993.

Schackburg, Dr. Richard. *Yankee Doodle.* Simon and Schuster, 1994.

Seuss, Dr. *Yertle the Turtle and Other Stories.* Random House, 1958.

Stevenson, James. *Yuck!* William Morrow, 1987.

Zolotow, Charlotte. *If It Weren't for You.* HarperCollins, 1987.

## Technology

*Nature Stories and Poem.* (Video includes *The Year at Maple Hill*); 11 min. Pied Piper/AIMS Multimedia, 9710 De Soto Ave., Chatsworth, CA 91311; 1-800-367-2567.

*Yearn 2 Learn: Snoopy.* (Software includes readiness skills); WIN; National School Products, 101 East Broadway, Maryville, TN 37804; 1-800-251-9124.

*Yummy, Yummy.* (Cassette and four paperbacks); Troll Associates, Catalog Sales Dept., 100 Corporate Dr., Mahwah, NJ 07498; 1-800-929-8765.

# Yellow Yarn Yo-Yo

Enlarge the following key picture by creating an overhead transparency of this page and projecting it onto laminated poster board. Spread glue over the yo-yo part of the projection or trace the yo-yo and then spread glue over it. Swirl yellow yarn over the glue, making it look like a yo-yo. Allow the glue to dry. Refer to the key picture each day, especially when you discuss the calendar (page 9). At the end of the week, tape the yarn yo-yo to a wall as part of an alphabet line-up.

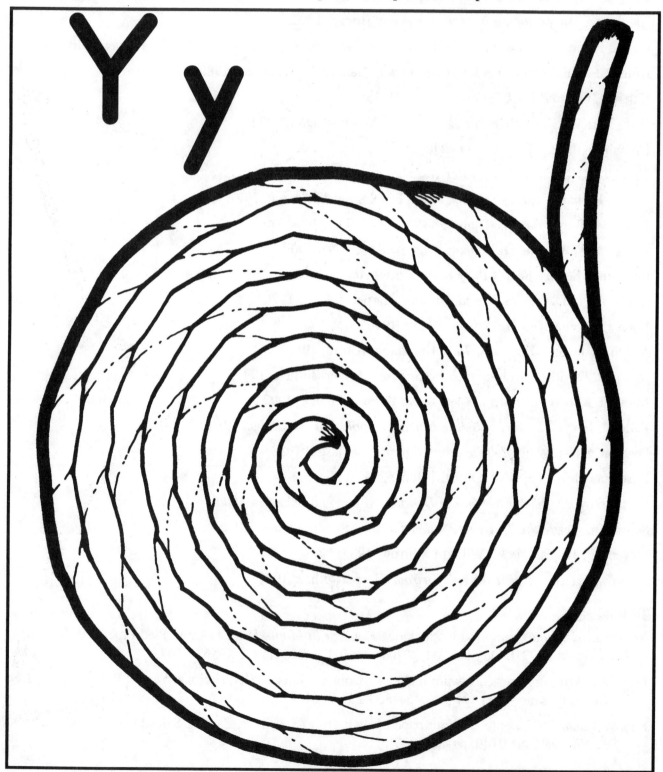

# Yellow Daffodil

Use yellow crepe or tissue paper to cut two copies of the pattern shown below.  Put one copy in front of the other, overlapping them as shown.  In the center, hold a small white or gold candy liner paper with a 1" (2.5 cm) bottom.  Poke a green chenille stem up through the center of the two crepe or tissue paper pieces and the candy liner.  Bend the end of the chenille stem to secure it.  Fold up the other end to make a leaf.

# Yankee Doodle Hat

**Directions:** Fold a section of the newspaper in half as shown.  Fold down the top corners.  Fold up the bottom on each side to form a hat.  Color.  Add a feather.

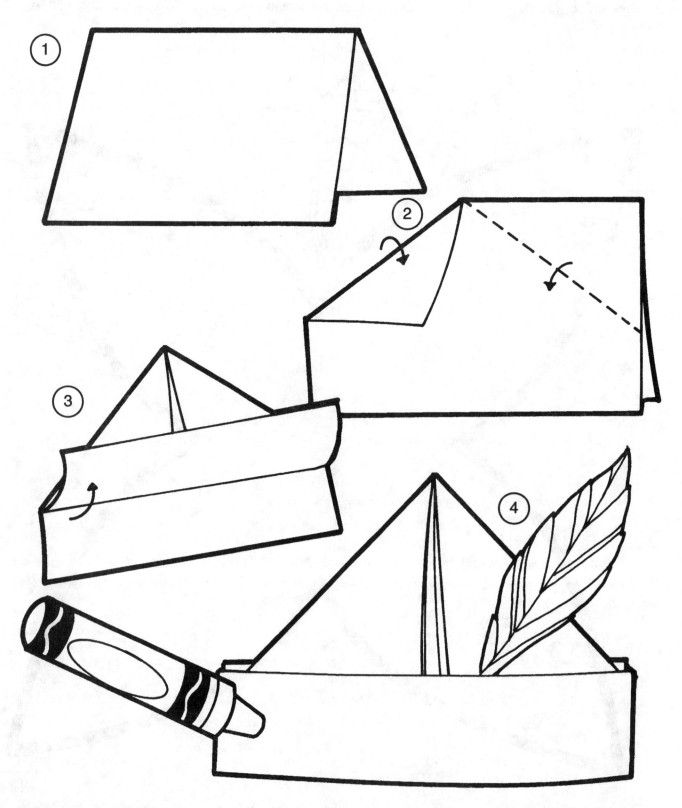

# The Letter L

- ### *MARCH*

  1. Review the following saying with students: "March comes in like a lion and goes out like a lamb." Discuss its meaning.

  2. Reproduce the heart patterns (page 211) on green paper for students. Invite them to make shamrock leaves for the Class Tree (page 9) by gluing three green hearts together.

- ### *LETTER OF THE WEEK*

Display the key picture of A Laughing Lion with a Lunchbox (page 209). Refer to it each day. During the week, have students make the letter **L** using a variety of materials such as lace, lemon drops or lollipops, lemon gelatin, etc.

- ### *LIONS AND LAMBS*

  1. Read aloud some lion and lamb books as students look at the pictures. See the bibliography (page 208) for suggestions. Discuss the behavior of each animal. (You may also wish to use the pictures provided on page 210.) Talk about lion and lamb weather. Ask: *Did March come in like a lion? Do you think it will go out like a lamb?* Make an opinion graph. Students may change their minds and the graph as the month progresses.

  2. Have students make some lambs for the right side of your Calendar bulletin board (page 9). Ask each student to do the following: Cut out a lamb face (page 210) and glue it in the center of a small paper plate. Use cotton recycled from medicine and vitamin bottles to glue around the edge of the paper plate. Stretch the cotton out a bit so it will look like lamb's wool.

  3. Bring in some of the herb "Lamb's Ear" for students to feel. Ask: *How do you think it got its name?*

  4. Have students recite or sing "Mary Had a Little Lamb" (*Nursery Rhymes: Book One*, TCM560). Review "Little Bo Peep" (*Nursery Rhymes: Book Three*, TCM562).

- ### *LITTLE AND LARGE*

Read aloud *The Lion and the Mouse* by Aesop (Troll, 1981). Ask students to make a list of large things and a list of little things. Ask: *How are large things important? How are little things important?* Have students draw something little and tell how it is important to them.

- ### *LUCKY LEAPING LEPRECHAUNS*

  1. Give students some green construction paper as well as other colors in addition to wallpaper samples and other art supplies. Let them create their own leprechauns. Show them how to fold green strips of paper accordion-style for the arms and legs. Hang the leprechauns from the ceiling using paper clips and string or put them on the Class Tree bulletin board (page 9). Students may also like to create leprechaun houses using the pattern on page 212.

  2. Take the class outside to look for lucky four-leaf clovers. Ask: *What would you do if you caught a leprechaun on St. Patrick's Day?* and *Might leprechauns be lavender?*

# The Letter L *(cont.)*

## • *LUCKY LEAPING LEPRECHAUNS (cont.)*

3. Allow students to use whatever materials they can find in the room (paper, blocks, manipulatives, etc.) to devise "Leprechaun Traps" the morning of, or the day before, St. Patrick's Day. This may be done cooperatively or individually. While you are at lunch, have someone put gold foil-wrapped chocolate coins or other individually wrapped candies in the inventions. If you prefer, put a "pot of gold" with candies in it in a prominent place in your classroom. Leave a green shamrock note next to the pot saying, "Sorry you could not catch me. I liked your Leaping Leprechauns, so I left you a special treat! Happy St. Patrick's Day! Lucky Leprechaun." Share the candies with students. Provide some lime green juice or gelatin for them to enjoy.

4. Make a Class Book entitled "The Day I Met a Leprechaun . . ."

## • *LAVENDER*

Bring in some lavender flowers or perfume for students to smell. Plant some English lavender seeds.

## • *LETTERS*

1. Work together to write a letter to your librarian thanking her or him for helping you learn to use the library. In the letter, tell the librarian what your students' favorite books and activities are.

2. Help each student write a letter to someone they love. In the letters, have students tell why they love the people they are writing to.

## • *LOVE*

1. Ask: *Whom or what do you love? What does love mean? How do your parents show you love? Do your parents love you when they punish you for doing what they asked you not to do? Do they love you when they do not allow you to cross the street alone?*

2. Have students draw or cut out pictures to make an "I Love" collage.

## • *LIVING THINGS*

1. Ask students to brainstorm a list of living things. Discuss the characteristics of living things. Examples: Living things move, grow and change, and have babies. They need food, water, air, sunshine, and shelter (a home). Explain that non-living things do not need the same things as living things. Examples: Tables and rocks do not move, grow, or have babies. They do not need food, water, air, sunshine, or shelter.

2. Have students cut out pictures of living things. On another day have them cut out pictures of non-living things. Make "Living Things" and "Non-living Things" collages. Discuss the characteristics of each thing depicted before students decide on which collage it belongs.

## • *LITTER*

Have students dispose of litter they find around the school. Ask: *Where should we put trash instead of throwing it on the ground? Why is this important? What things can be recycled?*

# The Letter L (cont.)

### • LOOK AND LISTEN

1. Take students on a "Look and Listen Walk." Ask them to look and listen for living and non-living things, signs of spring, and leaves. Ask: *What is happening to the trees now? They looked dead all winter, but were they?* Show them the flower bulbs they planted last fall. Ask: *Are they living or non-living? How can you tell?*

2. Return to the classroom and have students brainstorm lists of living and non-living things that they saw and heard outside. Ask: *What changes will spring bring*? Write down students' responses. Write the date when students first spot each thing on the list.

### • LISTENING

1. Have students listen to and follow 2- or 3-part simple directions. Examples: Walk to the door and knock three times. Walk to the table and touch your head. Hold up your yellow, orange, and red crayons. Allow students who listen successfully to take turns giving directions.

2. Make loud and soft sounds and ask students to identify the tone of each. Make high and low sounds and ask them to identify the pitch of each.

### • LIST OF "L" OPPOSITES

Make a list of opposites in which one or both words begin with **L**. Examples include little and large, long and short, loud and soft, left and right, light and dark, and like and dislike.

### • LACING

Have students practice lacing and tying shoes. Punch holes in clean plastic meat trays to make shapes for additional lacing practice.

### • LUNCH

1. Give each student a paper plate. Ask students to cut out pictures to show their favorite lunches. Before letting them glue their pictures onto the plates, remind them that they should have a meat or meat substitute (such as cheese or peanut butter), bread, fruit and/or vegetable, and milk for a healthful lunch.

2. Review lunchtime rules. Surprise those who remember with lemon lollipops.

### • LICORICE

Allow students to use various flavors of licorice lace to practice forming letters. Then they can enjoy eating the licorice when the practice session is over.

### • LEMONS AND LIMES

Have students look at some lemons and limes and compare them. Ask them to try to tell the difference between these fruits by smelling each one. Have students complete the following activities using lemons and limes: Dip halves in yellow and green paint to make prints; make some lemon-limeade, adding water and sugar to taste; fingerpaint with lemon pudding on paper plates or wax paper; and sprinkle powdered lemon and/or lime gelatin on **L** shapes.

# Bibliography

**Books**

Alda, Arlene. *Sheep, Sheep, Sheep, Help Me Fall Asleep.* Delacourte, 1992.

Allen, Pamela. *A Lion in the Night.* Putnam, 1986.

Berenstain, Stan and Jan. *The Berenstain Bears and the Truth.* Random House, 1983.

Bunting, Eve. *Clancy's Coat.* Viking Kistrel, 1984.

de Paola, Tomie. *Haircuts for the Woolseys.* Putnam, 1989.

de Paola, Tomie. *Jamie O'Rourke and the Big Potato.* Scholastic, 1992.

Eaton, Dave. *What Is Love?* Harvest House, 1986.

Ernst, Lisa. *Nattie Parsons' Good-Luck Lamb.* Puffin, 1988.

Fatio, Louise. *The Happy Lion.* Scholastic, 1986.

Giff, Patricia. *Lazy Lions, Lucky Lambs.* Delacorte, 1986.

Hale, Sarah Josepha. *Mary Had a Little Lamb.* Orchard, 1995.

Hoban, Tana. *Is It Larger? Is It Smaller?* Greenwillow Books, 1985.

Hoban, Tana. *Over, Under, and Through and Other Spatial Concepts.* Macmillan, 1973.

Hoban, Tana. *Push-Pull, Empty-Full: A Book of Opposites.* Macmillan, 1972.

Holloway, Judith and Clive Harper. *Living Things.* Modern Curriculum Press, 1990.

Hooks, William H. and Barbara Brenner. *Lion and Lamb.* Bantam, 1989.

John, Joyce, illus. *The Leprechaun's Treasure.* Nystrom, 1992.

Kimmel, Eric. *I Took My Frog to the Library.* Viking, 1990.

Kitamura, Satoshi. *When Sheep Cannot Sleep.* Farrar, Straus, & Giroux, 1986.

Offen, Hilda. *The Sheep Made a Leap.* Dutton, 1994.

Sanders, Scott Russell. *Warm as Wool.* Bradbury, 1992.

Scarry, Richard. *Big and Little.* Western, 1986.

Scarry, Richard. *Things to Love.* Western, 1987.

Schertle, Alice. *Jeremy Bean's St. Patrick's Day.* Lothrop, Lee, & Shepard, 1987.

Shaw, Nancy. *Sheep in a Jeep.* Houghton Mifflin, 1986.

Shaw, Nancy. *Sheep in a Shop.* Houghton Mifflin, 1991.

Shaw, Nancy. *Sheep on a Ship.* Houghton Mifflin, 1988.

Shaw, Nancy. *Sheep Out to Eat.* Houghton Mifflin, 1992.

Shaw, Nancy. *Sheep Take a Hike.* Houghton Mifflin, 1994.

Shute, Linda. *Clever Tom and the Leprechaun.* Scholastic, 1988.

Stevens, Janet. *Androcles and the Lion.* Holiday, 1989.

Sundgaard, Arnold. *Lamb and the Butterfly.* Orchard, 1988.

Watanabe, Shigeo. *What a Good Lunch!* Putnam, 1988.

**Technology**

*How the Leopard Got His Spots.* (Video); 11 min. Coronet/MTI Film and Video, P.O. Box 2649, Columbus, OH 43216; 1-800-321-3106.

*The Lion and the Mouse.* (Video); 10 min. Coronet/MTI Film and Video, P.O. Box 2649, Columbus, OH 43216; 1-800-321-3106.

# A Laughing Lion with a Lunchbox

Enlarge the following key picture by creating an overhead transparency of this page. Project and trace it onto yellow poster board. Color the lunchbox red and the lion's feet, mane, and the tip of its tail brown. Then laminate the lion. Refer to the key picture each day, especially when you discuss the calendar (page 9). At the end of the week, tape the lion to a wall as part of an alphabet line-up.

# Lamb and Lion Faces

**Lion**

**Lamb**

# Shamrock Leaves

Reproduce the patterns shown below on green paper. Cut them out. Glue the parts together as shown.
Students may decorate the Shamrock leaves with glitter and sequins if desired. After the glue has dried,
display the Shamrock leaves on the March Class Tree (page 9).

# Lucky Leaping Leprechaun Land

Students may decorate the leprechaun houses with crayons, markers, glitter, sequins, buttons, lace trims, colored glue, feathers, silk flowers, yarn, etc. Put some leaping Leprechauns and students' Leprechaun houses under the Shamrock Class Tree (page 211).

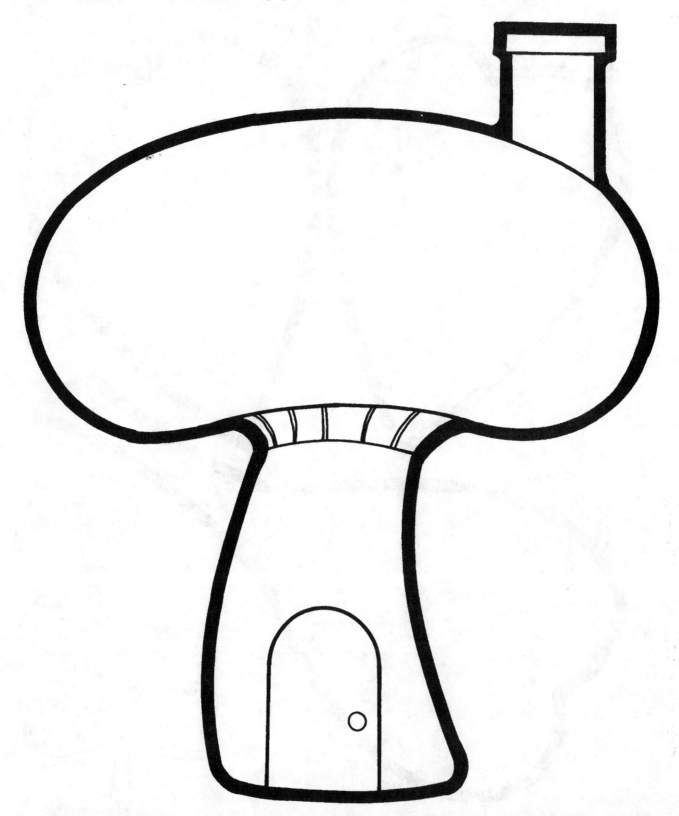

# Leprechaun Hat

Reproduce the hat pattern shown below. Have each student color and decorate a hat. Then help students cut out their hats. Staple each hat to a tagboard band. Adjust the band so that it fits a student's head, then staple it closed. Allow students to wear their Leprechaun hats on St. Patrick's Day (March 17).

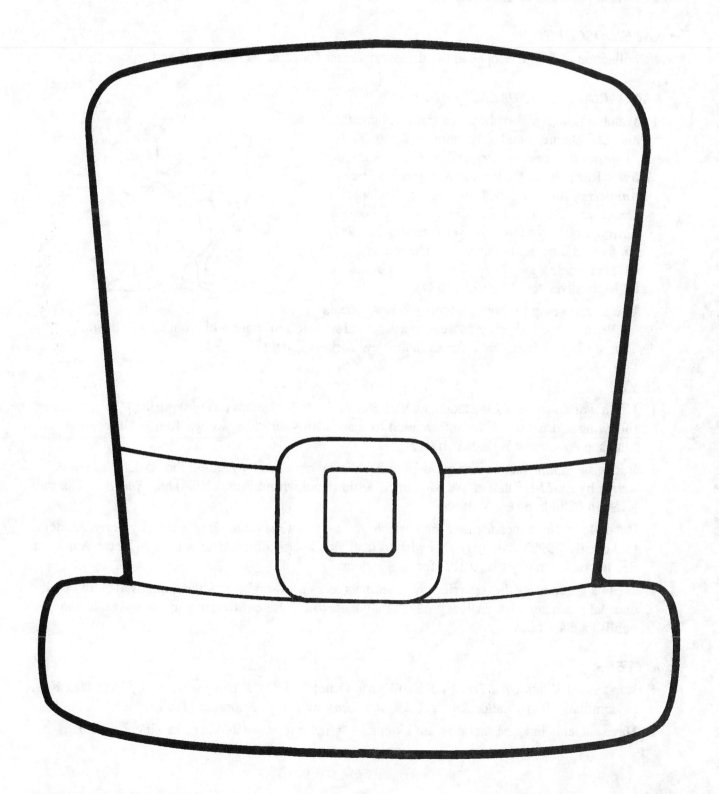

# The Letter K

- **LETTER OF THE WEEK**

Display the key picture, A Kaleidoscopic Kite (page 218). Refer to it each day. During the week, have students make the letter **K** using a variety of materials such as popcorn kernels, small kite shapes, ketchup (red paint can be substituted), etc.

- **KALEIDOSCOPE**

Put a collection of kaleidoscopes in the discovery center for students to explore and enjoy.

- **KANGAROOS AND KOALAS**

1. Watch a film or video about Australia. Name the animals that are found only there. Ask: *Is life in Australia the same or very different from where we live*? Read aloud *Koalas and Kangaroos: Strange Animals of Australia* by Toni Eugene (National Geographic Society, 1981), *What Do You Do with a Kangaroo?* by Mercer Mayer (Scholastic, 1987), *Kippy Koala* by Katherine Oana (University Classics, 1985), and *Kirby Koala Visits Grandma* by Ruth Silverstein (Antioch, 1984).

2. Use a world map to show students where Australia is. Write to the following address to ask for information to share with your class: Australian Tourist Commission, 489 Fifth Avenue, New York, NY 10117.

- **KENYA**

1. Use a world map to show students where Kenya is. It is a country in east Africa. Write to the following address to ask for information to share with your class: Kenya Tourist Office, 424 Madison Ave., New York, NY 10017.

2. Background information and pictorials may also be obtained by reading the books *We Live in Kenya* by Zulf M. Khalfan and Mohamed Amin (Bookwright Press, 1984) and *Kenya* by Conrad R. Stein (Childrens Press, 1985)

3. Read aloud *The Crocodile and the Ostrich: A Tale From the Akamba of Kenya* by Verna Aardema (Scholastic, 1992). You may also wish to read aloud some other African tales by Verna Aardema. See the bibliography (page 217) for suggestions.

4. Write a group story that describes how animals learn a lesson or how the animals acquired their unusual characteristics. Allow groups of students to illustrate different parts of your tale and publish a class book.

- **KITTENS**

1. Read aloud *Kitten Up a Tree* by Keiko Kanao (Knopf, 1987), *Kitten for a Day* by Ezra Jack Keats (Macmillan, 1974), and/or *Kitty . . . A Cat's Diary* by Robyn Supraner (Troll, 1986).

2. Have students imagine that they are kittens. Ask them to move and act like kittens would.

# The Letter K *(cont.)*

## • KING

1. Obtain crowns for all students from local fast food restaurants if possible. As an alternative, cut crowns from yellow construction paper, and allow students to decorate them with glitter and sequins. Adjust and staple each crown so that it fits a student's head. Let students wear their crowns while listening to stories about kings. See the bibliography (page 217) for suggestions.

2. Students may draw castles they might live in if they were king (or queen). Ask: *What is the difference between a king and queen? What would you do all day if you were a king or queen? What rules would you change if you were king or queen?*

3. Make your own "If I Were King (or Queen) . . . Big Book using the pattern on page 219. Enlarge the pattern by making it into an overhead transparency and projecting it onto yellow tagboard. Trace and cut out two copies of the pattern for the covers of the book. Write the title on the front of one tagboard crown. Laminate both tagboard crowns. Use large white paper to trace and cut out the crown pattern for each student. You may wish to have parent volunteers or older students help you do this. Give students the white crown patterns, and let them draw pictures to show what they would do if they were king or queen. Write the sentences on their crowns. Place students' pages between the tagboard covers. Punch two holes in the sides and bind the book with metal rings. Hang the book on the stick-on plastic hooks on your classroom door or in the library center.

4. Help students do research to find out which countries still have kings and/or queens.

## • KITES

1. Invite students to make "Kaleidoscopic Kites" to fly on a windy day. Have them cut kite shapes from butcher paper. (Students may choose shapes such as birds or fish.) Tell them to decorate both sides of their kites with crayons or markers. On each kite, do the following: punch a hole near a bottom edge, put hole reinforcers on each side, tie on a long piece of cord or yarn, and tape crepe paper streamers to the bottom. On a windy day, take students outside with their kites to watch them fly.

2. Tell the class to stand in a circle. Have students hold up their kites and watch the streamers. Ask: *What is making the streamers move? Can you see the wind? Can you feel it? Can you hear it? Which way is it blowing? Can you see anything else the wind is moving?* Lead students to conclude that air is all around us, but we cannot see it. Wind is air that is moving. It blows many things, including kites and clouds.

3. Take students and a real kite outside on a windy day. Allow them to take turns flying the kite. You may wish to have an older student help you watch your students while flying the kites.

4. Encourage students to draw pictures of what they would see if they were riding on a kite that was flying in the wind.

# The Letter K *(cont.)*

- ### *KIND*

    1. Ask: *How can you be kind to kittens and other animals? Should you ever hurt other living things?*

    2. Adopt the following as a class motto: Never hurt a living thing.

    3. Talk about being kind to animals and people. Have students draw pictures of themselves doing something kind.

- ### *KIDNEY BEANS*

    1. Have the class practice counting skills using kidney beans. Call out a number and ask students to count out that many beans onto their kites. Provide students with the numeral cards 0–10 and ask them to count the correct number of beans onto each card.

    2. Allow students to make **K**'s with some kidney beans.

- ### *KITCHEN*

Ask students to organize the objects in the housekeeping center. Ask: *Are all the plates together? Are all the cups together? Where do they go? Are the pots and pans together? Where should you put them?* Lead students to conclude that organizing things makes them easier to find. You may wish to discuss how they can organize their things at school.

- ### *KICKBALL*

Together, play kickball outside. Direct students to kick only balls or other non-living things.

- ### *"K" SNACKS*

Ask students to brainstorm a list of foods that begin with the letter **K**. If possible, prepare some of these foods for students to taste. For example, you can peel and slice kiwi fruit for students to enjoy.

- ### *KEY*

    1. Bring a variety of keys for students to examine. Working together, have them sort the keys according to like characteristics.

    2. Have students practice fine-motor skills by tracing keys onto construction paper.

    3. Discuss the need to keep house keys in a safe place.

- ### *KIDS*

Show students pictures of baby goats and pictures of children. Ask if they know what baby goats and children have in common. Lead students to conclude that they are both called "kids."

# Bibliography

## Books

Aardema, Verna. *Ananse Finds a Fool.* Dial, 1992.

Aardema, Verna. *Bimwili and the Zimwi: A Tale from Zanzibar.* Dial, 1985.

Aardema, Verna. *The Crocodile and the Ostrich.* Scholastic, 1992.

Aardema, Verna. *Oh, Kojo! How Could You!: An Ashanti Tale.* Dial, 1985.

Aardema, Verna. *Princess Gorilla and a New Kind of Water: A Mpongwe Tale.* Dial, 1988.

Aardema, Verna. *Traveling to Tondo.* Knopf, 1991.

Brenner, Peter. *King for One Day.* Scroll, 1987.

Brown, Margery W. *Afro-bets: Book of Shapes.* Just Us Books, 1991.

Ellis, Veronica Freeman. *Afro-bets First Book About Africa: An Introduction for Young Readers.* Just Us Books, 1989.

Feelings, Muriel. *Moja Means One: A Swahili Counting Book.* Dial, 1971.

Gackenbach, Dick. *King Wacky.* Crown, 1984.

Geography Department. *Kenya in Pictures.* Lerner, 1988.

Grifalconi, Ann. *The Village of Round and Square Houses.* Little, Brown, 1986.

Hadithi, Mwenye. *Hot Hippo.* Little, Brown, 1986.

Haley, Gail E. *A Story, A Story.* Atheneum, 1970.

Heide, Florence Parry and Judith Heide Gililand. *The Day of Ahmed's Secret.* Lothrop, Lee & Shepard, 1990.

Hillig, Chuck. *The Magic King.* Stillpoint, 1984.

Hudson, Cheryl Willis. *Afro-bets 123 Book.* Just Us Books, 1987.

Kanao, Keiko. *Kitten Up a Tree.* Knopf, 1987.

Keats, Ezra Jack. *Kitten for a Day.* Macmillan, 1974.

Khalfan, Zulf M. and Mohamed Amin. *We Live in Kenya.* Bookwright Press, 1984.

Kipling, Rudyard. *The Elephant's Child.* Follett, 1969.

Knutson, Barbara. *How the Guinea Fowl Got Her Spots: A Swahili Tale of Friendship.* Lerner/Carolrhoda, 1990.

Mayer, Mercer. *What Do You Do with a Kangaroo?* Scholastic, 1987.

McKee, David. *King Rollo's Spring; King Rollo's Winter.* Penguin Books, 1989.

Oana, Katherine. *Kippy Koala.* University Classics, 1985.

Payne, Emmy. *Katy No-Pocket.* Houghton Mifflin, 1973.

Peters, Lisa W. *Serengeti.* Crestwood House, 1989.

Sendak, Maurice. *In the Night Kitchen.* Harper & Row, 1985.

Silverstein, Ruth. *Kirby Koala Visits Grandma.* Antioch, 1984.

Stein, Conrad R. *Kenya.* Childrens Press, 1985.

Stelson, Caren. *Safari.* Carolrhoda, 1988.

Steptoe, John. *Mufaro's Beautiful Daughters.* Scholastic, 1987.

Stock, Catherine. *Armien's Fishing Trip.* Morrow, 1990.

Supraner, Robyn. *Kitty . . . A Cat's Diary.* Troll, 1986.

Williams, Karen Lynn. *Galimoto.* Lothrop, Lee & Shepard, 1990.

Wood, Audrey. *Koala Lou.* HBJ, 1988.

Yolen, Jane. *Emperor and the Kite.* Putnam, 1988.

# A Kaleidoscopic Kite

Enlarge the following key picture by creating an overhead transparency of this page and projecting it onto poster board.  Trace and cut out the kite shape.  Decorate the kite by gluing a variety of poster board cutouts onto it.  Allow the glue to dry, then laminate the kite.  Use tape to attach a long string and crepe paper streamers to the back at the bottom of the kite.  Refer to the key picture each day, especially when you discuss the calendar (page 9).  At the end of the week, tape the kite to a wall as part of an alphabet line-up.

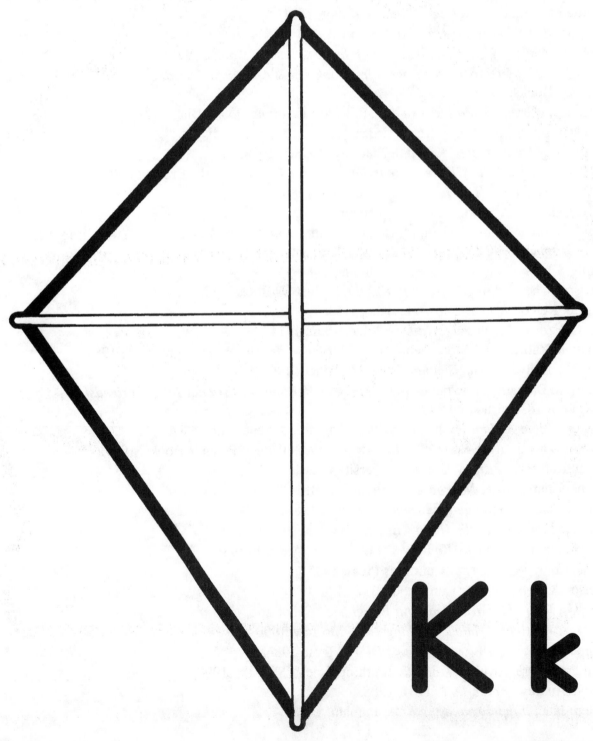

# King Shape Book

Create a Big Book, using the directions on page 215 and the pattern shown below.

If I were king (queen), I would _____

_____ .

# The Letter G

• *LETTER OF THE WEEK*

Display the key picture, Grasshopper in the Growing Green Grass (page 224). Refer to it each day. During the week, have students make the letter **G** using a variety of materials such as green or gold glitter, gravel and glue, washed grape seeds, gumdrops, real or cellophane grass, green grits, green crayon shavings, etc.

• *GREEN GRASS GROWING IN THE GARDEN*

1. Point out that plants are living things. They need water, air, sunshine, and minerals from the ground to make their own food in their leaves. Take students outside to look for green growing things. Ask: *Can you see leaves beginning to grow back on the trees? Is the grass getting green?* After returning to the classroom, ask students to list all the plants they saw while taking their walk.

2. Purchase several different packages of seeds (grass, radish, green bean, lima bean, lettuce, carrot, marigold). Put some seeds on wet paper towels. Seal them in reclosable plastic bags. Staple on the seed package or use permanent marker to write the name of the seeds enclosed in each plastic bag. Students can watch the seeds grow. Put some seeds on a dry paper towel. Ask: *Will they grow? Why or why not?*

3. Plant some of the pumpkin seeds that you saved during the fall. Have students place the seeds in recycled cups with a drainage hole in the bottom. Put one cup in a dark cabinet to show that plants need sun. Withhold water from another cup to show that plants need water.

4. Place a sweet potato in water to watch the vine grow.

5. If available, clip philodendron or wandering Jew vines and put them in water to watch the roots grow.

6. Stick carrot tops in a shallow pan of water to watch the tops grow.

7. Put celery stalks in clear glasses with different food coloring added to the water. Have students watch as the water moves up the stalk and colors the leaves. Explain that this is how water moves up plant stems into the leaves. Cut a slice from the bottom of a celery stalk for students to see the "tubes" where the water moves up to the leaves.

8. Have students learn "Mary, Mary, Quite Contrary" (*Nursery Rhymes: Book Four,* TCM 563). Ask: *What does your garden grow?* Invite parents to send empty seed packs to school if they plant gardens. Tape the packages to a piece of poster board. Help students determine which packages are for vegetables and which are for flowers. Ask: *What do we have the most of? What do we have the least of?* Make a graph to show the data.

9. Cut out pictures of plants and make a collage entitled "Plants Are Living Things."

10. Ask a school administrator for permission to have a vegetable garden on the school grounds. Have students plan what they want to grow and how to organize the garden. Then help them plant the vegetables and care for them until they are ready to harvest.

# The Letter G *(cont.)*

## • *GRAPH*

Make several graphs during the week. Ask questions about each and allow students to draw in their responses and write their names. Topics for graphs include the following questions: *Are you a guy or a gal? Are your eyes green, gray, blue, or brown? How will you go home today?*

## • *GROW UP*

Talk about different jobs that people have. Have students draw what they want to be when they grow up. Ask them to dictate sentences as you write them on strips of paper for a bulletin board entitled "You Can Be Anything You Want to Be." If you prefer, the sentences can be written on construction paper and made into a class book with the same title.

## • *GRASSHOPPERS AND OTHER BUGS*

1. Read several information books about insects. See the bibliography (page 223) for suggestions. In addition, read aloud from the Scholastic Big Book Magazine *Insects*. Take students outside on a bug hunt. Help students try to identify any bugs that they find. Ask: *Where do they live? What do they eat?* Tell students to draw what they saw in a "Bug Journal" and label each bug. If they did not see any bugs, ask them why they think the bugs were not visible. Make plans to go on another bug hunt later when the weather warms up.

2. Tell students that bugs and insects are living things. They are animals. An insect has three body parts (head, chest, and stomach) and six legs. Insects do not have bones like people, but rather a hard shell-like covering. Spiders are arachnids. They have eight legs and spin webs. Some insects like aphids, grasshoppers, and some beetles are harmful because they eat the plants in our gardens. Other bugs like ladybugs, spiders, and praying mantis are helpful because they eat harmful insects.

3. Read aloud Eric Carle's *The Grouchy Ladybug* (Crowell, 1986), *The Very Busy Spider* (Putnam, 1984), *The Very Quiet Cricket* (Philomel, 1990), and *The Very Hungry Caterpillar* (Philomel, 1969).

4. Point out that some insects, like butterflies, are beautiful to look at. Read *Flutterby* by Stephen Cosgrove (Price Stern Stone, 1984). Display some pictures of butterflies. Ask students to design the most gorgeous butterfly in the world (page 225). Encourage them to use all the colors they can or to tear pieces of multi-colored tissue paper and make a collage like Eric Carle's. Arrange the tissue paper on the butterfly pattern and brush with liquid laundry starch or thinned white glue. Hang the butterflies on paper clips tied to strings attached to the ceiling. Let them flutter in the breeze.

5. Have students sequence the butterfly's life cycle by following these steps: Divide a paper plate into fourths. Draw eggs on a leaf on one section, a caterpillar eating the leaf in the next section, a cocoon in the third section, and a butterfly in the last section.

6. Direct students to create new insects, draw diagrams of them, and name them.

7. Invite students to draw their five favorite bugs and dictate a sentence about each. Make a ladybug-shaped class book.

# The Letter G *(cont.)*

**• *GOOD HEALTH***

Review what is necessary for good health: healthful foods (meats or meat substitutes, breads and cereals, fruits, vegetables, milk products) and healthful snacks (low in sugar); plenty of rest, exercise, cleanliness, and clean teeth.

**• *GEORGE***

Read aloud several of H.A. and Margret Rey's books about a mischievous monkey named George.

**• *GLOBE***

1. Ask a volunteer to find water and land on a globe. Ask: *Is there more land or water? Can you find any mountains? Can you find an ocean?*

2. Help students locate your city, state, and country, and any other countries that you have learned about. Ask: *What other places would you like to learn about?*

3. Talk about the differences between maps and globes. Ask: *When would a globe be more useful? When would a map be more useful?*

4. Find the North Pole and the South Pole where it is always cold. Explain that on a globe, north is up and south is down. Find the equator around the center of the globe. Tell students that it is always hot there.

**• *GRANDPARENTS***

Invite students' grandparents to visit your class during the week. You may wish to arrange it so they can come to lunch one day. Students might like to draw themselves doing a special activity with their grandparents and dictate stories or make greeting cards as gifts to present to their grandparents when they arrive. Students whose grandparents live far away should be encouraged to mail their gifts or write letters. If possible, round up volunteers to be "adopted" by students who do not have grandparents. Ask grandparents to share some childhood memories.

**• *GROCERY STORE***

Set up a grocery store in the housekeeping center. Include clean empty food boxes, coupons, and paper and pencils for grocery lists.

**• *GUITAR***

Listen to a demonstration or a tape of different types (classical, rock, country) of guitar music.

**• *GREEN EGGS AND HAM***

Read *Green Eggs and Ham* by Dr. Seuss (Random House, 1987). Use food coloring to cook green eggs and green grits.

**• *GOOD SNACKS***

Allow students to enjoy honey on graham crackers, grapes or grape juice, and sugarless gum.

# Bibliography

## Books

Berenstain, Michael. *The Butterfly Book.* Western, 1992.

Berenstain, Stan and Jan. *The Berenstain Bears and the Week at Grandma's.* Random House, 1986.

Carle, Eric. *The Grouchy Ladybug.* Crowell, 1986.

Carle, Eric. *The Very Busy Spider.* Putnam, 1984.

Carle, Eric. *The Very Hungry Caterpillar.* Philomel, 1969.

Carle, Eric. *The Very Quiet Cricket.* Philomel, 1990.

Ehlert, Lois. *Planting a Rainbow.* HBJ, 1988.

Elkington, John. *Going Green: A Kid's Handbook to Saving the Planet.* Viking, 1990.

Farrand, John, Jr. *Butterflies.* W. H. Smith, 1990.

Fischer-Nagel, Heiderose and Andreas. *Life of the Ladybug.* Carolrhoda, 1986.

Fleming, Denise. *In the Tall, Tall Grass.* Holt, 1991.

Gibbons, Gail. *Monarch Butterfly.* Holiday House, 1989.

Grimm, Brothers. *The Golden Goose.* Troll, 1981.

Howe, James. *I Wish I Were a Butterfly.* Gulliver, 1987.

Katz, Bobbi. *The Creepy Crawly Book.* Random House, 1989.

Keats, Ezra Jack. *Goggles!* Macmillan, 1987.

Mattern, Joanne. *Insects.* Troll, 1991.

Mayer, Mercer. *Just Grandpa and Me.* Western, 1985.

Oechsli, Helen and Kelly Oechsli. *In My Garden: A Child's Gardening Book.* Macmillan, 1985.

O'Toole, Christopher. *Discovering Bees and Wasps.* Bookwright Press, 1986.

Pallotta, Jerry. *The Icky Bug Alphabet Book.* Charlesbridge, 1986.

Parker, Nancy and Joan Wright. *Bugs.* Greenwillow, 1987.

Pearce, Fred. *The Green Book.* Grosset and Dunlap, 1991.

Seuss, Dr. *Green Eggs and Ham.* Random House, 1987.

Still, John. *Amazing Butterflies and Moths.* Knopf, 1991.

Wilkes, Angela. *My First Green Book.* Knopf, 1991.

## Technology

*The Gingerbread Boy.* (Video); 8 min. Troll Associates, Catalog Sales Dept., 100 Corporate Dr., Mahwah, NJ 07498; 1-800-929-8765.

*Goggles.* (Videotape/Videodisc); Coronet/MTI Film and Video, P.O. Box 2649, Columbus, OH 43216; 1-800-321-3106.

*Goofy Ghost.* (Cassette); Troll Associates, Catalog Sales Dept., 100 Corporate Dr., Mahwah, NJ 07498; 1-800-929-8765.

*What's It Like to Be a Grocer?* (Cassette); Troll Associates, Catalog Sales Dept., 100 Corporate Dr., Mahwah, NJ 07498; 1-800-929-8765.

# Grasshopper in the Growing Green Grass

Enlarge the following key picture by creating an overhead transparency of this page and projecting it onto poster board. Then trace each part to make different colored bugs and the green grass. Cut out the poster board pieces and glue them together. Allow the glue to dry. Use a black marker to draw facial features on the bugs and write the letters. Then laminate the grass scene. Refer to the key picture each day, especially when you discuss the calendar (page 9). At the end of the week, tape the grass scene to a wall as part of an alphabet line-up.

# Gorgeous Butterfly

**Directions:** Make this the most gorgeous butterfly in the world.

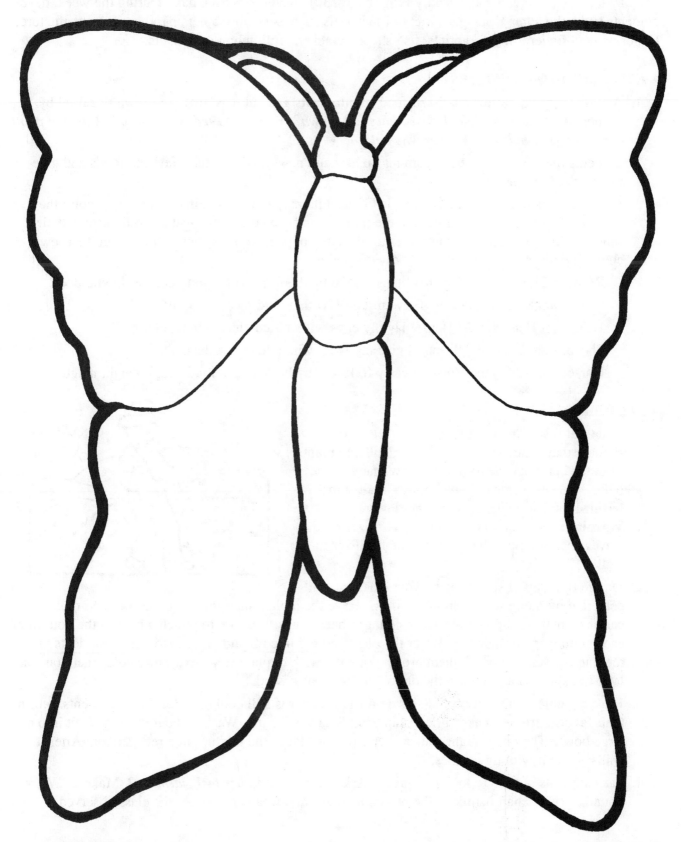

# The Letter F

• **LETTER OF THE WEEK**

Display the key picture, A Fat Friendly Frog (page 230).  Refer to it each day.  During the week, have students make the letter **F** using a variety of materials such as small feathers purchased at a craft store, finger-painted fingerprints, footprints, fish-shaped crackers, foil, fabric scraps, etc.

• **FARMERS AND RANCHERS**

1. Ask student to brainstorm a list of foods, both plants and animals, that are grown or raised by farmers and ranchers.  Ask: *How is that food grown?  Where do seeds come from?  Can you plant corn and get tomatoes?  Why or why not?*

2. Students may cut out pictures from magazines and newspapers of their favorite foods and glue them onto **F**-shaped cutouts.

3. Have students make Five Farm Friends Finger Fitters (page 232).  First, tell them to color the animals.  Then have students cut out the puppets and glue the ends together to fit around their fingers.  Students can learn the verses to make the puppets talk, or they can make up their own conversation.  A few examples are provided below.

    Rooster: I am Brewster the Rooster.  I wake up the farm with a loud cockle-doodle-doo.

    Cow: I am Maude the Cow.  I give my milk with a loud moo, moo, moo.

    Hen: I am Henrietta the Hen.  I lay my eggs with a loud cluck, cluck, cluck.

    Sheep: I am Daisy the Sheep.  I give my wool with a loud baa, baa, baa.

    Horse: I am Boris the Horse.  I carry folks on my back with a loud neigh, neigh, neigh.

• **FLOWERS**

1. Point out that some farmers also grow flowers.  Explain that is how people get spring bulbs to plant.  Take the class outside to find out how many of the bulbs students planted are blooming.  Take some fertilizer and sprinkle it around the flowers.  **Warning:** Be careful not to put any fertilizer on the leaves or it will burn them.  Water the fertilizer in well.

2. On the first day of spring, invite your class to celebrate by doing some "Spring Things." Have them plant marigold seeds in recycled milk cartons, small yogurt containers, or cottage cheese cups.  Be sure to punch a hole in the bottom of each container for drainage.  Water the plants with diluted liquid plant food.  Have students put them in the sun and watch them grow.  You may wish to plant some extra marigolds that you can later transplant outside when the danger of frost has passed.

3. Have a picnic.  This can be done inside if the weather is still cool outside.  Invite students to bring their favorite fruit to make "Friendship Fruit Salad" to share.  Wash and cut it up the fruit into a large bowl.  Then pour orange juice over the fruit.  Place the mixture in a refrigerator.  After it chills, serve it with fig cookies.

4. Take students outside to look for spring.  Ask: *Does the weather feel warm yet?*  Make a "We Found Spring" chart listing all the plants, animals, and weather changes the class observed.

# The Letter F *(cont.)*

## • *FEET OR FINS?*

Show pictures of ocean and land animals. Have students classify them according to whether they have fins or feet. You may wish to reproduce the animals in the following pages for this activity: 39–41, 172, 175, 255–261, and 283–292.

## • *FINGERPRINTS*

1. Have students draw some flowers surrounded by ink fingerprint bugs and other creatures.

2. Put paper towels with flowers printed on them at an easel for students to paint. The towel absorbs the paint to make bright pictures. Put large feathers in paint on the other side of the easel with which students can experiment.

3. Ask students to cut out flowers from seed catalogs and magazines. Tell them to glue the flowers to a spring bulletin board covered with green butcher paper grass. Allow students to draw and color other signs of spring in the grass. They may like to draw their favorite springtime activities and dictate stories.

4. Make learning games with pages from flower notepads. Have students match two different kinds of flowers or match flowers with butterflies or bees.

## • *FLAG*

1. Look at your country's flag. Ask: *What colors do you see? What shapes do you see? What do the shapes and colors mean? What does the flag symbolize for our country? What is the name of our country?* If you live in the United States, put your right hand over your heart and teach the "Pledge of Allegiance."

2. Display pictures of flags used by other countries. Invite students to create their own personal flag. Ask: *What does it mean?*

## • *FREE*

Get a book from the library, *Free Stuff for Kids* by The Free Stuff Editors; Meadowbrook Press, Deephaven, MN 55391, that lists free things children can order. Ask parents to send stamps to school or provide some yourself. Allow each student to choose one thing to order. Ask: *What does free mean? Is it really free?*

## • *FEEL*

Set up a "Feel Center" that includes fabrics, fake fur, feathers, felt, flannel, and foil. Let students decide if these objects feel hard or soft, rough or smooth. Ask if they can name any other words that describe how something feels such as sticky, slimy, wet, dry, hot, and cold.

## • *FEELINGS*

Discuss how everyone feels happy, sad, and angry. Encourage students to draw pictures that show what makes them feel happy, sad, and angry.

# The Letter F *(cont.)*

## • *FROGS EAT FLIES*

1. Tell students that frogs are living things, and they are animals. They have smooth skin and lay eggs. Frogs, toads, newts, and salamanders are called amphibians. That means that they breathe with gills and live in the water during the first part of their lives. When they reach adulthood, they have developed lungs and live the rest of their lives on land. Frogs lay their eggs in the water, and tadpoles hatch from them.

2. If possible, obtain some tadpoles and raise them in an aquarium so students can watch the frogs grow. Consider ordering some frog eggs from a biological supply house if you are unable to locate tadpoles in your area.

3. Reproduce the pictures of the frog (page 230) and its life cycle (page 231). Sequence the frog development pictures: egg, tadpole, grows legs, loses tail, frog. Students may paste them in order on a strip. Color the frog green and the fly yellow. Cut slits in the frog. Pull the strip through and tell how the frog develops.

4. Read aloud a book about frogs. See the bibliography (page 229) for suggestions. Have students make frog-shaped books entitled "My Frog Friend and Me." Ask them to draw pictures and dictate sentences about their favorite things to do together.

## • *A FABULOUS FRIDAY WITH FRIENDS*

Read aloud a story about friends. See the bibliography (page 229) for suggestions. Talk about how to make friends. Ask: *What do you like to do with your friends? How do you make new friends? How do you keep old friends?* Have students celebrate their friends on a Friday by doing their favorite fun activities together.

## • *FAIRY*

Display pictures of fairies. Ask students to draw fairies and dictate a class story.

## • *FOLDED FRACTIONS*

Have students practice folding paper into halves. Stress that one of two pieces is $\frac{1}{2}$. Tell them to color $\frac{1}{2}$ of their papers and write $\frac{1}{2}$ on each half. Show how to fold another piece of paper into fourths. Remind students that one of four pieces is $\frac{1}{4}$. Have them color $\frac{1}{4}$ of the paper and write $\frac{1}{4}$ on each fourth.

## • *FUNNY FEET*

Trace students' feet on butcher paper and cut them out. Allow students to decorate their cutouts with craft feathers, fabric scraps, fake fur, foil, fingerpaints, etc. Tell them to add wiggly eyes. Invite students to "walk" their funny feet across the room.

## • *FUR OR FEATHERS?*

Look at pictures of animals (birds and mammals). Ask if they are covered with fur or feathers. Students may sort the pictures. Name an animal and let students tell you whether it has fur or feathers on its body. Remind them that if it has feathers, it is a bird.

# Bibliography

**Books**

Adams, Pam. *There Was an Old Lady Who Swallowed a Fly.* Playspaces, 1973.

Arnosky, Jim. *Watching Foxes.* Lothrop, 1984.

Baker, Jeannie. *Where the Forest Meets the Sea.* Scholastic, 1987.

Barbaresi, Nina. *A Fox Jumped Up One Winter's Night.* Western, 1985.

Berenstain, Stan and Jan. *The Berenstain Bears and the Trouble with Friends.* Random House, 1987.

Berenstain, Stan and Jan. *The Berenstain Bears Get in a Fight.* Random House, 1987.

Carle, Eric. *Do You Want to Be My Friend?* Harper, 1987.

Clark, Barry. *Amazing Frogs and Toads.* Knopf, 1990.

Cooney, Barbara. *Chanticleer the Fox.* Crowell, 1958.

Gibbons, Gail. *Fire! Fire!* Harper & Row, 1987.

Gibbons, Gail. *Frogs.* Holiday, 1993.

Grimm, Brothers. *The Frog Prince.* Troll, 1979.

Heine, Helme. *Friends.* Macmillan, 1986.

Hoban, Russell. *Best Friends for Frances.* Harper & Row, 1969.

Hoban, Tana. *Is It Rough? Is It Smooth? Is It Shiny?* Greenwillow, 1984.

Horth-Sander, Irmtraut. *Will You Be My Friend?* North-South, 1986.

Johnson, Sylvia A. *Tree Frogs.* Lerner, 1986.

Johnston, Ginny. *Slippery Babies.* Morrow, 1991.

Kanno, Wendy. *The Funny Farm House.* ARO, 1984.

Kellogg, Steven. *Best Friends.* Dial Books, 1986.

Lacey, Elizabeth A. *The Complete Frog.* Lothrop, Lee & Shepard, 1989.

Lionni, Leo. *Fish Is Fish.* Knopf, 1987.

Lobel, Arnold. *Days with Frog and Toad.* Harper & Row, 1979.

Lobel, Arnold. *Frog and Toad All Year.* Harper & Row, 1976.

Lobel, Arnold. *Frog and Toad Are Friends.* Harper & Row, 1970.

Lobel, Arnold. *Frog and Toad Together.* Harper & Row, 1972.

Mahy, Margaret. *Making Friends.* Macmillan, 1990.

Majewski, Joe and Maria. *A Friend for Oscar.* Dial, 1988.

McMillan, Bruce. *Dry or Wet?* Lothrop, Lee & Shephard, 1988.

Munro, Leaf. *The Story of Ferdinand.* Viking, 1938.

Pallotta, Jerry. *The Flower Alphabet Book.* Charlesbridge, 1988.

Pallotta, Jerry. *The Frog Alphabet Book.* Charlesbridge, 1990.

Pallotta, Jerry. *The Furry Alphabet Book.* Charlesbridge, 1991.

Rey, Margret. *Curious George at the Fire Station.* Houghton Mifflin, 1985.

Rockwell, Anne. *Fire Engines.* E. P. Dutton, 1986.

Seuss, Dr. *The Foot Book.* Random House, 1968.

Vissey, A. *Princess and the Frog.* Little Brown, 1985.

Walsh, Ellen Stoll. *Hop Jump.* HBJ, 1993.

# A Fat Friendly Frog

Enlarge the following key picture by creating an overhead transparency of this page and projecting it onto green poster board.  Then trace and cut out the frog.  Then laminate the frog.  Refer to the key picture each day, especially when you discuss the calendar (page 9).  At the end of the week, tape the frog to a wall as part of an alphabet line-up.

Use this pattern for the activity described on page 231, as well.

# Frog Life Cycle

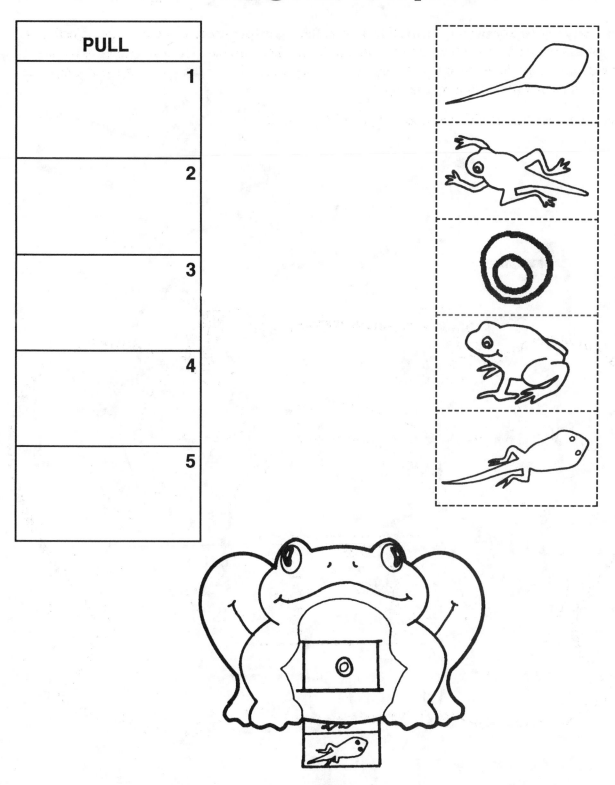

| PULL | |
|---|---|
| | 1 |
| | 2 |
| | 3 |
| | 4 |
| | 5 |

**Directions:** Color the big frog and the pictures.  Cut the boxes on the dotted lines.  Put the pictures in the correct sequence.  Glue them in the boxes on the left.  Do not glue over the numbers.  Pull the pictures through the two slits in the frog's stomach.

# Five Farm Friends Finger Fitters

**Directions:** Color, cut out, and make the finger puppets.

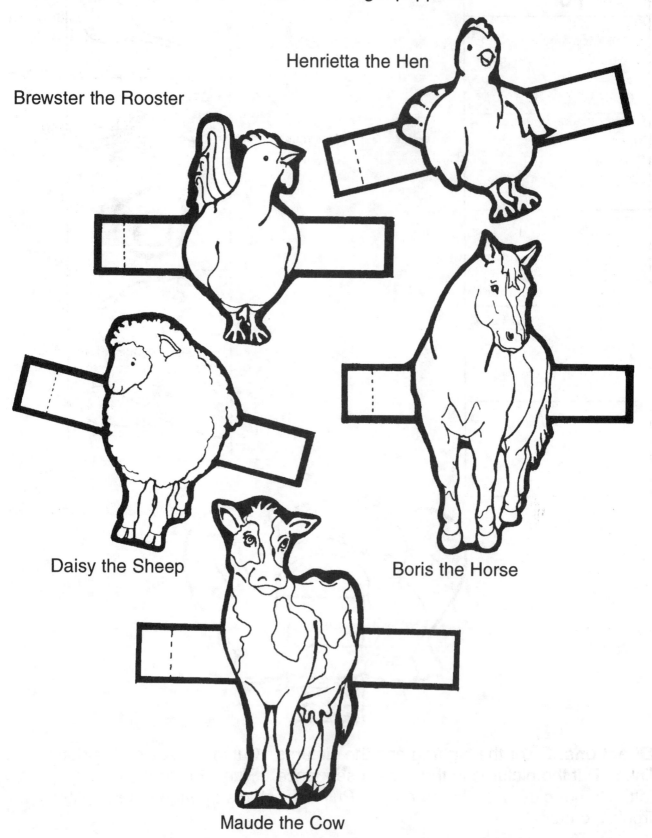

Henrietta the Hen

Brewster the Rooster

Daisy the Sheep

Boris the Horse

Maude the Cow

# The Letter U

## • APRIL

Reproduce the Dogwood Blossom patterns (page 237) on white construction paper. Have students cut out all three pieces. Tell them to color the circle yellow. Help them glue the pieces together as shown on page 237. Then place the flowers on the Class Tree (page 9).

## • LETTER OF THE WEEK

Display the key picture, The Unicorn Umbrella Is Up (page 236). Refer to it each day. During the week, have students make the letter **U** using a variety of materials such as elbow macaroni, bent pipe cleaners, small horseshoe prints, etc.

## • UMBRELLA

1. Reproduce the umbrella child patterns (pages 238 and 239) on pastel-colored construction paper. Have students cut out all three parts. Help them use brads to join the pieces together at the dots. Place the umbrella children on a spring bulletin board entitled "April Showers Bring May Flowers." Invite a group of students to add a rainbow to the bulletin board sky using crayons, markers, chalk, or paint.

2. Read several books about umbrellas. See the bibliography (page 235) for suggestions. Ask students to design their own umbrellas. Then tell them to draw pictures showing themselves carrying their umbrellas to school. Ask: *What will you do with your umbrella?*

3. Each student should make a list of his or her favorite indoor things to do on rainy days. Ask: *Can you think of some new things to do?*

## • UNICORN

1. Read some stories about unicorns. See the bibliography (page 235) for suggestions. Ask: *What is a unicorn? Are they real or imaginary? Are there any unicorns living today? Do you think there ever were any real unicorns? What happened to them?*

2. Make an "I Believe in Unicorns" class book. Students may draw pictures of themselves with their pet unicorns. Prompt students to dictate stories using the following: *What is its name? Where does it live?* Tell a story about an adventure you had with your unicorn. Reproduce the unicorn picture (page 240) for the covers of the book. Ask volunteers to color the unicorn pictures. Mount the pictures on tagboard and laminate. Place students' stories between the covers and staple them together to make the class book.

3. As an alternative to the writing activity described above, reproduce the unicorn picture (page 240) for students. Tell them to color the pictures. Then write the story each student dictates on the back of his or her paper.

## • UNIQUELY US

Talk about ways in which we are all unique (different) and ways in which we are all alike. Make a book entitled "Uniquely Us." Have students draw pictures of themselves. Ask each student to dictate a sentence telling something she or he does or does not like to do. Tell them to include some of those things in their pictures.

# The Letter U *(cont.)*

- ***UNCLE***

Ask: *What is an uncle? Do you have any uncles? What are their names? How is an uncle related to your mother or father? What is an aunt? Do you have any aunts? What are their names? How is an aunt related to your mother or father?* Invite students to bring pictures of uncles and aunts to share with the class.

- ***UNIFORM***

Discuss what a uniform is and the reasons people wear them. Provide magazines and blunt scissors for students to cut out pictures of people wearing uniforms. Have them use the pictures to make a class uniform collage. After the collage has been completed, review the types of uniforms shown in the pictures and identify the jobs those people do.

- ***"UN" WORDS***

Encourage students to name as many words as possible that begin with the prefix "un." Examples include *unlock, untie, unzip, unbutton, unwrap,* and *uncover.* Ask volunteers to demonstrate each word and its opposite. Point out that the prefix "un" means *not.* Ask: *How does this prefix change the meaning of each word?*

- ***UPSIDE-DOWN CAKE***

Be sure to ask parents if their children have any food allergies or dietary restrictions. Pour one stick melted margarine and 1 cup (250 mL) brown sugar in a greased 9" x 13" (23 cm x 33 cm) cake pan. Arrange pineapple slices in the pan with maraschino cherries in the centers. As an alternative, you can cut the brown sugar to $^1/_2$ cup (125 mL) and substitute one 21-ounce (800 g) can of cherry or apple pie filling. Mix yellow cake mix according to the directions on the package. You can use the pineapple liquid for all or part of the water, if desired. Pour the cake batter in the pan. Bake the cake at 350° F (175° C) for 50-60 minutes or until it is done. When it is through cooking, run a knife along the sides between the cake and the pan. Then invert the cake onto a cookie pan or tray. Before allowing students to eat the cake, ask: *Why do you think this is called an upside-down cake?*

- ***UPSIDE-DOWN SUNDAE***

Provide a variety of sundae ingredients for students to use. Direct them to make ice cream sundaes by completing the steps in reverse order. Tell them to put cherries, sprinkles, and whipped cream in their dish first. Have them add sauces, syrups, and/or fruit. Scoop ice cream and place it on top of students' other ingredients.

- ***UNDER***

1. Ask students to name things in the classroom that are under something else.
2. Provide "under" directions for students to follow. Examples: *Put your hands under the table. Put your pencil under your chair. Put your right hand under your left foot.*

# Bibliography

## Books

Andersen, Hans Christian. *The Ugly Duckling.* Troll, 1979.

Drescher, Henrik. *The Yellow Umbrella.* Bradbury, 1987.

Feczko, Kathy. *Umbrella Parade.* Troll, 1985.

Gibbons, Gail. *Sun Up, Sun Down.* HBJ, 1987.

Gibbons, Gail. *Up Goes the Skyscraper!* Macmillan, 1986.

Hartley, Deborah. *Up North in Winter.* Viking, 1986.

Howe, James. *There's a Monster Under My Bed.* Atheneum, 1986.

Kanao, Keiko. *Kitten Up a Tree.* Knopf, 1987.

Kaplan, C. *Underground Tea Party: A Tale About Overcoming Fear.* Miliken, 1990.

Lewis, Jean. *Glow in the Dark Under the Sea.* Western, 1991.

Loewen, Iris. *My Mom Is So Unusual.* Pemmican, 1991.

Mayer, Mercer. *There's an Alligator Under My Bed.* Dial, 1987.

Mayer, Mercer. *Unicorn Alphabet.* Viking, 1989.

Mitchell, Margaree King. *Uncle Jeb's Barber Shop.* Simon and Schuster, 1993.

Monsell, Mary Elise. *Underwear!* Albert Whitman, 1993.

Pallotta, Jerry. *Underwater Alphabet Book.* Charlesbridge Publishing, 1991.

Seuss, Dr. *Great Day for Up!* Random House, 1974.

Yorinks, Arthur. *Ugh.* Farrar, Strauss & Giroux, 1993.

Ziefert, Harriet and Richard Brown. *Nicky Upstairs and Down.* Viking, 1994.

Ziefert, Harriet and Suzy Mandel. *Under the Water.* Viking, 1990.

Zolotow, Charlotte. *The Unfriendly Book.* Harper & Row, 1975.

## Technology

*Chuck, the Unlucky Duck.* (Cassette and four paperbacks); Troll Associates, Catalog Sales Dept., 100 Corporate Dr., Mahwah, NJ 07498; 1-800-929-8765.

*Come On Up!* (Cassette and four paperbacks); Troll Associates, Catalog Sales Dept., 100 Corporate Dr., Mahwah, NJ 07498; 1-800-929-8765.

*The Ugly Duckling.* (Video); 11 min. Troll Associates, Catalog Sales Dept., 100 Corporate Dr., Mahwah, NJ 07498; 1-800-929-8765.

*Umbrella Parade.* (Video); 8 min. Troll Associates, Catalog Sales Dept., 100 Corporate Dr., Mahwah, NJ 07498; 1-800-929-8765.

*Underwater Life.* (Cassette and four paperbacks); Troll Associates, Catalog Sales Dept., 100 Corporate Dr., Mahwah, NJ 07498; 1-800-929-8765.

*What's Under the Ocean?* (Video); 8 min. Troll Associates, Catalog Sales Dept., 100 Corporate Dr., Mahwah, NJ 07498; 1-800-929-8765.

# The Unicorn Umbrella Is Up!

Enlarge the following key picture by creating an overhead transparency of this page and projecting it onto poster board. Then trace each part to make a red umbrella top and a black handle. Cut out the poster board pieces and glue them together. Allow the glue to dry and laminate. Refer to the key picture each day, especially when you discuss the calendar (page 9). At the end of the week, tape the unicorn to a wall as part of an alphabet line-up.

# Dogwood Blossom

**Directions:** Cut out all three parts. Color the circle yellow. Then glue the blossom together.

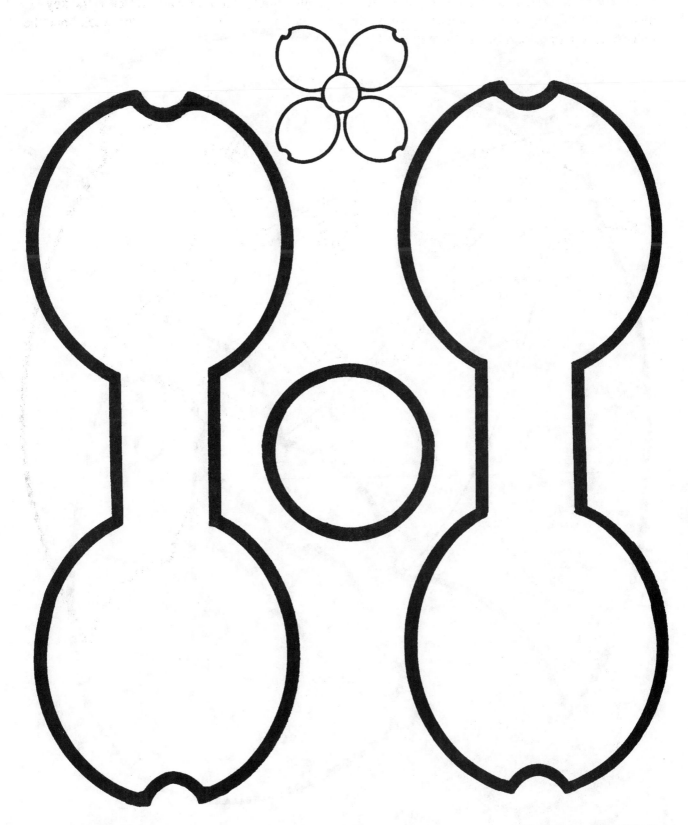

# Umbrella Child

Reproduce the patterns (pages 238 and 239) on construction paper. Have students cut out the patterns. Then help them use brads to join the pieces of the umbrella child at the dots.

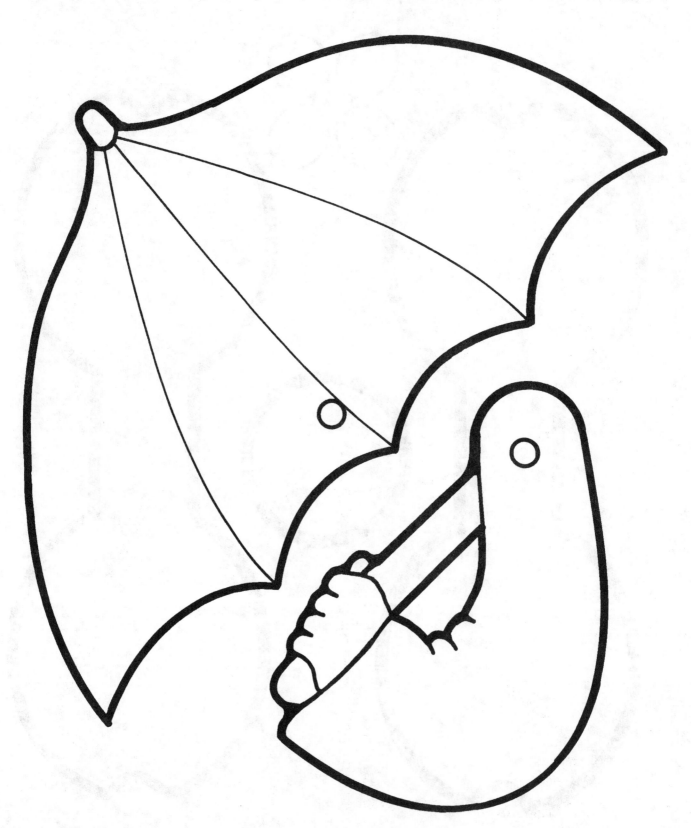

# Umbrella Child *(cont.)*

# Unicorn

# The Letter R

**• LETTER OF THE WEEK**

Display the key picture, A Racing Rabbit with a Red Rose (page 246). Refer to it each day. During the week, have students make the letter **R** using a variety of materials such as red rice, raisins, ribbon, rick-rack, etc.

**• RABBITS**

1. Read aloud *The Tale of Peter Rabbit* (Troll, 1979) and *The Tale of Benjamin Bunny* (Troll, 1981) both by Beatrix Potter while students enjoy some cinnamon raisin (currant) buns or carrot raisin cake. Ask: *Have you ever done anything your mother told you not to and gotten into trouble? What should Peter have done? What do you think he will do next time?*

2. Read aloud Margery Williams' *The Velveteen Rabbit* (Avon, 1975) and/or watch the video (Rabbit Ears Productions and Random House Home Video, 1985). Ask students to decide which of their toys they would like to become real. Have them draw their toys and dictate stories about what they would do with their real toys. Display students' work on a bulletin board.

3. Have students make recycled red rice rabbit texture collages using the following directions: Put red food coloring in enough water to cover some rice. Soak for about three hours or until the desired color is reached. Drain the rice and place it on paper towels to dry overnight. Reproduce the rabbit on page 247 on white construction paper. Have students cut out their rabbits and glue them onto clean recycled Styrofoam® meat trays. Tell them to spread glue all over the rabbits. First have them add wiggly eyes, then let them thickly spread red rice all over the rabbit. When the glue is dry, ask students to shake off any excess rice. Each student can glue on two long pieces of recycled Styrofoam® packing material for the ears, cotton recycled from a medicine bottles for the tail, and a small pink pom pon nose. Talk about how the different parts of their rice rabbits feel. Ask: *Does it feel like a real rabbit? Why or why not?*

4. Serve pink marshmallow rabbits. Ask how they feel. Explain that we feel with nerves that are all over our bodies. Our sense of touch helps protect us from extreme hot and cold.

**• RED RICE**

1. Put extra red rice in a dishpan with containers of varying sizes for students to practice pouring, measuring, and comparing.

2. Read *Chicken Soup with Rice* by Maurice Sendak (Scholastic, 1987). Have each student to draw a picture of his/her favorite month and dictate a sentence to tell what he/she likes to do during that month. Together, enjoy some canned chicken soup with rice.

3. Write to the Government of India Tourist Bureau (page 80) to provide more information to your class. Ask a volunteer to locate India on a globe.

**• RAIN**

Ask: *Where do you think the butterflies go when it rains in the rain forest?* Reproduce the raindrop pattern (page 248) on light blue paper. Have students draw pictures on the raindrop to show where a butterfly goes when it rains and dictate sentences to go with their pictures.

# The Letter R *(cont.)*

## • *RAINBOW*

1. Show students a rainbow in a prism that is held up to the light. Have them draw rainbows. Teach the sequence of colors as red, orange, yellow, green, blue, indigo, purple. Drop red, yellow, and blue food coloring in a jar of water and tell students to watch a rainbow form.

2. Read aloud *A Rainbow of My Own* by Don Freeman (Penguin, 1978) and/or *Skyfire* by Frank Asch (Prentice-Hall, 1984). Ask: *What would you do if you had your own rainbow? What would your rainbow look like?* Have students draw pictures to make a rainbow-shaped book. Ask: *How many words can you make that include the word rain?* Examples: *rain hat, raincoat, rain cloud, rainstorm, rain boots, raindrop.* Tell students to draw pictures and write the words.

3. Show students how to make rainbow ribbons using the following directions: Mix cherry, orange, lemon, lime, blueberry, and grape gelatin according to the speed-set directions on the packages. Layer the flavors, beginning with grape, in a 9" x 13" (23 cm x 33 cm) clear glass casserole dish. Make the flavors one at the time, chilling each layer until it is firm. Chill the rainbow ribbons overnight. Serve this treat with whipped topping "clouds."

## • *RAIN FOREST*

1. Explain that a rain forest is defined as an area with a thick growth of tall trees, vines, shrubs, flowers, and other plants. It gets over 80 inches (200 cm) of rainfall per year. It is filled with birds, reptiles, amphibians, mammals, fish, and insects. Rain forests grow in four layers: The **Forest Floor** is where ferns and other smaller plants grow. Humidity is almost 100 percent. Very little sunlight reaches this layer because of the taller trees above. Termites, ants, beetles, and worms constantly recycle fallen debris into the thin soil to provide nourishment for the plants growing there. The **Understory** is a layer of young trees, shrubs, and palms. The **Canopy** has larger trees that measure up to 100 feet (30 m). Most of the plants and animals live in the canopy or the understory. The **Emergent Layer** contains trees growing as high as 250 feet (75 m). The harpy eagle and other birds of prey live at this layer.

2. Point out that tropical rain forests occur in a band around the equator in Hawaii, Central and South America, Africa, Southeast Asia, and Australia. The largest rain forests occur in Brazil in the Amazon basin of South America, in Zaire in central Africa, and in Indonesia. Ask volunteers to locate these areas and the equator on a map or globe. Tell students that rain forests once covered about 20 percent of the earth's land surface. Today they cover less than 7 percent.

3. A good starting point for a rain forest study is the story *The Great Kapok Tree* by Lynne Cherry (HBJ, 1990). Together read the book, stopping on each page to enjoy the richness of the illustrations and to discuss the reasons the animals give for not cutting down the tree.

4. Transform a bulletin board into a rain forest. You may wish to transform the Class Tree (page 9) into a great kapok tree. Have students paint yellow paper with green tempera paint. Allow the paint to dry. Then have students trace and cut the leaf patterns (pages 249–253) using the painted paper. Cut additional tree trunks and branches from crumpled brown paper bags. Staple them to the bulletin board. Ask students to cover the branches with the painted leaves. Alternatively, you can have students use the patterns to cut various leaves from different shades of green tissue paper.

# The Letter R (cont.)

• **RAIN FOREST** (cont.)

5. Have students cut smaller ground plants, decorating some with brightly colored markers. Staple these to the forest floor. Allow students to make flowers using the patterns on page 254 or by following these directions: layer two or more pieces of brightly colored tissue paper; cut squares; gather the tissue paper in the center; cut off the corners to round the edges of the flowers. Staple the flowers to the trees. Provide students with a variety of rain forest animal patterns by reproducing pages 255–261. Have them color and cut out the animals for the bulletin board. Staple various shades of green crepe paper streamers to the trees. If desired, you can form a canopy by winding the streamers across the classroom and taping them to the wall opposite the bulletin board. Play a tape of jungle sounds as you transform your classroom. (*Tropical Jungle* may purchased from The Nature Company, P.O. Box 2310, Berkeley, CA 94702.) Use rain forest leaf-shaped sponges and different shades of green tempera paint to make foliage on your windows. Then fill in the spaces with the brightly colored animals and flowers.

6. Make a Rain Forest Terrarium in a gallon jar or old aquarium. Layer gravel, charcoal, and potting soil. Help students add small house plants. Water them sparingly. Loosely cover the terrarium with plastic wrap. Water will condense on the plastic and "rain" into the "forest."

7. Name the kinds of products that come from the rain forest: medicines; mahogany, rosewood, sandalwood, bamboo, rattan; avocados, bananas, coconuts, grapefruit, oranges, lemons, limes, tangerines, guava, mangoes, papayas, pineapples; Brazil nuts, cashews, macadamia nuts; coffee, cola, chocolate, tea; tapioca, vanilla, and most spices. Discuss the problems of deforestation and the loss of species that may be helpful to people such as plants with anti-cancer properties.

8. Invite students to make rain forest cookies. Help them mix a batch of chocolate chip cookie dough. Line a cookie sheet with aluminum foil. Each student should place a spoonful of dough on the foil and write his or her name beside the cookie on the foil with a fine-point non-toxic marker. They may add cinnamon, coconut, cashews, Brazil, or macadamia nuts as desired. Bake the cookies according to the directions. Have students make Tropical Fruit Treats. Bring several tropical fruits and have students identify them. Cut the fruit into bite-sized pieces, and mix them in a large bowl. Add coconut if desired. Serve with the Rain Forest Cookies or alone.

• **REPTILES**

1. Talk about reptiles. They are cold-blooded animals with scaly skin. Most lay eggs. Reptiles include snakes, turtles, lizards, crocodilians (alligators, crocodiles, gavial, caimans), and tuataras. Read *The Yucky Reptile Alphabet Book* by Jerry Pallotta (Charlesbridge, 1989).

2. If possible, bring different kinds of turtles, small lizards, and harmless snakes to school for students to observe. Encourage students to visit a pet store or a nature museum where handlers allow them to see and touch reptiles. Teach about the benefits of having reptiles.

3. Challenge students to make colorful reptiles (or other rain forest animals) using equal amounts of colored glue, flour, and cornstarch. Mix and knead the dough until it is well-blended. Encourage students to use several colors for their creations. Allow the dough to dry for 24 hours, turning the reptiles several times.

# The Letter R *(cont.)*

- ### *REDUCE, REUSE, RECYCLE*

    1. Talk about the meaning of these three words and why they are important. Ask: *What can be recycled in your area?* Examples include aluminum cans, paper, glass bottles, plastic drink bottles and milk jugs. Ask: *Where can they be taken for recycling?* Point out that we can save trees from being cut if we reuse and recycle paper.

    2. Have a "Recycling Contest" and have participants come up with new ways to recycle products that they use at home. Give a prize for the best idea.

    3. Have a "Recycling Picnic" where all the items brought must be reused and recycled.

    4. Ask students to work with partners to make posters that encourage recycling.

- ### *ROCKS*

    1. Let students eat some Rocky Road ice cream while you read aloud *Alexander and the Wind-Up Mouse* by Leo Lionni (Pantheon, 1969).

    2. Invite students to make rock collections in clean recycled egg cartons, making sure they wash the rocks. Allow them to use magnifying glasses to examine and identify their specimens according to a simple rock manual. Then request that students sort them into groups.

    3. Make "Pet Rock Critters" by painting rocks, then adding features with markers and fabric scraps. Write stories about them. Create names and homes for them.

 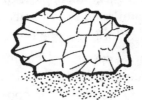 

- ### *RIDICULOUS RHYMING RIDDLES*

    Review some nursery rhymes and poems that students have learned. Identify the rhyming words and think of other words that rhyme. Try to write some rhymes, first as a class, then individually. Allow students to share some riddles, then have them try to write some that rhyme.

- ### *RIGHT AND LEFT*

    Use "The Hokey Pokey" and "Simon Says" to practice right and left discrimination.

- ### *RACING RELAYS*

    Set up for an Alphabet Relay. Have each student race down, match up an alphabet card to a grid with letters printed on it, then race back. You may want to have them name the letters, too.

- ### *RAISIN RICE PUDDING AND OTHER RECIPES*

    1. Stir up a favorite recipe or use a package to make raisin rice pudding.

    2. Send notes home asking parents to share their families' favorite recipes. Compile the recipes into books for Mother's Day gifts. Let each student illustrate one for his or her mom.

- ### *RESTAURANT*

    Set up a restaurant in the housekeeping center. Ask local restaurants to donate supplies. Include play money for paying the bills. Students can practice writing skills by taking food orders.

# Bibliography

**Books**

Althea. *Rainforest Homes.* Cambridge, 1985.

Catterwell, Thelma. *Aldita and the Forest.* Houghton Mifflin, 1989.

Cherry, Lynne. *The Great Kapok Tree.* HBJ, 1990.

Chinery, Michael. *Rainforest Animals.* Random House, 1991.

Cowcher, Helen. *Rain Forest.* Farrar, Straus & Giroux, 1988.

Craig, Janet. *Wonders of the Rain Forest.* Troll, 1989.

Dorros, Arthur. *Rainforest Secrets.* Scholastic, 1990.

Galdone, Paul. *Rumpelstiltskin.* Houghton Mifflin, 1985.

Ganeri, Anita. *Explore the World of Exotic Rainforests.* Western, 1992.

George, Jean Craighead. *One Day in the Tropical Rain Forest.* HarperCollins, 1990.

Grimm, Brothers. *Rapunzel.* Troll, 1979.

Grimm, Brothers. *Rumpelstiltskin.* Troll, 1979.

Keller, Holly. *Will It Rain?* Greenwillow, 1984.

Landan, Elaine. *Tropical Rain Forests Around the World.* Watts, 1990.

Lauber, Patricia. *Get Ready for Robots!* Harper & Row, 1987.

Ling, Mary. *Amazing Crocodiles and Reptiles.* Knopf, 1991.

Lobel, Arnold. *The Rose in My Garden.* Greenwillow, 1984.

Martin, Bill, Jr., and John Archimbault. *Listen to the Rain.* Holt, 1988.

Mitgutsch, Ali. *From Rubber Tree to Tire.* Carolrhoda, 1986.

Newman, Arnold. *Tropical Rainforest.* Facts On File, 1990.

Pallotta, Jerry. *The Yucky Reptile Alphabet Book.* Charlesbridge, 1989.

Potter, Beatrix. *The Tale of Peter Rabbit.* Troll, 1979.

Selsam, Millicent E. and Joyce Hunt. *A First Look at Rocks.* Walker, 1984.

Taylor, Barbara. *Rain Forest.* Kindersley, 1992.

Uchitel, Sandra. *Endangered Animals of the Rain Forest.* Price, Stern, Sloan, 1992.

Williams, Margery. *The Velveteen Rabbit.* Avon, 1975.

Willow, Diane. *At Home in the Rain Forest.* Charlesbridge, 1991.

Wood, John N. and Kevin Dean. *Nature Hide & Seek: Jungles.* Knopf, 1987.

**Technology**

*Rumpelstiltskin.* (Video); 8 min. Troll Associates, Catalog Sales Dept., 100 Corporate Dr., Mahwah, NJ 07498; 1-800-929-8765.

*Ten Little Robots.* (Software); PC; National School Products, 101 East Broadway, Maryville, TN 37804; 1-800-251-9124.

*What Good Are Rocks?* (Video); 12 min. Coronet/MTI Film and Video, P.O. Box 2649, Columbus, OH 43216; 1-800-321-3106.

*What Is a Reptile?* (Video); 8 min. Troll Associates, Catalog Sales Dept., 100 Corporate Dr., Mahwah, NJ 07498; 1-800-929-8765.

# A Racing Rabbit with a Red Rose

Enlarge the following key picture by creating an overhead transparency of this page and projecting it onto poster board. Then trace each part to make a white rabbit, pink inner ears, a red rose, and a green flower stem. Cut out the poster board pieces and glue them together. Allow the glue to dry and laminate the rabbit. Then glue on a pink pom pom nose or color the nose pink. Refer to the key picture each day, especially when you discuss the calendar (page 9). At the end of the week, tape the rabbit to a wall as part of an alphabet line-up.

# Red Rice Rabbit

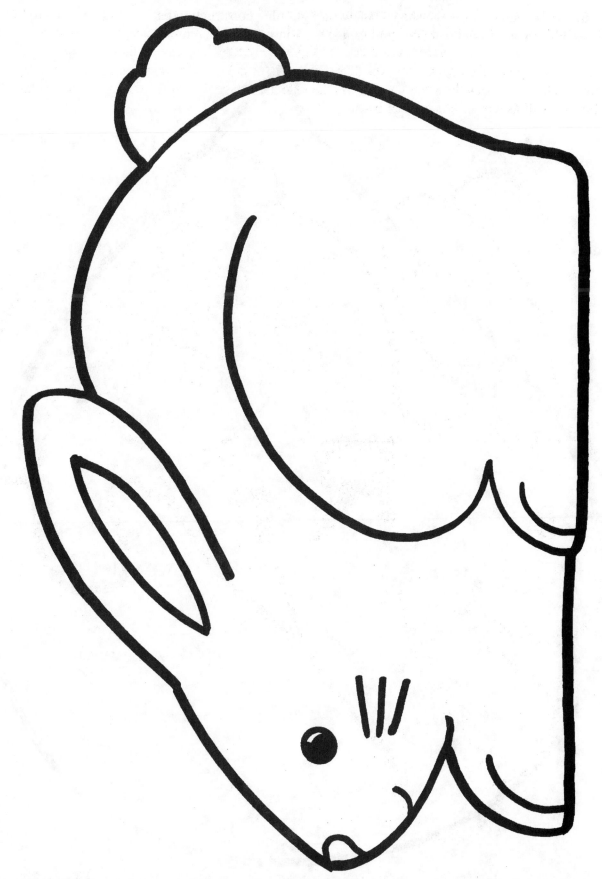

# Raindrop

Reproduce the raindrop pattern shown below on light blue construction paper. Ask students to draw pictures that show where butterflies go when it rains in the rain forest.

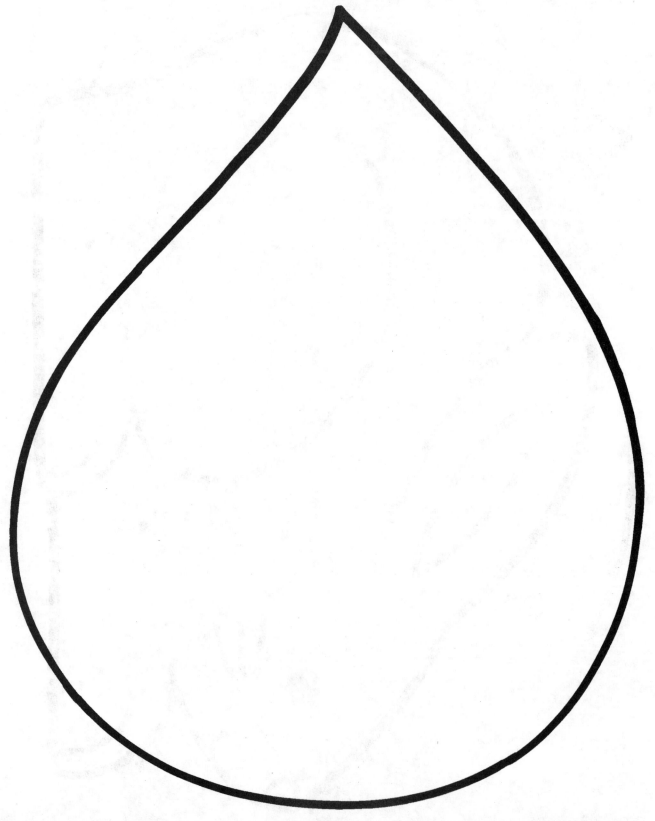

# Rain Forest Plants

**Directions:** Paint the leaves green.  Use a pink marker to draw the veins.  Cut out the leaves.  Then cut fringe on the sides.  Have an adult staple several leaves together for the forest floor plants.

# Rain Forest Plants *(cont.)*

**Directions:** Paint the leaves green.  Use pink markers to outline the leaves.
Then cut out the leaves.

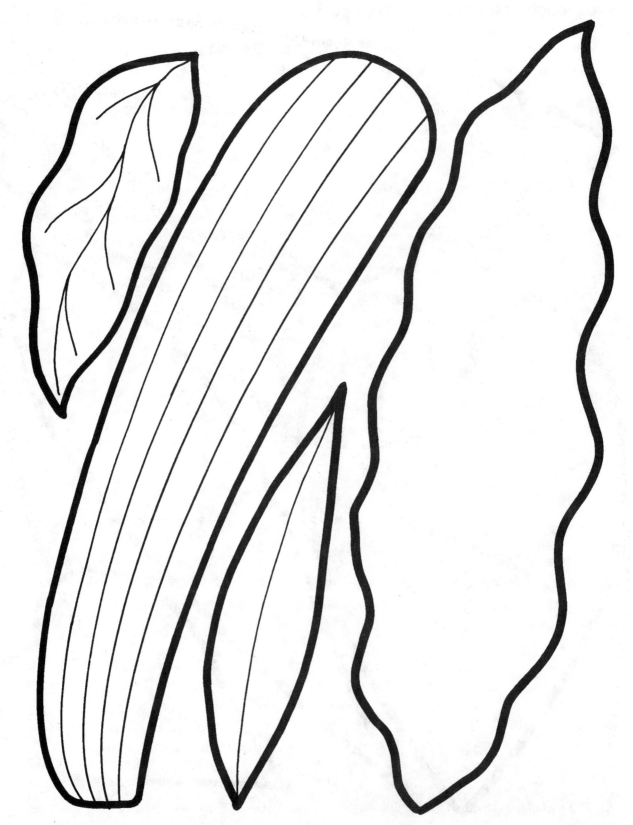

250

# Rain Forest Plants *(cont.)*

**Directions:** Paint the leaves green.  Cut them out.  Have an adult staple several leaves together to make a palm-tree shape.

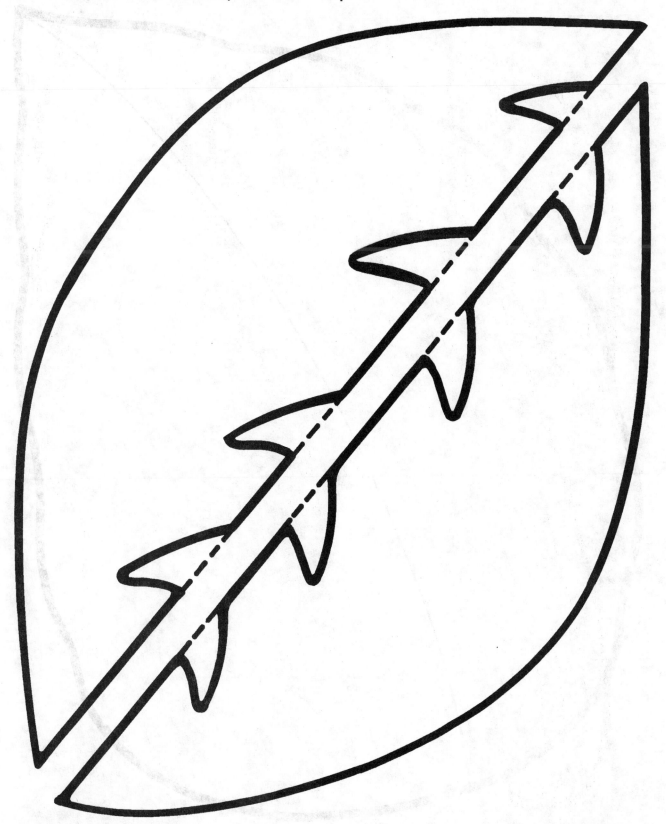

# Rain Forest Plants *(cont.)*

**Directions:** Paint the leaf green.  Then cut it out.

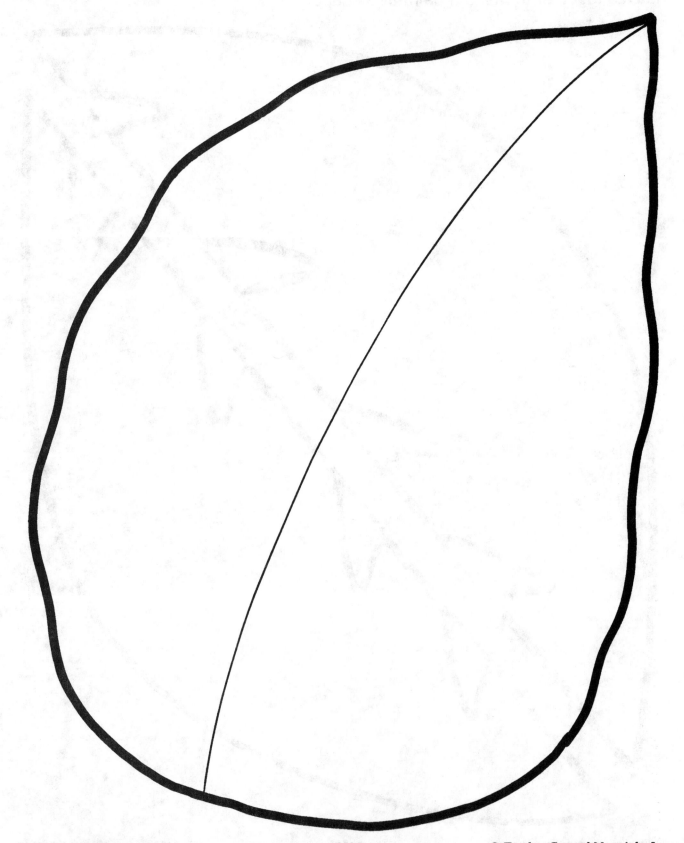

# Rain Forest Plants *(cont.)*

**Directions:** Paint the leaf green.  Then cut it out.

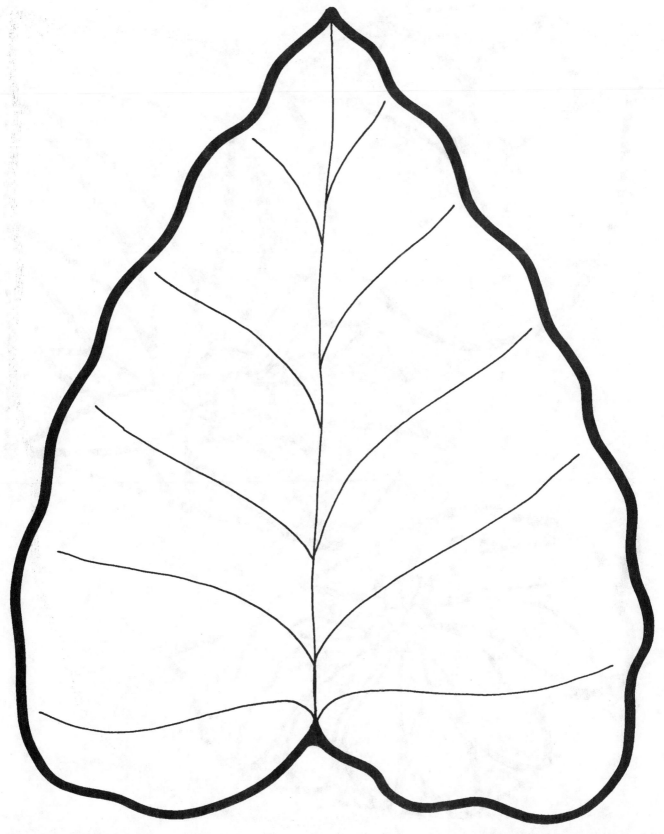

# Rain Forest Plants *(cont.)*

**Directions:** Use bright colors to paint the flowers.  Then cut them out.

# Rain Forest Animals

Have students color and cut out the rain forest animals shown on pages 255–261.

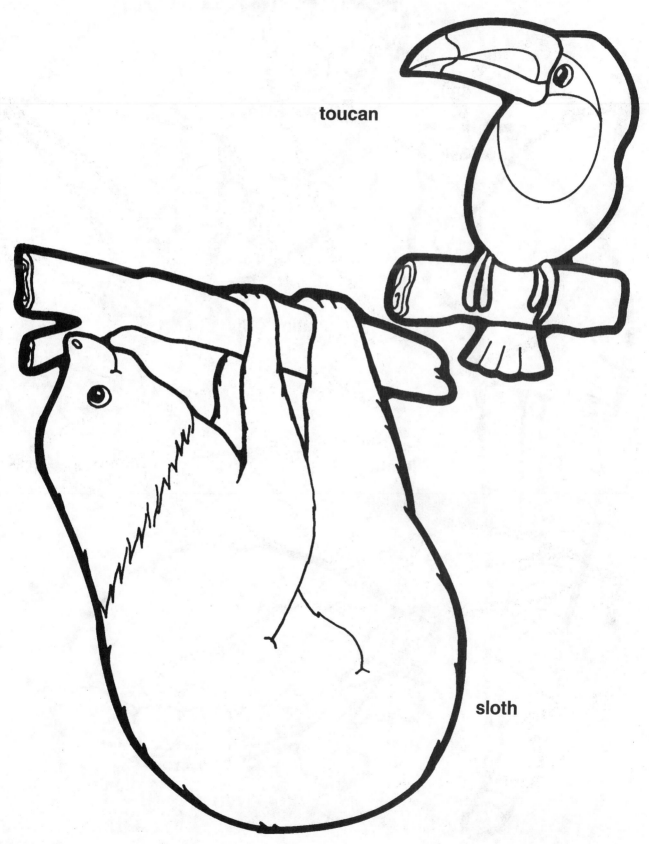

toucan

sloth

# Rain Forest Animals *(cont.)*

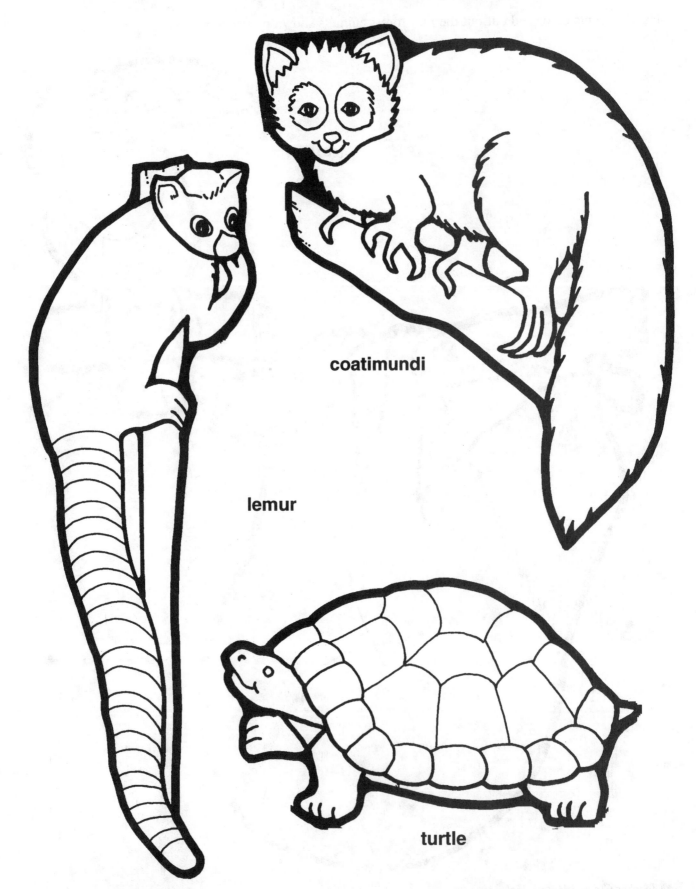

coatimundi

lemur

turtle

# Rain Forest Animals *(cont.)*

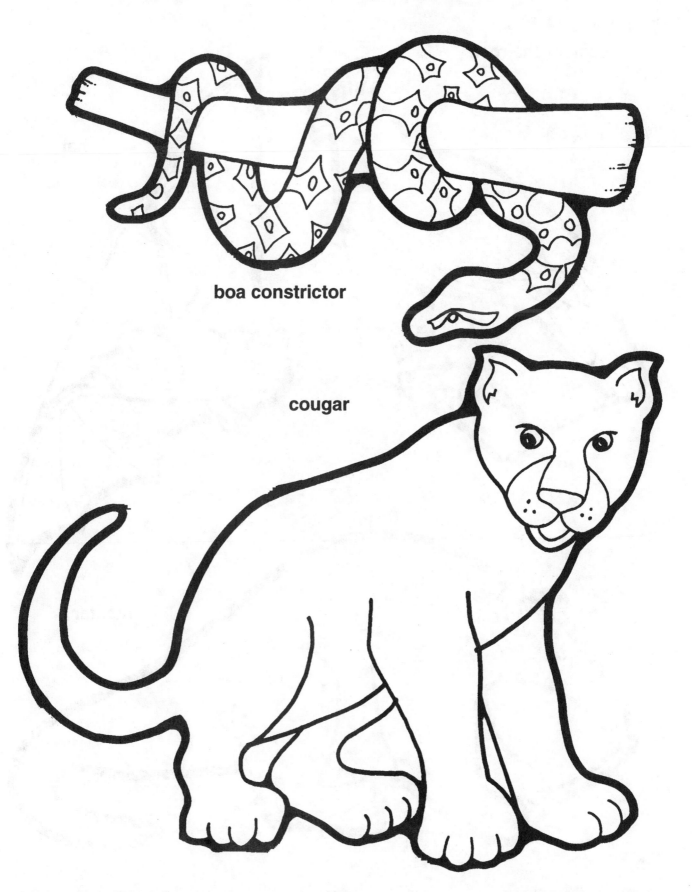

boa constrictor

cougar

# Rain Forest Animals *(cont.)*

**cock-of-the-rock**

**bat**

**anteater**

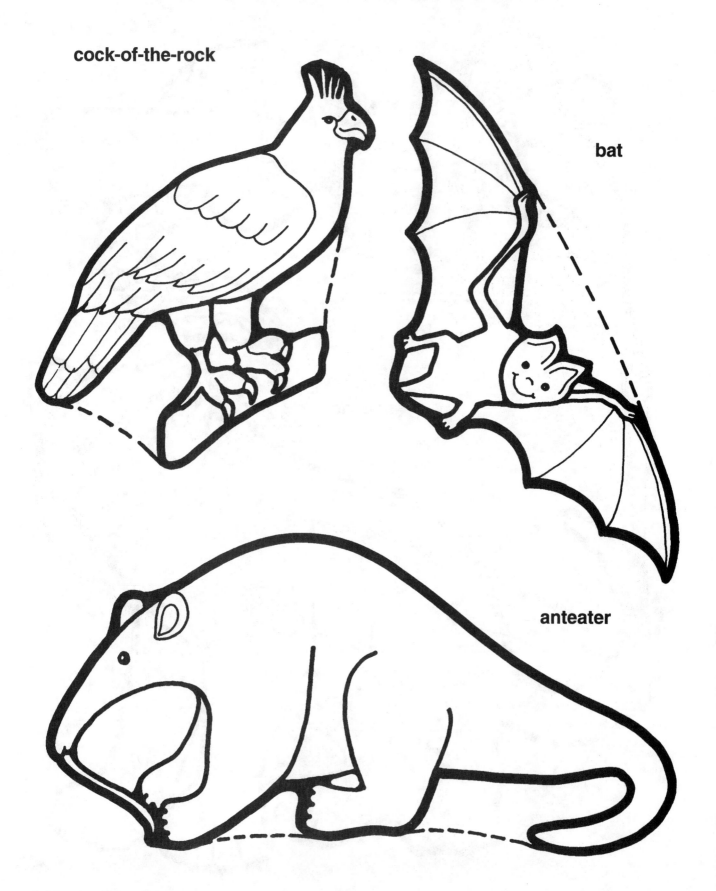

# Rain Forest Animals *(cont.)*

**macaw**

**salamander**

**tree frog**

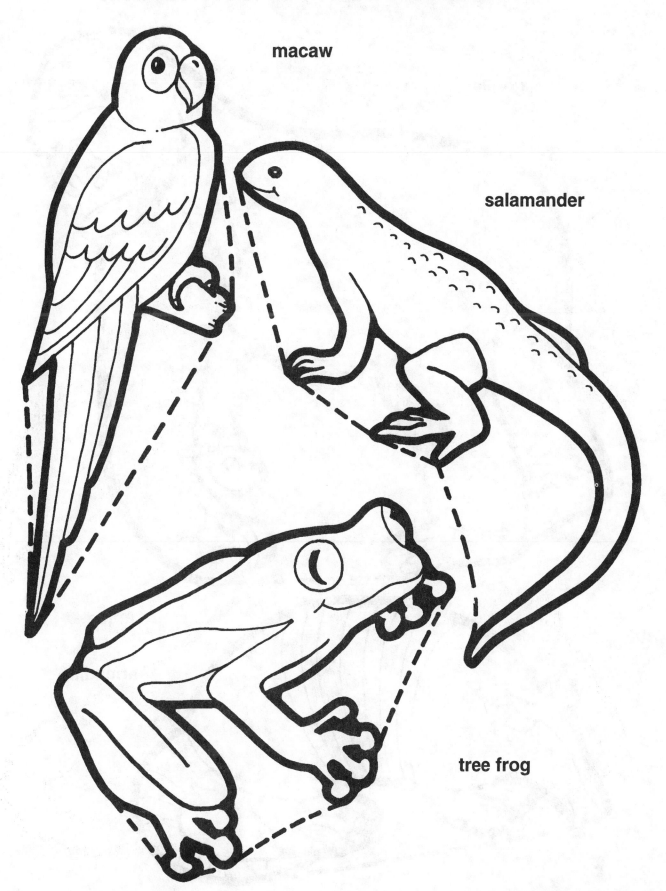

# Rain Forest Animals *(cont.)*

**gorilla**

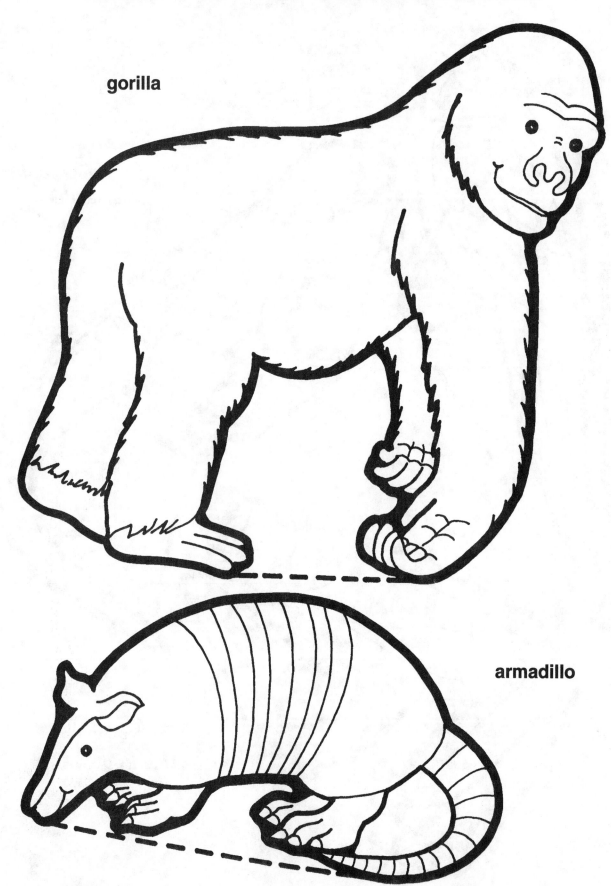

**armadillo**

# Rain Forest Animals *(cont.)*

howler monkey

monkey

# The Letter E

## • *LETTER OF THE WEEK*

Display the key picture, An Elegant Egg (page 267).  Refer to it each day.  During the week, have students make the letter **E** using a variety of materials such as cleaned and crushed eggshells, emery boards, mathematical equations, bits of eraser, etc.

## • *EMERGENT LAYER*

Drape green crepe paper streamers above your rain forest bulletin board to represent the emergent layer. Tape on birds which students have colored.

## • *ELEPHANTS*

Read several books on elephants.  See the bibliography (page 266) for suggestions.  Add elephants colored by students to your rain forest.

## • *EAT*

Read aloud *Eating the Alphabet* by Lois Ehlert (HBJ, 1989).  Work together to make an ABC book of food.  Ask students to cut out pictures of foods from magazines and newspapers, beginning with each letter of the alphabet.  Students may draw pictures of foods they are unable to locate.  Write the names of the foods under the pictures.

## • *EGGS*

1. Read aloud a story about eggs such as *An Egg Is an Egg* by Nicki Weiss (Putnam, 1990).  Ask students to brainstorm a list of animals that hatch from eggs.  Have them make an egg-shaped class book.  Students draw, stencil, or cut out pictures of animals that hatch from eggs.  For each picture, have them complete the sentence: A _____ hatches from an egg.

2. With the help of a local 4-H or agricultural extension service, hatch some eggs in an incubator. Return the chicks to a farm after they hatch.  Students may enjoy imagining they are chicks and dramatizing how they hatch out of their eggs.

3. Have cooperative learning groups list ways we use eggs.  Make a graph that shows students' favorite ways to have their eggs cooked.  Read *Green Eggs and Ham* (Random House, 1960) and *Scrambled Eggs Super!* (Random House, 1953), both by Dr. Seuss.  Scramble eggs with a little green food coloring and some chopped ham.  Save the crushed eggshells to use in Elegant Easter Eggs (page 264).  Make some deviled eggs for students to taste, as well.

4. Read *Horton Hatches the Egg* by Dr. Seuss (Random House, 1940).  Ask: *Where did the egg come from?  Can an elephant lay an egg?  What hatches from a bird egg?  What hatches from a snake egg?*

5. Try conducting relay races in which students balance boiled eggs in spoons.

## • *EASTER EGG COOKIES*

Slice refrigerated sugar cookie dough and shape into oval egg shapes.  Bake the dough according to the directions.  Have students frost the cookies with canned frosting, mixed with food coloring, and decorate them with tubes of decorator icing and various candies.

# The Letter E *(cont.)*

## • *EARTHY EASTER EGGS*

1. Use plants to dye Easter eggs the natural way. Put eggs in a single layer in an enamel saucepan. Cover with water. Add a teaspoon (5 mL) of vinegar. Add plant materials to get the desired color: red cabbage leaves for blue, spinach for golden-pink, carrot tops for green, yellow Delicious apple peelings for lavender, onion skins for orange, and orange peelings for yellow. Experiment with other plants and flowers. Bring the mixture to a boil and reduce the heat. Simmer for about 15 minutes. Remove the plant materials when the desired color is reached. To get a darker color, put the eggs in a bowl and cover them with the dye water. Refrigerate the bowl overnight. **Warning**: Do not eat eggs that have been out of the refrigerator for longer than an hour.

2. Have students practice listening and following directions as they have an Easter egg hunt. Write each direction shown below on a separate slip of paper. Put the slips in plastic eggs and hide them around the room. Reproduce the incomplete picture (page 269) for students. Tell them to listen carefully to the directions. As they find each egg, read the directions once for the whole class to follow. Only some of the directions will be used to complete the picture.

| | |
|---|---|
| 1. | Stand on your right foot and clap your hands three times. |
| 2. | Color the boy's shirt blue. |
| 3. | Draw a basket for the girl to carry her Easter eggs in. |
| 4. | Hop three times, clap your hands twice, and blink your eyes once. |
| 5. | Touch your shoulders, your knees, and then your feet. |
| 6. | Walk to your desk, sit down, then get up. |
| 7. | Put your hands on your head, clap your hands once, then touch your nose. |
| 8. | Color the tree green. |
| 9. | Clap your hands, slap your knees, then snap your fingers. |
| 10. | Draw two flowers in the grass. |
| 11. | Color the grass green. |
| 12. | Hold your hands over your head, clap twice, then touch your ears. |
| 13. | Color the roof of the house purple. |
| 14. | Draw another ear on the Easter Bunny. |
| 15. | Hide four Easter eggs in the picture. |
| 16. | Walk around your chair three times and wiggle your nose. |
| 17. | Color the butterfly orange. |
| 18. | Stand up and shake all over. |
| 19. | Walk around a table and clap your hands. |
| 20. | Draw a blue door on the house. |
| 21. | Raise your hands, snap your fingers twice, then touch your nose. |
| 22. | Touch a window, a chair, and a door. |
| 23. | Draw a yellow sun in the sky. |
| 24. | Color the girl's dress red. |

# The Letter E (cont.)

## • ELEVEN EASTER EGGS

Help students create 11 different kinds of Easter eggs by doing the following:

1. Make a chick in an egg (page 268).

2. Gelatin eggs: Put halves of washed plastic eggs in egg cartons. Fill them with gelatin. Chill the gelatin until it is firm. Briefly run the eggs under water to remove the gelatin from the mold. Put the gelatin halves together with whipped topping.

3. Elegant Easter Eggs: Ask students to bring in washed eggshells during the month before Easter. Dye crushed eggshells with a purchased egg dying kit. Put the eggshells in the dye and leave them there until the desired color is reached. Drain the shells and dry them on paper towels. Trace a large egg shape on construction paper. Spread glue inside the shape. Sprinkle crushed eggshells over the glue randomly or in a design or pattern. Spread the shells evenly and press down slightly. When the glue is dry, shake off any loose eggshells and proudly display the Easter egg.

4. Decorate an egg shape with dark crayon designs. Then paint over the crayon with a tempera wash.

5. On a construction paper egg outline, glue torn pieces of tissue paper using liquid laundry starch or thinned white glue. Slightly overlap the tissue scraps for a stained glass effect.

6. Brush a piece of egg-shaped drawing paper with water. Put a piece of tissue paper down and take it up. The color will remain. Do the whole egg, overlapping two colors in some places to make new combined colors.

7. Place a paper egg-shaped pattern, plain or with designs, on a table and cover it with clear plastic wrap. Outline the egg with colored glue. Make a design inside with additional colored glues, or randomly drizzle colors inside the outline. Let the glue dry for at least 24 hours. Peel off the plastic wrap. This colorful decoration will adhere to flat, smooth surfaces such as windows and refrigerators.

8. Blow up a small balloon. Dip string in glue thinned with a little water. Wrap the string around the balloon. Sprinkle it with glitter. Hang the balloon until it is dry. Pop the balloon. Hang the string egg shape in the classroom or cut a hole in the front and decorate it with grass, eggs, and silk flowers.

9. Put egg-shaped paper at the easel and create designs with paint or chalk.

10. Put clean eggshell halves in egg cartons. Punch a small hole in the bottom of each eggshell. Fill the eggshells with dirt and plant marigold seeds in them. Take the plants home or replant them outside, eggshell and all, to beautify the school grounds.

11. Put clean eggshell halves in egg cartons. Punch a small hole in each shell and draw faces on the front with permanent markers. Fill the eggshells with dirt and plant grass seed in them. Watch "hair" grow. Give the "Eggheads" "haircuts" by snipping off some grass with a pair of scissors.

## • EGG CARTONS

Ask: *How many ways can you think of to recycle egg cartons?* Allow students to cut egg cartons into individual cups to make flowers or into halves to make caterpillars.

# The Letter E *(cont.)*

### • *EGG CARTON MATH*

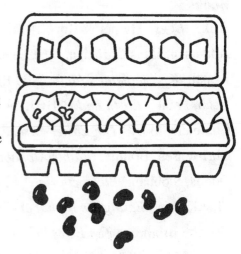

1. Provide clean egg cartons for students to use when practicing math skills such as counting, adding, and subtracting. Give each student an egg carton and ten large, dry beans. They may put some or all of the beans in the egg carton, close it, and shake the carton. Have them count the beans in the top row and write down the number. Then tell them to count the beans in the bottom row and write the number under the first one. Show students how to put a plus sign to the left of the bottom number and draw a line under that number. Ask them to count all the beans in the carton and write the answer under the line. To subtract, students may put in some beans, count them, and write down the number. Then direct them to take out some or all of the beans, count them, and write the number under the first number. Have them draw a line under the bottom number and place a minus sign on the left side of that number. Ask students to count the beans left in the carton to determine the answer and write it under the line.

2. An alternative method would be to give each student an egg shape with a line in the center separating it in half crosswise. Write an addition problem on the board such as $2 + 3 =$ _____. Students put 2 beans (or jelly beans) on the top half and 3 beans on the bottom half. They can count the beans to discover that $2 + 3 = 5$. Write a subtraction problem on the board, such as $5 - 3 =$ _____. Students can put 5 beans on the egg and take away 3 to determine that $5 - 3 = 2$.

3. Egg cutouts and beans could also be used for counting practice if students are not ready for addition and subtraction. Instruct students to count out 5 beans on each of 8 egg cutouts. If they are able to do this successfully, increase the number until they can consistently count out 10 on each cutout. Then give them number cards 1–10 and ask them to match the number card to the correct number of beans.

4. Have students use jelly eggs as counters instead of dry beans.

### • *EQUAL*

Ask students to count out equal numbers of beans on each half of the egg cutouts (page 268). Then ask them to count out more or less on the top part of their eggs.

### • *ESTIMATE*

Place some jelly eggs in a small jar. Allow students to estimate or guess the number of eggs in the jar. Award the eggs to the student who comes closest to the correct number.

### • *EASY EXERCISES*

Prepare a simple exercise tape for students to use on rainy days.

### • *EARTH AS AN ECOSYSTEM: ECOLOGY*

Ask students to find out what *ecosystem* and *ecology* mean. Tell them to make posters with environmental messages to display around your school.

# Bibliography

## Books

Aliki. *Eggs.* Harper & Row, 1994.

Andersen, Hans Christian. *The Emperor's New Clothes.* Troll, 1979.

Appelt, K. *Elephant's Aloft.* HBJ Big Book, 1995.

Asch, Frank. *Earth and I.* HBJ, 1994.

Chalmers, Mary. *The Easter Parade.* Harper & Row, 1988.

Christensen, Bonnie. *Edible Alphabet.* Dial, 1994.

Dodds, Siobhan. *Elizabeth Hen.* Little, Brown, 1987.

Ehlert, Lois. *Eating the Alphabet: Fruits and Vegetables from A to Z.* HBJ Big Book, 1989.

Grimm, Brothers. *The Elves and the Shoemaker.* Troll, 1981.

Heine, Helme. *The Most Wonderful Egg in the World.* Macmillan, 1987.

Joyce, William. *Bently and Egg.* Scholastic, 1992.

Lewis, K. *Emma's Lamb.* Macmillan, 1991.

Lionni, Leo. *An Extraordinary Egg.* Knopf, 1994.

McGovern, Ann. *Eggs On Your Nose.* Macmillan, 1987.

Petrash, Carol. *Earthways: Simple Environmental Activities for Young Children.* Gryphon, 1992.

Pfeffer, Pierre. *Elephants: Big, Strong, and Wise.* Young Discovery, 1987.

Polacco, Patricia. *Rechenka's Eggs.* Philomel, 1988.

Roberts, S. *Ernie's Big Mess.* Random House, 1992.

Schlein, Miriam. *Elephants.* Aladdin, 1990.

Seuss, Dr. *Green Eggs and Ham.* Random House, 1960.

Seuss, Dr. *Horton Hatches the Egg.* Random House, 1940.

Seuss, Dr. *Scrambled Eggs Super!* Random House, 1953.

Weiss, Nicki. *An Egg Is an Egg.* Putnam, 1990.

Wolf, Winifred. *The Easter Bunny.* Dial, 1986.

Zoobooks Magazine. *Elephants.* Wildlife Education, 1986.

## Technology

*Easter Parade.* (Cassette); Troll Associates, Catalog Sales Dept., 100 Corporate Dr., Mahwah, NJ 07498; 1-800-929-8765.

*Electro Dog's First Reader and Writer CD.* (Software for beginning reading skills); MPC. National School Products, 101 East Broadway, Maryville, TN 37804; 1-800-251-9124.

*Elephants.* (Video); 5 min. Coronet/MTI Film and Video, P.O. Box 2649, Columbus, OH 43216; 1-800-321-3106.

*Uncle Elephant.* (Video); 25 min. Pied Piper/AIMS Multimedia, 9710 De Soto Ave., Chatsworth, CA 91311; 1-800-367-2567.

# An Elegant Easter Egg

Enlarge the following key picture by creating an overhead transparency of this page. Project and trace it onto white poster board. Color the egg. Then laminate the egg. Glue fabric down to create the design. Allow the glue to dry. Refer to the key picture each day, especially when you discuss the calendar (page 9). At the end of the week, tape the egg to a wall as part of an alphabet line-up.

# Chick Egg

**Directions:** Color the chick. Cut out both pieces. Then use a brad to put them together.

# Following Directions

**Directions:** Look for eggs in your classroom. Follow the directions to complete the picture.

# The Letter W

### • *LETTER OF THE WEEK*

Display the key picture, A Wonderful Wet Watermelon (page 275). Refer to it each day. During the week, have students make the letter **W** using a variety of materials such as washed watermelon seeds or black circles punched from construction paper, wallpaper, pasta wheels, wax paper, etc.

### • *WATER*

1. Tell students that water is a liquid. It takes the shape of the container it is in. If you put water in the freezer, it freezes into a solid that holds its shape when taken out of its container. Put several ice cubes in a plastic glass and put the glass in the sun. Discuss how the ice melts and becomes water again. Put the glass of water in the freezer. After it freezes, ask: *What shape is the ice now? What happened to the ice cubes?* Put the ice in a pan on a stove or hot plate. **Warning**: Never let students near a stove or hot plate. Show the class that the ice (a solid) turns to water (a liquid), then boils and turns to steam (a gas). Ask: *Where does the steam go?* Reproduce The Water Cycle (page 276). Allow students to color their pictures and other details.

2. Give students large clean paintbrushes and water. Go outside on a warm, windy day and "paint" a sidewalk with water. Ask: *Where does it go?* Explain that it evaporates into the air and that the warmth and wind speed up the evaporation process. Put a full glass of water on a windowsill in the sun and tell students to observe how the water evaporates over a period of time.

3. Provide a water table or a dishpan full of water on a plastic-covered table for water exploration activities. Ask children to wear plastic smocks. Put containers and measuring cups of different sizes and shapes in the water for experimenting with volume. Ask: *Which holds more water—a tall, narrow container or a short, wide container? Can you always tell which container holds more water just by looking at it?* After students have had the opportunity to explore volume, replace the containers with small classroom objects such as paper clips, cork, chalk, crayon, etc. Write "Float" on one clean Styrofoam® meat tray and "Sink" on another. Students should experiment then sort the objects onto the trays.

### • *WALNUT SHELL BOATS*

1. Have each student put a small piece of clay in half of a walnut shell. (Save the walnuts to make Waldorf Salad.) For each boat, thread a toothpick in and out of a small triangle sail and stick one end in the clay. Have sailboat races. Students make the "wind" by blowing on the sails.

2. Point out that some things dissolve in water and some do not. Invite students to try to dissolve salt, sugar, honey, oil, sand, clay, crayons, a pencil, a peppermint candy, a piece of regular Styrofoam® packing, and some of the new biodegradable packing.

3. Mix equal amounts of cornstarch and water for students to play with. Sometimes the mixture is a solid and sometimes it is a liquid. Add more water as it dries out.

### • *WALDORF SALAD*

Mix diced apples, chopped walnuts, raisins, sunflower seeds in desired quantities. Moisten with a small amount of mayonnaise or plain or vanilla yogurt. This makes a healthful, delicious snack!

# The Letter W (cont.)

- ## WEATHER

  1. Talk about the different kinds of weather you have each day. Make a picture graph with symbols for each type of weather.

  2. Display a picture of the Water Cycle (page 276). Point out that water evaporates from lakes, oceans, rivers, and mud puddles into the air. As it goes up, it cools, forms clouds, and then falls as precipitation (rain, sleet, snow, hail). The cycle continues again. Have students note condensation (water in the air) from a glass of ice water. Tell them this is how clouds form.

  3. Talk about the dangers of thunderstorms and tornadoes. Remind students that they should go inside when they see dark clouds forming in the sky or if they hear thunder. Students should not stand under a tree because they attract lightning. People struck by lightning (which is electricity) may be killed. If there is a tornado, tell students that they should go in rooms or closets with no windows, preferably in the center of their houses.

  4. Ask: *How has the weather changed since you have been in school this year? How should you dress for different kinds of weather? What is your favorite type of weather? How do plants and animals react to different types of weather?*

  5. Read aloud *It Looked Like Spilt Milk* by Charles Green Shaw (Harper, 1947). Take students outside to look at the clouds. Ask: *What do the clouds look like?* Make a class book. Have students cut out white shapes and glue them onto light blue paper. Then they can dictate and complete the sentences: "It looked like a _____. But it wasn't a _____." The last page of your class book should correspond to the last page in Shaw's book.

- ## WIND AND WINDWHEELS

  Explain that air is all around us and it occupies space. To prove this, put cups upside down in water and slowly release the air bubbles inside. Point out that wind moves air from place to place. Have students watch as the wind moves the clouds. Ask: *What else does it move?* Help students make windwheels using the pattern on page 277. Have them take the windwheels outside.

- ## A WONDERFUL WEDNESDAY WALK IN THE WOODS

  1. On a Wednesday take a walk, preferably in the woods. Ask students to tell what they see, hear, feel, and smell. Ask how the trees have changed. Find some flowers for students to smell. Have students whistle, whisper, wink, wave, and/or waddle while they walk.

  2. Taste some cold and wonderful wet watermelon. (Save the seeds.)

  3. Back inside the classroom, make "Five Senses" booklets. For each student, staple together six half sheets of paper, write "A Walk in the Woods" on the front, and then write *See, Hear, Feel, Smell, Taste* on the other five pages. Students can draw and write about what they experienced with their five senses while on the walk.

- ## WEBS

  Ask students to observe spiders they find. Watch the video of *Charlotte's Web* (Paramount Home Video, 1972) and read stories about spiders. See the bibliography (page 274) for suggestions.

# The Letter W (cont.)

- **WATERMELON WONDERS**

1. If watermelon is unavailable in your area, make your own. Soften 1 quart (0.95 L) of lime sherbet (add green food coloring if desired), and spread inside of a 4-quart (3.8 L) melon mold or round bowl lined with plastic wrap. Freeze the mold. Spread 1 quart (0.95 L) of softened vanilla ice cream over the lime sherbet. Freeze the mold. Soften ½ gallon (1.9 L) of raspberry sherbet or strawberry ice cream. Mix in 1 cup (250 mL) chocolate chips (for seeds) and red food coloring if desired. Fill the mold and refreeze it. Turn the mold upside down to remove the "watermelon." Cut it into slices and allow students to enjoy eating it.

2. Make some Watermelon Popsicles for students. Mix watermelon pieces with a splash of orange juice in a blender or food processor. Freeze the mixture in cups with craft sticks inserted. If you prefer, students can make Watermelon Wigglers using watermelon gelatin.

3. Make 10 tagboard watermelon slices (page 275). Number the slices 1–10. Have students put them in numerical order. Then they can count out the correct number of "seeds" (clean watermelon seeds, black beans, buttons, pom pons, or punched paper circles) on each slice. Give each student a watermelon slice (page 275) to color. Name the number to be counted, or hold up number cards. Have students practice counting out seeds onto the watermelon slices. To practice addition, say: *Put three seeds on one side of your slice and two seeds on the other side.* Ask: *How many seeds do you have on your slice of watermelon? Write 3 + 2 = 5 on the board.* To practice subtracting, say: *Put five seeds on your watermelon. Take 2 seeds off. How many seeds do you have left?* Write $5 - 2 = 3$ on the board. Chocolate chips can be used for watermelon seeds. Then have students practice subtracting by eating the "seeds" **Warning:** Remind students not to eat real watermelon seeds.

- **WOOD**

1. Have students brainstorm a list of things made of wood. Ask them to identify things in the classroom that are made of wood. Ask: *Where does wood come from? How long does it take for a tree to grow? Why should we care if wood is wasted?*

2. Collect wood scraps from lumberyards or carpenters. Provide wood glue and allow students to make their own "Word Works" and name their creations.

- **WILD WEST DAY**

Invite the class to come dressed in western wear. Play western country music.

- **WHALES**

Show pictures of a blue whale and an Orca (pages 166 and 167). Allow students to pretend they are whales living in the ocean. Ask: *What adventures can you have?*

- **WEEK**

Count the number of days in a week and help students learn the names and sequence of the days. Ask: *Which day is your favorite? Why? What day was yesterday? What day will tomorrow be?*

# The Letter W *(cont.)*

## • *WEIGH*

Ask students to use balance scales to discover which of two small classroom objects weighs more than the other. Tell students to make predictions before they weigh the objects. Place the scales in the discovery center for further exploration. Caution students not to place too much weight on either side of the scales or they will break.

## • *WORMS*

Make a worm farm. Dig up some worms in a wooded or landscaped area. Put them in a large jar with some soil. Cover the jar with black paper and leave it undisturbed for a few days. Remove the paper and allow students to watch the worms digging tunnels through the dirt. Discuss how they eat plant decay and add to the soil. Read aloud stories about worms, such as *The Big Fat Worm* by Nancy Van Laan (Knopf, 1987), while students eat some gelatin-candy worms. Be sure to put the real worms back outside when students have completed making their observations.

## • *WOLF*

Read aloud any traditional version of *Little Red Riding Hood* and *The Three Little Pigs*. Compare the wolves in these two stories. Then read *The True Story of the Three Little Pigs* by Jon Sciezka (Scholastic, 1989); and *The Three Little Wolves and the Big Bad Pig,* by Eugene Trivizas (Scholastic, 1993). Ask students to compare/contrast the different versions.

## • *WISH*

Read *The Three Wishes* by Margot Zemach (Farrar, Straus, Giroux, 1986) and *Sylvester and the Magic Pebble* by William Steig (Windmill, 1969). Students may make a class "Wish Book" by drawing pictures of what they would wish for if they each had one wish. They should write or dictate sentences.

## • *"WYNKEN, BLYNKEN, AND NOD"*

Read aloud the poem "Wynken, Blynken, and Nod" by Eugene Field (Viking, 1982). If possible, compare different versions of the poem. Invite students to learn parts of the poem. Divide the class into six cooperative learning groups. Divide the poem into six parts, copying each part on an 18" x 24" (46 cm x 61 cm) piece of yellow or light blue butcher paper. Give each part of the poem to a group to illustrate using markers, glitter, foil stars, etc. Put the poem back together and display it as a mural. Outline large letters on another piece of paper for a title.

## • *WORDS*

Practice using the **W** question words: *Who? What? When? Where? Why?*

## • *WONDERFUL STORIES*

1. Watch the video *The Wizard of Oz* (MGM/UA Home Video, 1939).
2. Read aloud Kenneth Grahame's *The Wind in the Willows* adapted by Janet Palazzo-Craig (Troll, 1982).

# Bibliography

**Books**

Andersen, Hans Christian. *The Wild Swans.* Troll, 1981.

Bunting, Eve. *Wednesday Surprise.* Houghton Mifflin, 1989.

David, Gibbs. *Walter's Lucky Socks.* Bantam Books, 1991.

Drexler, Carol Joan, adapted by. *The Wizard of Oz.* Educational Reading Service, 1970.

Field, Eugene. *Wynken, Blynken, and Nod.* Viking, 1982.

Fowler, Allan. *It Could Still Be Water.* Childrens Press, 1992.

Fowler, Allan. *What's the Weather Today?* Childrens Press, 1991.

Hort, Lenny. *The Boy that Held Back the Sea.* Dial, 1987.

Humphries, Gillinan and Francis Thatcher. *Sam Cat: A Book About Weather.* Childrens Press, 1984.

Jennings, Terry. *Earthworms.* Gloucester, 1988.

Keats, Ezra Jack. *Whistle for Willie.* Penguin, 1977.

Kerber, Karen. *Walking is Wild, Weird, and Wacky.* Landmark, 1985.

Kraus, Robert. *Squirmy's Big Secret.* Silver, 1990.

Noll, Sally. *Watch Where You Go.* Viking, 1993.

Palazzo-Craig, Janet, adapted by. *Kenneth Grahame's The Wind in the Willows,* Volumes 1, 2, 3, and 4. Troll, 1982.

Perrault, Charles. *The Three Wishes.* Troll, 1979.

Polacco, Patricia. *Thunder Cake.* Philomel, 1990.

Pollock, Penny. *Water Is Wet.* Putnam, 1985.

Scieszka, Jon. *The True Story of the Three Little Pigs! By A. Wolf.* Scholastic, 1989.

Seidler, Tor. *Wainscott Weasel.* HarperCollins, 1993.

Steig, William. *Sylvester and the Magic Pebble.* Windmill, 1969.

Trivizas, Eugene. *The Three Little Wolves and the Big Bad Pig.* Scholastic, 1993.

Van Laan, Nancy. *The Big Fat Worm.* Knopf, 1987.

Walt Disney Editors. *Winnie the Pooh.* Warner Brothers Big Book, 1986.

Zemach, Margot. *The Three Wishes.* Farrar, Straus, Giroux, 1986.

**Technology**

*An Alphabet of Weather.* (Video); 13 min. Coronet/MTI Film and Video, P.O. Box 2649, Columbus, OH 43216; 1-800-321-3106.

*What Makes the Weather?* (Video); 8 min. Troll Associates, Catalog Sales Dept., 100 Corporate Dr., Mahwah, NJ 07498; 1-800-929-8765.

*Why Do Spiders Spin Webs?* (Video); 11 min. Coronet/MTI Film and Video, P.O. Box 2649, Columbus, OH 43216; 1-800-321-3106.

*Winnie the Pooh's ABC of Me.* (Video by Disney Entertainment Productions); 12 min. Available from Coronet/MTI Film and Video, P.O. Box 2649, Columbus, OH 43216; 1-800-321-3106.

# A Wonderful Wet Watermelon

Enlarge the following key picture by creating an overhead transparency of this page. Project and trace it onto white poster board. Paint the inside of the watermelon red and the outside of it green. Leave the inner rind white. Allow the paint to dry. Cut out seeds from black construction paper and glue them onto the melon. Cut out the letters from white construction paper or poster board. Glue them onto the melon. Allow the glue to dry. Then laminate the watermelon. Refer to the key picture each day, especially when you discuss the calendar (page 9). At the end of the week, tape the watermelon to a wall as part of an alphabet line-up.

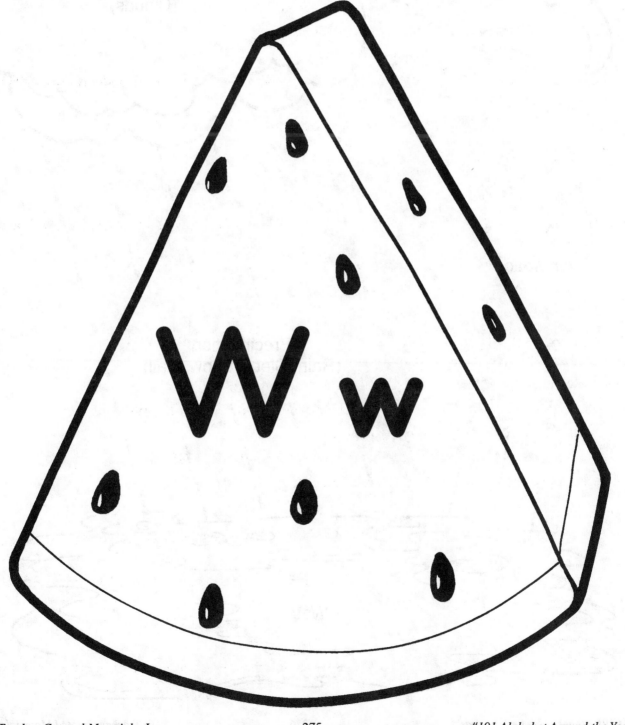

# The Water Cycle

**Directions:** Color the picture.  Add more things to it.

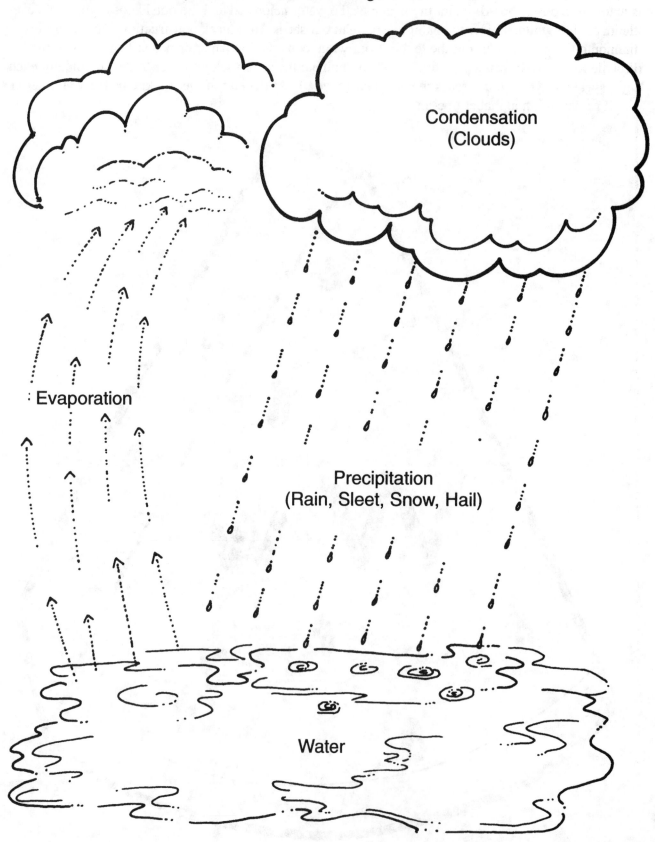

Condensation
(Clouds)

Evaporation

Precipitation
(Rain, Sleet, Snow, Hail)

Water

# Windwheel

Reproduce the windwheel pattern shown below. Have each student do the following: Cut out the square and color both sides of it. Cut along the diagonal lines starting at each corner. Carefully bend the corners marked with **W**'s until they are over the **X** in the center of the square. Push a straight pin or thumb tack through each corner and the **X**. Then attach the windwheel to the pencil on an eraser. Provide assistance as needed.

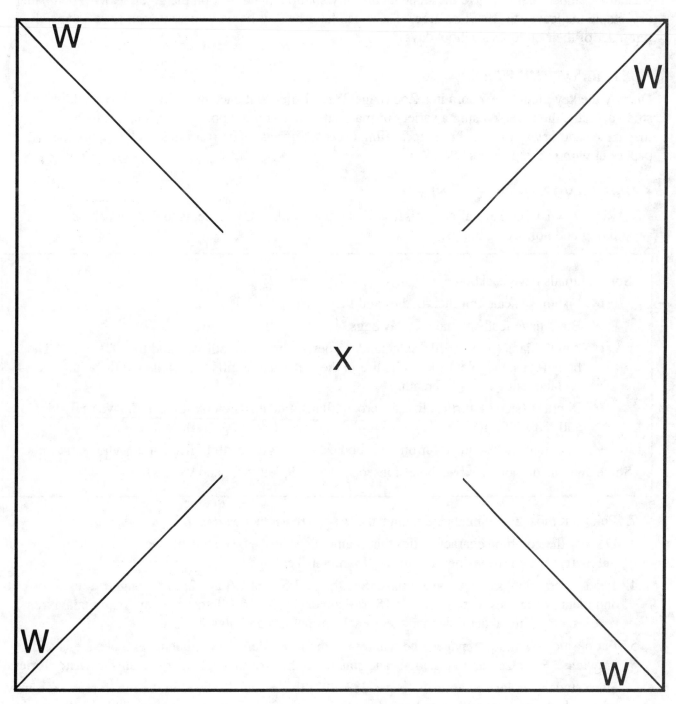

# The Letter Z

### • *MAY*

The Class Tree becomes a "Friendship Tree" during the last month of school. Draw two leaf patterns on one page. Reproduce the patterns on green construction paper. Cut out the patterns and provide one for each student. One at a time, paint each student's right hand with his or her favorite color of washable tempera paint. Have the student carefully stamp a handprint on the green leaf. When paint is dry, staple the leaves to the Class Tree. These can later be sent home so parents can have a special reminder of their children's school days.

### • *LETTER OF THE WEEK*

Display the key picture, A Zebra in a Zoo (page 282). Refer to it each day. During the week, have students make the letter **Z** using a variety of materials such as old zippers, zeros cut out from magazines and newspapers, zebra stripes, zinnia seeds, zigzags made from rick-rack or construction paper cut with pinking shears, etc.

### • *ZEBRA AND OTHER ZOO ANIMALS*

1. Review what you have already discussed about animals. Ask students to distinguish between living and non-living things.

---

Some animals have backbones:

- ✔ Fish have scales on their bodies and they lay eggs.
- ✔ Birds have feathers and they lay eggs.
- ✔ Amphibians (frogs, toads, salamanders, newts) have smooth skin and they lay eggs. The baby (eggs, tadpoles) spends its life in the water using gills to breath, and the adult lives on land using lungs to breath.
- ✔ Reptiles (snakes, turtles, lizards, crocodilians, tuatara) are cold-blooded, have scaly skin, and most lay eggs.
- ✔ Mammals have hair or fur on their bodies. They give birth to live babies who drink milk.

Some animals do not have backbones: insects, shellfish, jellyfish, and worms.

---

2. Point out most zoo animals are mammals. Ask: *Are we mammals? How do you know?*

3. Discuss the common characteristics that mammals share. Have students work with partners to cut out pictures from magazines and make "Mammals" collages.

4. Read several books about zoo animals. See the bibliography (page 281) for suggestions. Look at and identify pictures of zoo animals. Sort them according to whether they are mammals, birds, reptiles, etc. Talk about how many legs each animal has and how it moves.

5. Put plastic zoo animals, paper, and markers in the block center for students to make signs and drawings. Place zoo animal stencils and stamps in the writing center for students to write stories.

6. Have students color zoo animals (pages 283–292) that originally lived in the rain forest. You may wish to have students add these animals to the rain forest bulletin board (page 242). Tell students that zoos help protect animals and provide a safe place for us to see them. Explain that most people will not be able to travel to far away countries to see these animals, but they may be able to go to a nearby zoo.

# The Letter Z *(cont.)*

## • *ZOOSCAPE*

1. Create a zoo mural. Cover a bulletin board with green background paper. Have students work cooperatively to decide what kind of a zoo they think their animals would like to live in. Suggested questions for discussion: *If you were a zebra, would you prefer a concrete cage with steel bars or a grassy meadow where you could run and play with other zebras and perhaps some giraffes? Would you like to be in the same cage as some lions? Why or why not?* Allow students to decide which animals could live together and how many animals should be put in each area of the zoo.

2. Divide the Zooscape into different areas. Allow students to decide which animals will live in the different sections of the zoo. To make the zoo animals, students may color the patterns on pages 283-292 or draw some of their own. Tell students to make signs with the names of the animals on them. Tell them to decide how each group of animals will be confined. Ask: *How will you separate them from people who come to visit them? What special provisions will you need to make for the animals?* Read about the native habitats for the animals students have chosen to put in their zoo. Ask: *Can you provide ice for the polar bears and penguins? Are all the animals in the zoo mammals? Are there any reptiles, birds, fish, amphibians, or insects?*

3. If there is a real zoo nearby, take students there for a visit. Ask them to compare the real zoo to the one they designed.

## • *ZOOBOOK*

Have students create pictures and stories for a class zoobook using one of the following topics: "If I Were a Zookeeper," "If I Were A Zoo Animal, I Would Be. . .," or "My Pet Zoo Animal."

## • *ABC ZOO ANIMALS*

Make a class list of animals beginning with each letter of the alphabet. Allow each student to draw or color an animal and dictate facts about it for a ABC Zoo Animals Book. Suggestions include: alligator, baboon, camel, deer, elephant, fox, giraffe, hippopotamus, iguana, jaguar, koala, lion, moose, newt, otter, penguin, quail, rhinoceros, seal, tiger, umbrella bird, vulture, walrus, ox (ends with **x**), yak, zebra.

## • *ZANY ZIGZAG ZOO*

Allow students to create "Zany Zoo Animals" using construction or butcher paper, yarn, sequins, craft feathers and other scraps. Enclose the creatures in zigzag fences on a bulletin board. Have students name their animals.

## • *ZOOM ZIGZAGS*

Invite students to carefully zoom around the classroom in zigzags.

## • *ZERO*

To help students understand the concept of zero, ask nonsense questions. Example: *How many lions are there walking around the room?*

# The Letter Z *(cont.)*

## • *ZOO GAMES*

Have students play the following zoo games to practice the skills they are learning. Match capital and small letters on pictures of mother and baby animals. Put numerals on pictures of monkeys. Count out correct number of banana-shaped counters. Pair rhyming words by matching pictures on peanuts with pictures of elephants on a game board. Match pictures of zoo animals to the correct beginning letters on alphabet cards. Count out plastic zoo animals into numbered plastic berry baskets. Play Monkey See, Monkey Do using the same rules as Simon Says. Toss peanuts into a shoebox with a picture of an elephant on the front.

## • *ZANY ZOO SNACKS*

1. Mix bear-shaped graham crackers, animal crackers, animal-shaped chewy fruit snacks, peanuts, and banana chips. Serve in reclosable plastic bags.

2. Have students make zoo cookies by using refrigerated sugar cookie dough to create zoo animals. Allow them to decorate their cookies with sprinkles and bake them according to the directions on the package.

## • *ZUCCHINI*

1. Make some zucchini bread for students to taste.

2. Ask students to try raw zuchini with a Zesty Dip made by combining a packet of ranch salad dressing mix with 1 cup (250 mL) of yogurt and 1 cup (250 mL) of sour cream.

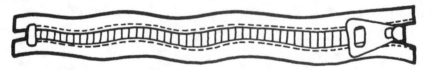

## • *ZIPPERS*

1. Give students reclosable plastic bags. In each bag, put some vanilla pudding and a drop or two of different food colors. Ask students to guess what color their pudding will be after it is mixed with the colors. Have them gently mix the contents as they practice zipping and unzipping their bags. They may practice making letters and numbers, especially zeros, by carefully "writing" these on the outside of their bags with their fingers. Tell them to gently rub the bags to erase the "writing." When practice time is over, students can eat the pudding.

2. On another day, mix up some Peanut Butter Clay. Combine equal amounts of peanut butter, honey, and powdered milk. Students can use the clay to practice making all of the ABC's. Then they can eat some and take the rest home in reclosable plastic bags for further practice.

3. Colored glue dough, made from equal amounts of colored glue, flour, and cornstarch, can be stored in reclosable plastic bags for several weeks for letter and number practice.

## • *ZITHERS AND ZINNIAS*

Allow students to listen to a real zither or some taped music as they plant some zinnia seeds outside. Tell them to water the plants and watch them grow.

## • *ZIP CODE*

Allow students to sign a large **Z** on the laminated house (page 51) as they learn their zip codes.

# Bibliography

## Books

Arnold, Caroline. *Elephant.* Morrow, 1993.

Arnold, Caroline. *Giraffe.* Morrow, 1987.

Baker, Eugene. *Wild Animals.* Zachary's Workshop, 1989.

Brennan, John and Leonie Kearney. *Zoo Day.* Carolrhoda, 1989.

Browne, Anthony. *Zoo.* Knopf, 1993.

Butterfield, Moira. *1000 Facts About Wild Animals.* Grisewood & Dempsey, 1992.

Campbell, Rod. *Dear Zoo.* Penguin, 1987.

Cooper, Jason. *Zoos.* Rourke, 1992.

Dowell, Philip. *Zoo Animals.* Aladdin, 1991.

Ehlert, Lois. *Color Zoo.* Lippincott, 1989.

Emberly, Rebecca. *Jungle Sounds.* Little, 1989.

Evans, Lisa Gollin. *An Elephant Never Forgets Its Snorkel.* Crown, 1992.

Florian, Douglas. *At the Zoo.* Greenwillow, 1992.

Fowler, Alan. *It Could Still Be a Mammal.* Childrens Press, 1990.

Gibbons, Gail. *Zoo.* Harper & Row, 1987.

Goennel, Heidi. *Heidi's Zoo: An Un-Alphabet Book.* Tambourine, 1993.

Greeley, Valerie. *Zoo Animals.* Bedrick/Blackie, 1984.

Hadithi, Mwenye. *Greedy Zebra.* Little, Brown, 1984.

Hallmark Cards. *Safari Adventure: A Troll Pop-Up Book.* Troll, 1988.

Hoban, Tana. *A Children's Zoo.* Morrow, 1985.

Irvine, Georgeanne. *Endangered Species at the San Diego Zoo.* Scholastic, 1990.

Jones, Teri Crawford, ed. *Zoo Animals.* Publications International, 1991.

Kherdian, David. *Animal ABC.* Random House, 1984.

Kilpatrick, Cathy. *Zoo Animals.* Treasure, 1990.

Kindersley, Dorling. *Zoo Animals.* Macmillan, 1991.

Moss, Miriam. *Zoos.* Bookwright, 1989.

O'Neill, Michael. *Zoobabies.* Villard, 1991.

Pienkowski, Jan. *Zoo.* David and Charles, 1985.

Relf, Patricia. *Follow the Zookeeper.* Merrigold, 1984.

Rey, Margret and Allan J. Shalleck. *Curious George Visits the Zoo.* Houghton Mifflin, 1985.

Roffey, Maureen. *I Spy at the Zoo.* Aladdin, 1987.

Sayles, G. *My First Visit to the Zoo.* Barron's, 1990.

Schneck, Marcus. *Zoo Animals.* W.H. Smith, 1990.

Sharmat, Marjorie Weinman. *Helga High-Up.* Scholastic, 1987.

Sheppard, Jeff. *The Right Number of Elephants.* Harper, 1990.

Silverstein, Shel. *Who Wants a Cheap Rhinoceros?* Macmillan, 1964.

Stadler, John. *Three Cheers for Hippo!* HarperCollins, 1990.

West, Colin. *Pardon Said the Giraffe.* Lippincott, 1986.

Whitcombe, Bobbie. *Animals in Danger.* Brimax, 1988.

Whitehead, Pat. *Let's Go to the Zoo.* Troll, 1985.

Ziefert, Harriet. *Zippity Zap! A Book About Dressing.* Penguin, 1984.

# A Zebra in a Zoo

Enlarge the following key picture by creating an overhead transparency of this page. Project and trace it onto white poster board. Paint or color the zebra's black stripes and the grass green. If paint is used, allow it to dry. Then laminate the zebra. You may wish to glue some black yarn onto the zebra's mane and the end of its tail. Refer to the key picture each day, especially when you discuss the calendar (page 9). At the end of the week, tape the zebra to a wall as part of an alphabet line-up.

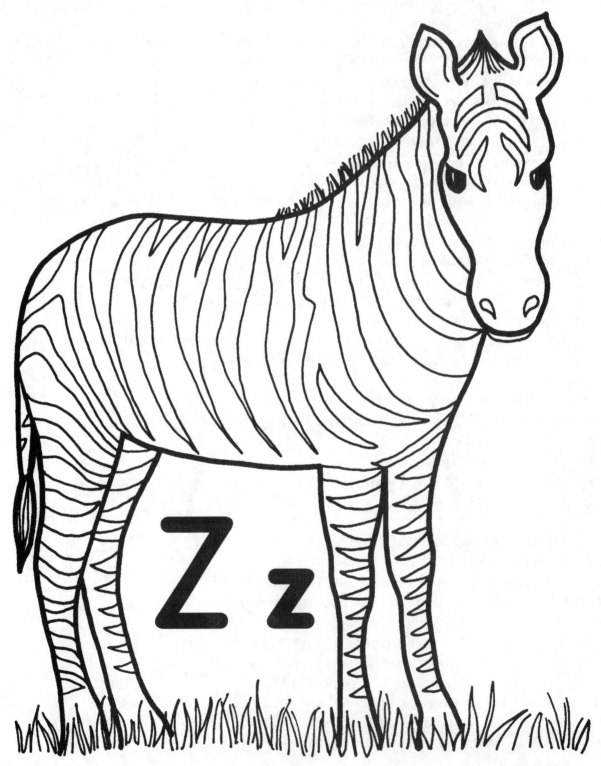

# Zoo Animals

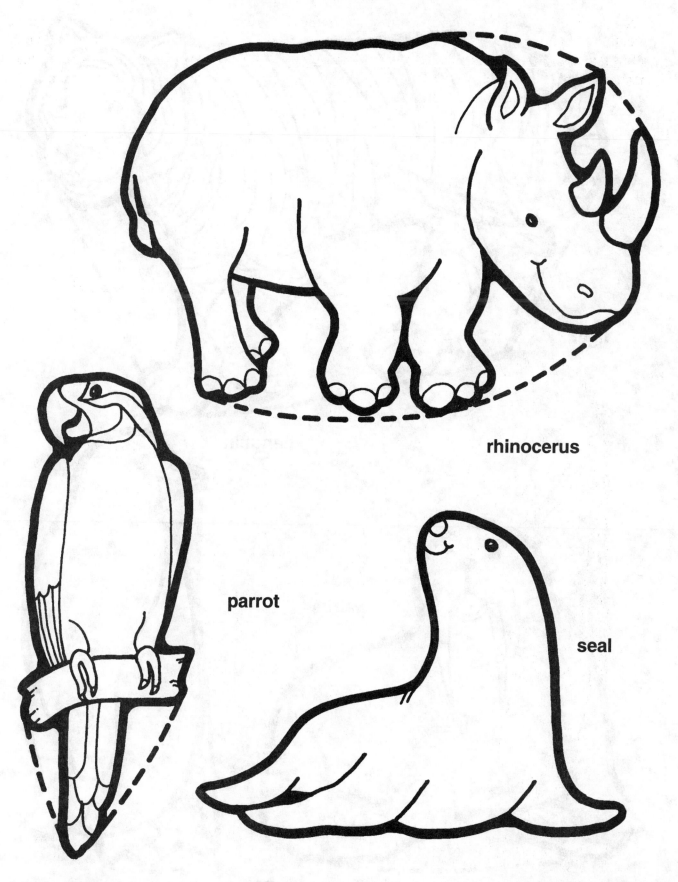

rhinocerus

parrot

seal

# Zoo Animals (cont.)

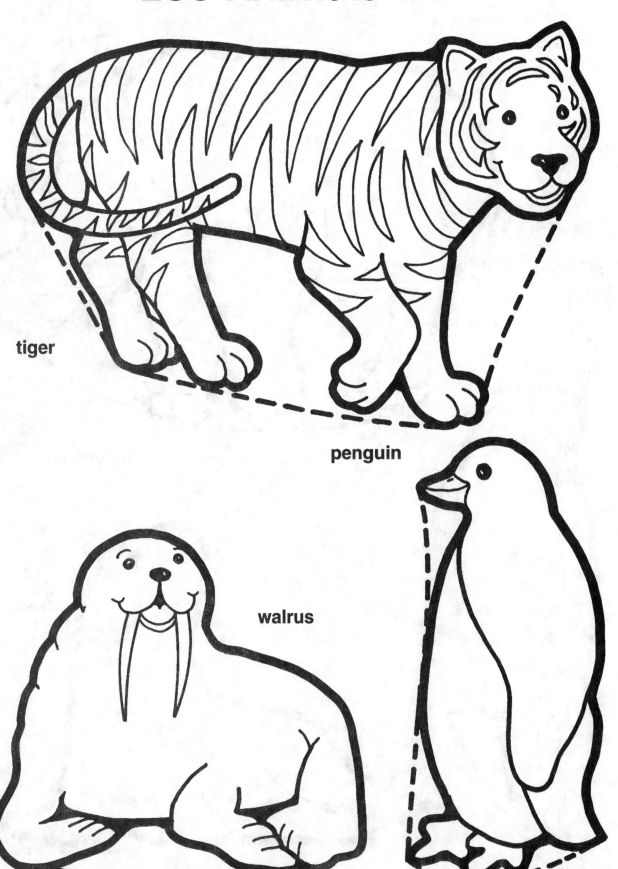

tiger

penguin

walrus

# Zoo Animals *(cont.)*

lion

vulture

kangaroo

# Zoo Animals *(cont.)*

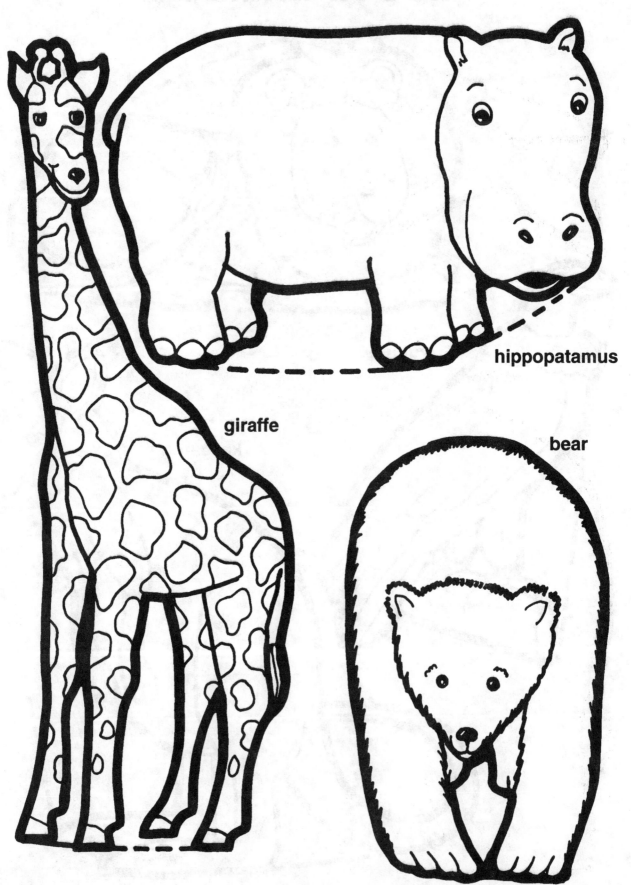

hippopatamus

giraffe

bear

# Zoo Animals *(cont.)*

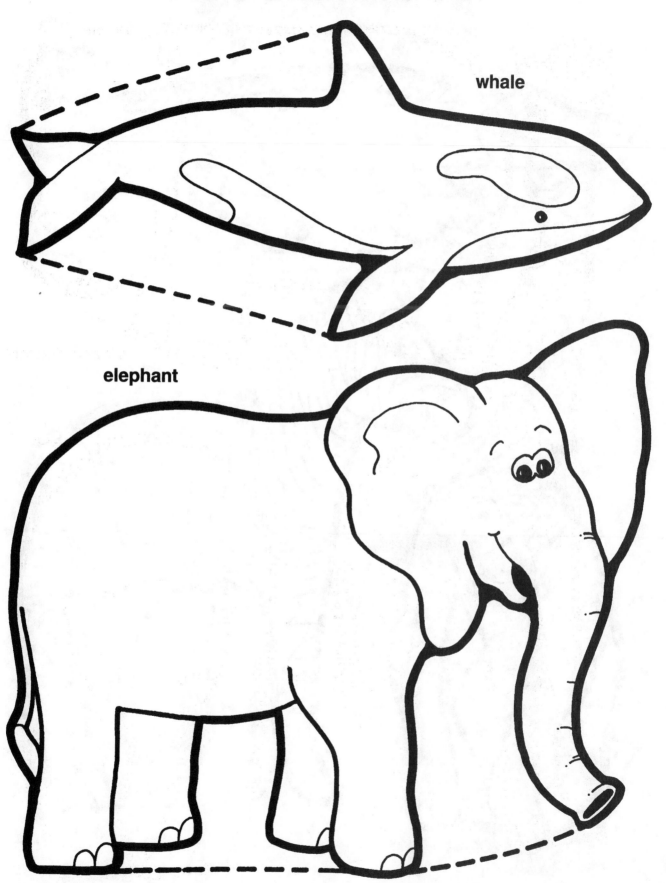

whale

elephant

# Zoo Animals (cont.)

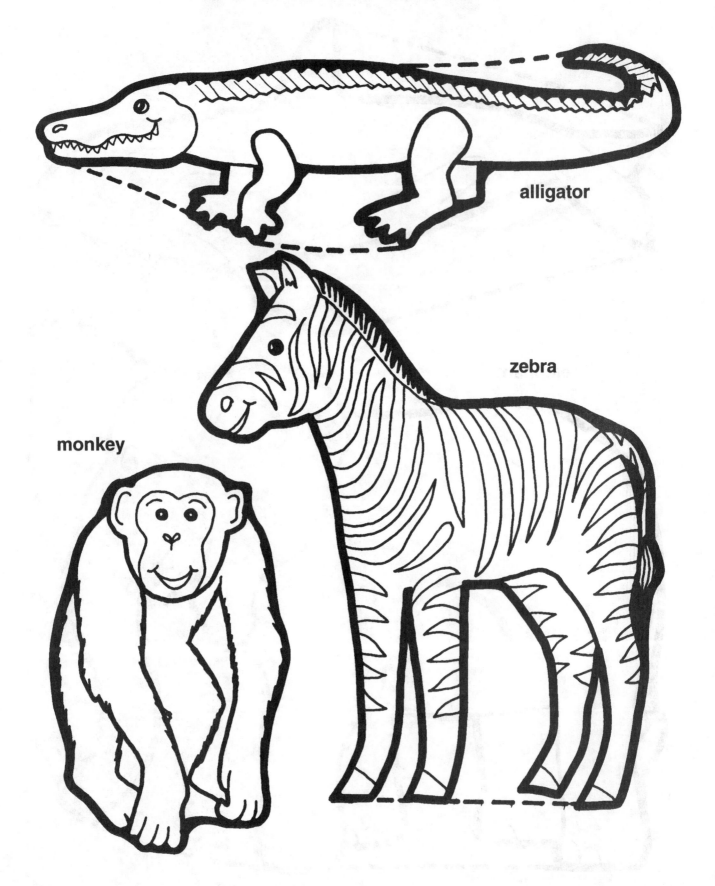

alligator

zebra

monkey

# Zoo Animals (cont.)

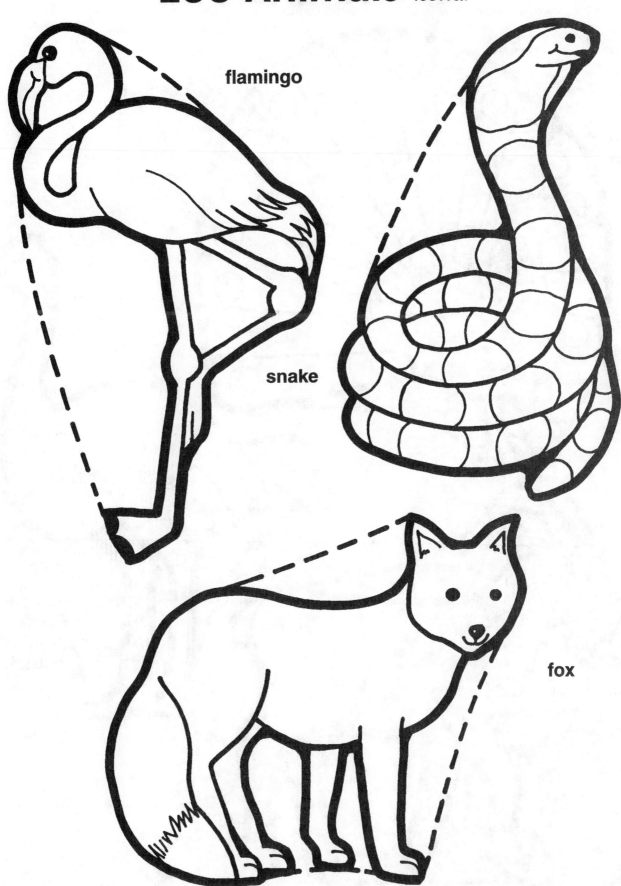

flamingo

snake

fox

# Zoo Animals *(cont.)*

peacock

ostrich

goat

# Zoo Animals *(cont.)*

**wolf**

**gorilla**

# Zoo Animals *(cont.)*

**dolphin**

**beaver**

**polar bear**

# The Letter D

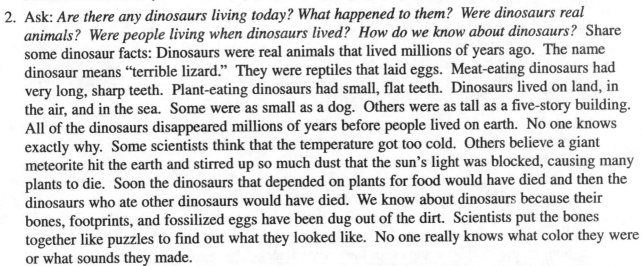

• *LETTER OF THE WEEK*

Display the key picture, A Dancing Dinosaur (page 298). Refer to it each day. During the week, have students make the letter **D** using a variety of materials such as construction paper or stick-on dots, dirt, dime rubbings, etc.

• *DINOSAURS*

1. Introduce the class to dinosaurs, by sharing one or more of the following books: *What Happened to Patrick's Dinosaur?* by Carol Carrick (Clarion, 1986), *The Dinosaurs* (Random House, 1984) and *The Day of the Dinosaurs* (Random House, 1987) both by Stan and Jan Berenstain, and *King of the Dinosaurs: Tyrannosaurus Rex* by Michael Berenstain (Western, 1989). See the bibliography (page 297) for additional suggestions.

2. Ask: *Are there any dinosaurs living today? What happened to them? Were dinosaurs real animals? Were people living when dinosaurs lived? How do we know about dinosaurs?* Share some dinosaur facts: Dinosaurs were real animals that lived millions of years ago. The name dinosaur means "terrible lizard." They were reptiles that laid eggs. Meat-eating dinosaurs had very long, sharp teeth. Plant-eating dinosaurs had small, flat teeth. Dinosaurs lived on land, in the air, and in the sea. Some were as small as a dog. Others were as tall as a five-story building. All of the dinosaurs disappeared millions of years before people lived on earth. No one knows exactly why. Some scientists think that the temperature got too cold. Others believe a giant meteorite hit the earth and stirred up so much dust that the sun's light was blocked, causing many plants to die. Soon the dinosaurs that depended on plants for food would have died and then the dinosaurs who ate other dinosaurs would have died. We know about dinosaurs because their bones, footprints, and fossilized eggs have been dug out of the dirt. Scientists put the bones together like puzzles to find out what they looked like. No one really knows what color they were or what sounds they made.

3. Help students make "Dinosaur Dictionaries." Reproduce the dinosaurs on pages 299–303. Instruct students to color the dinosaurs and dictate important facts that they have learned about each dinosaur. The following information can be used for the dictionaries:

   **Brontosaurus** means "thunder lizard." The earth must have shook when a brontosaurus walked, because it was one of the largest land animals that ever lived. It was about 70 feet (21 m) long. It was a plant-eater that stayed in or near the water most of the time for protection.

   **Tyrannosaurus Rex** means "king of the tyrant lizards." It was about 50 feet (15 m) in length and had sharp, six-inch (15 cm) long teeth. There is no doubt that it terrorized the dinosaur world. It was a meat eater.

   **Triceratops** means "three-horned face." It was a plant-eater with a horn on its nose, a horn over each eye, and a ruffled bony plate around its neck for protection. It was one of the last dinosaurs to die off.

   **Stegosaurus** was another plant-eater with large, bony plates down its back and sharp spikes on its tail for protection. It was about 25 feet (7.5 m) long.

   **Trachodon** was a duckbill dinosaur. It measured about 30 feet (9 m) long and had about 2000 teeth. It had webbed feet which allowed it to walk in the mud along bodies of water and scoop up water plants and animals in its flat mouth.

# The Letter D *(cont.)*

- ### DINOSAURS *(cont.)*

**Pteranodon** means "winged and toothless." It was a flying reptile, not a bird. Its wingspan was 20 feet (6 m). It flew over water and swooped down to catch fish, which it swallowed whole.

**Allosaurus** was a meat-eater with a large head, sharp claws and teeth. It was about 35 feet (7.5 m) long. It would attack other dinosaurs more than seven times its own weight.

**Brachiosaurus** was the largest of the dinosaurs, at about 90 feet (27 m) long. It was much like a brontosaurus. It had nostrils on top of its head so it could hide under water and still breathe.

4. Put dinosaur stencils and stamps in the writing center, and allow students to create dinosaur pictures and write stories about them.

5. Have each student draw a picture and dictate a story on dinosaur-shaped paper to tell which dinosaur he or she would like to have for a pet. Include such topics for discussion as where the dinosaur would live, what it would be fed, what its name would be, what problems might occur having a dinosaur as a pet, and what students would like to do with their pet dinosaurs. Combine the stories into a class book entitled "My Pet Dinosaur."

6. Select some or all of the dinosaur patterns (pages 299–303) to enlarge. Make transparencies of the patterns and trace two enlarged, identical copies of each dinosaur on white butcher paper. Staple the two identical dinosaur pieces together all around the sides, leaving a small opening. Let students decorate both sides of each dinosaur with crayons or markers. Remind them that no one knows what color the dinosaurs actually were. They should use their imaginations to decide what the dinosaurs looked like. Then have them crumple newspaper and stuff inside through the small opening in the seam. Staple the opening closed. Have students work in cooperative learning groups to choose names for the pet dinosaurs. Use colored glue to write each pet dinosaur's name. Allow the glue to dry overnight.

7. "Day of the Dinosaurs" display: Transform the Rain Forest bulletin board into Dinosaurland. Replace the rain forest animals with colorful stuffed dinosaurs designed by students (described above).

8. Mix equal amounts of flour, cornstarch, and colored glue. Allow students to use different colored dough to mold dinosaurs. Display the dinosaurs with the mural.

9. Digging for Dinosaurs: Hide assorted plastic dinosaurs in a sandbox. Allow students to discover them by digging them up.

10. Dinosaur Fossils: Collect, wash, and cut off the tops of 8-ounce (225 g) milk cartons. Mix plaster of Paris according to directions on the package. For each student, fill a milk carton about ¾ full. Allow students to rub petroleum jelly over small plastic dinosaurs and gently press them halfway down into the plaster. Let the plaster harden overnight. Tell students to carefully remove the plastic dinosaurs so they can see the "fossils." If students would like, they can cover the outside of their milk cartons with dinosaur print gift wrap or contact paper.

11. Color dinosaur macaroni in reclosable plastic bags with about 1 tablespoon (15 mL) of alcohol and several drops of food coloring. Allow the macaroni to dry on wax paper overnight. Have students use the dinosaur macaroni for counting, addition, and subtraction practice.

# The Letter D *(cont.)*

- ## *DINOSAUR DAY*

  1. Watch a dinosaur video such as *The Land Before Time* (Universal City Studios & U-Drive Productions, 1988), *The Land Before Time II* (Universal Cartoon Studios, 1994), or *The Land Before Time III* (Universal Cartoon Studios, 1995). Then have students, create a "Dinosaur Dance" with the Pet Dinosaurs.

  2. Help students paint T-shirts with dinosaur patterns using the direction shown on page 146. Encourage them to wear their T-shirts for the day.

  3. Enjoy making dinosaur cookies with the class. Mold the dough into dinosaurs or use cookie cutters and refrigerated sugar cookie dough. If you prefer, students can frost and decorate dinosaur-shaped graham crackers. Let them use jelly beans for dinosaur eggs.

- ## *DINOSAUR DIARIES*

Students may take their Pet Dinosaurs home on Friday. On Monday, students may dictate stories and draw pictures of their weekend activities to make a class book entitled "Dinosaur Diaries."

- ## *DAISY AND DANDELION*

Obtain a wildflower field guide and take students outside to look for daisies and dandelions. Try to identify any other wildflowers that they find. Instill in students the importance of leaving wildflowers where they find them, unless there is an abundance of a particular species.

- ## *DAYS*

Instruct students to name the days of the week and tell which day is their favorite and why.

- ## *DICTIONARY*

Have students practice finding words in various picture dictionaries. In order to find the words in the dictionaries, they need to decide what letter the word begins with and whether that letter is in the beginning, middle, or end of the alphabet.

- ## *DIRT DOES NOT DISSOLVE*

  1. Ask students to dig up some dirt and examine it using magnifying glasses. Talk about what they found in it. Have them name some creatures that might live in the dirt.

  2. Fill a jar half full of dirt and then fill it with water. Shake to mix it. Allow students to watch as the dirt settles to the bottom in layers. Explain that dirt is made up of tiny pieces of rock (sand) and bits of decayed plant and animal matter.

  3. Challenge students to dissolve various things, such as sugar, salt, dirt, pencils, etc., in water. Obtain some packing material that will dissolve in water and compare it to Styrofoam® packing that will not dissolve. Talk about which is better and why.

- ## *DOCTOR/DENTIST*

If possible, invite parents who are doctors and dentists to the class to talk about their professions.

# The Letter D *(cont.)*

## • *DRAGONS*

Read several books about dragons. See the bibliography (page 297) for suggestions. Watch a video such as *The Reluctant Dragon* (Walt Disney Home Video, 1987). Discuss whether dragons are real or imaginary creatures. The class might enjoy telling about imaginary pet dragons.

## • *DIAMOND DESIGNS*

Suggest that students make designs by fitting diamond-shaped pattern blocks together. They may wish to trace the blocks and color in their designs.

## • *DRAW DOODLES*

Model how to draw doodles and color the insides using different colors. Then let students try.

## • *DOT-TO-DOTS, DICE, AND DOMINOES*

1. Use dot-to-dot coloring book pages to provide letter and number sequencing practice.
2. Provide dice and dominoes for counting, addition, and subtraction practice. Roll two dice and count, add, or subtract the numbers. Count, add, or subtract the dots on the dominoes. Teach students how to play dominoes.

## • *DELICIOUS*

Supply students with magazines, white construction paper, and blunt scissors. Tell them to cut out pictures of "Delicious Things" to make an individual collage.

## • *DOLPHIN*

Have students color, cut out, and name a dolphin (page 168).

## • *A DOZEN DELICIOUS DONUTS OR DATE NUT BREAD*

Share one or two dozen mini donuts with the class. Ask: *How many are in a dozen? How many dozens do we need for everyone in the class to have one? What other things come in dozens?* If you prefer, students can help you make some date nut bread. Then they can enjoy eating it.

## • *DIRT DESSERT*

Invite volunteers to help you mix two packages of instant chocolate pudding according to the directions on the packages. Fold in an 8-ounce (225 g) container of whipped topping. Ask each student to crumble up a chocolate wafer cookie in the bottom of a clear plastic cup. Crumble up any remaining cookies into the pudding mixture to represent the "dirt." Add "rocks" (nuts and/or chocolate chips) if desired. Put some of the mixture in each cup and chill for about an hour. Put a surprise gelatin-candy worm in each cup before serving them.

## • *DODGE BALL AND "DUCK, DUCK, GOOSE"*

Allow students to enjoy playing Dodge Ball or Duck, Duck, Goose during P.E. time!

# Bibliography

## Books

Berenstain, Michael. *King of the Dinosaurs: Tyrannosaurus Rex.* Western, 1989.

Berenstain, Stan and Jan. *The Berenstain Bears Go to the Doctor.* Random House, 1987.

Berenstain, Stan and Jan. *The Day of the Dinosaurs.* Random House, 1987.

Berenstain, Stan and Jan. *The Dinosaurs.* Random House, 1984.

Blumenthal, Nancy. *Count-a-Saurus.* Scholastic, 1989.

Carrick, Carol. *What Happened to Patrick's Dinosaurs?* Clarion, 1986.

Cosgrove, Stephen. *Dragolin.* Price Stern Sloan, 1984.

Cosgrove, Stephen. *Persnickety.* Price Stern Sloan, 1988.

Crews, Donald. *Ten Black Dots.* Greenwillow, 1986.

D'Argo, Laura. *Learn About Dinosaurs.* New Seasons, 1990.

Donnelly, Liza. *Dinosaur Beach.* Scholastic, 1989.

Donnelly, Liza. *Dinosaur Garden.* Scholastic, 1990.

Eastman, Philip D. *The Cat in the Hat Beginner Book Dictionary.* Random House, 1984.

Grahame, Kenneth. *The Reluctant Dragon.* Troll, 1988.

Hoban, Tana. *Dots, Spots, Speckles, and Stripes.* Greenwillow, 1987.

James, Sara. *The Littlest Dinosaur.* Watermill, 1989.

Kellogg, Steven. *Prehistoric Pinkerton.* Dial, 1987.

Miller, M.R. *Dinosaurs.* Checkerboard, 1988.

Most, Bernard. *Whatever Happened to the Dinosaurs?* HBJ, 1984.

Muller, Romeo. *Puff the Magic Dragon.* Avon, 1963.

Nemes, Claire. *Dinosaurs.* Troll, 1990.

Norman, David, Ph.D. and Angela Milner, Ph.D. *Dinosaur.* Knopf, 1989.

Ottenheimer Publishers. *Dragons: A Pop-Up Book.* Ottenheimer, 1987.

Pallotta, Jerry. *The Dinosaur Alphabet Book.* Charlesbridge, 1991.

Pulver, Robin. *Mrs. Toggle and the Dinosaur.* Scholastic, 1991.

Whipple, Laura, compiled by. *Eric Carle's Dragons & Other Creatures That Never Were.* Philomel, 1991.

Whitehead, Pat. *Dinosaur Alphabet Book.* Troll, 1985.

Wildsmith, Brian. *Daisy.* Pantheon, 1984.

## Technology

*An Alphabet of Dinosaurs.* (Video by Christianson Productions, Inc.); 15 min. Coronet/MTI Film and Video, P.O. Box 2649, Columbus, OH 43216; 1-800-321-3106.

*Dinosaurs.* (Software with five games); PC; National School Products, 101 East Broadway, Maryville, TN 37804; 1-800-251-9124.

*Learn About Dinosaurs* by Learningways, Inc. (Software about nine dinosaurs); MAC; Available from Sunburst, P.O. Box 100, Pleasantville, NY 10570; 1-800-321-7511.

*More About Dinosaurs.* (Video); 8 min. Troll Associates, Catalog Sales Dept., 100 Corporate Dr., Mahwah, NJ 07498; 1-800-929-8765.

# A Dancing Dinosaur

Enlarge the following key picture by creating an overhead transparency of this page. Project and trace it onto white poster board. Color the dinosaur green or gray and cut it out. Then laminate the dinosaur. Refer to the key picture each day, especially when you discuss the calendar (page 9). At the end of the week, tape the dinosaur to a wall as part of an alphabet line-up.

# Dinosaurs

## tyrannosaurus rex

# Dinosaurs (cont.)

**triceratops**

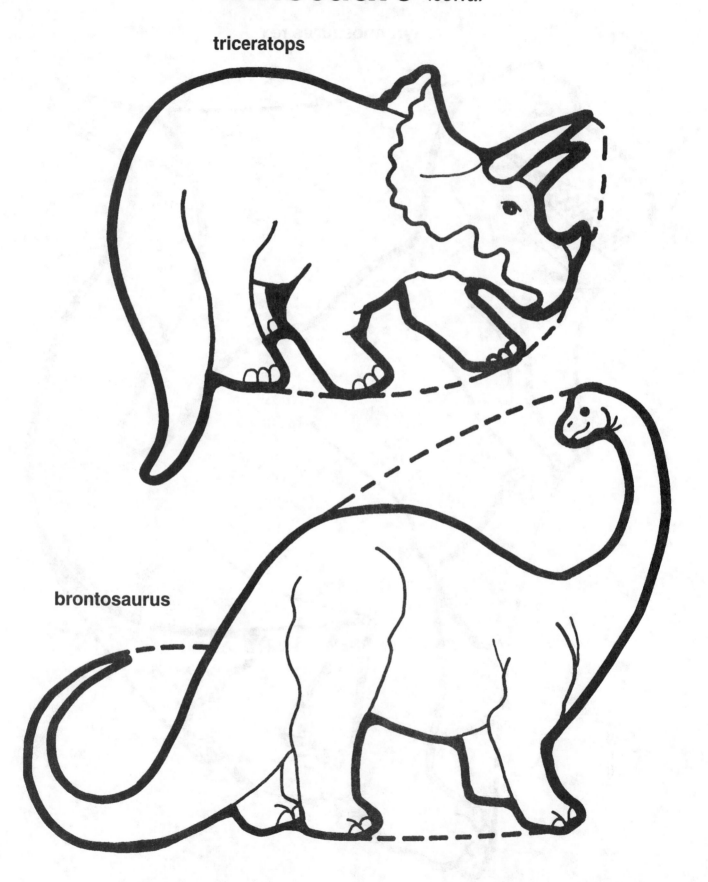

**brontosaurus**

# Dinosaurs *(cont.)*

**stegosaurus**

**trachodon**

# Dinosaurs *(cont.)*

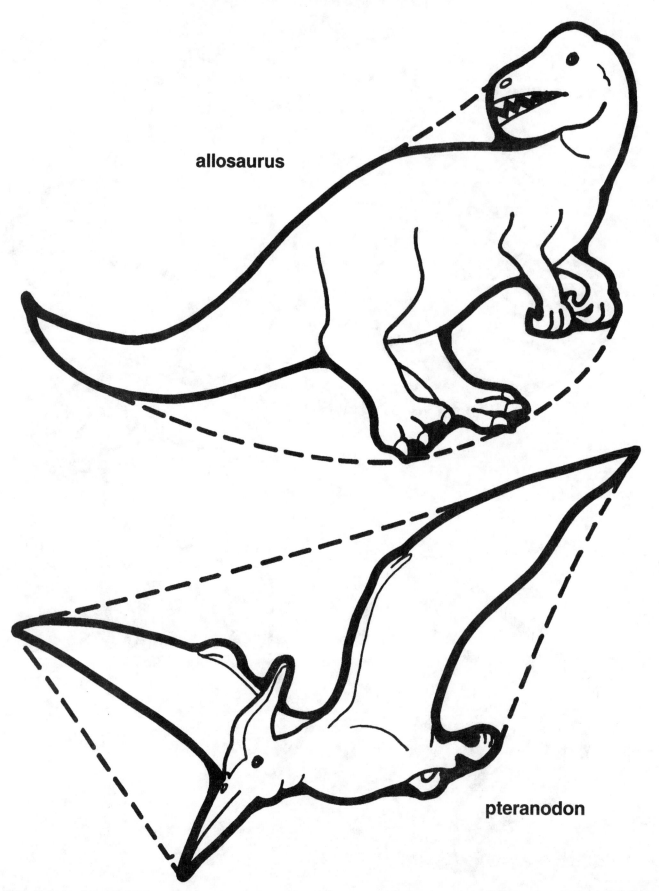

**allosaurus**

**pteranodon**

# Dinosaurs (cont.)

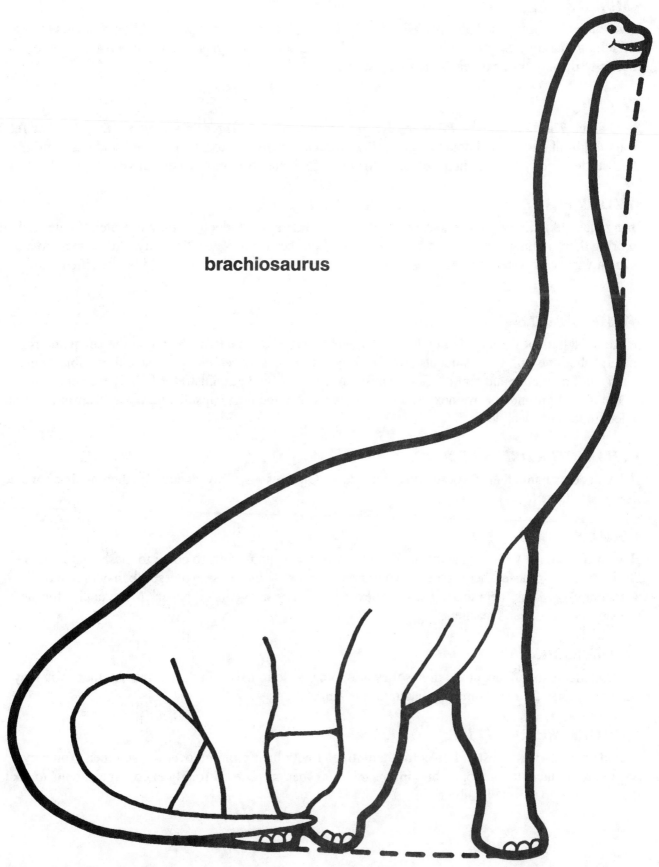

**brachiosaurus**

# End of the Year

### • *MURALS*

Divide the class into small groups. Give each group a piece of butcher paper. Allow students to draw something that they enjoyed doing or learning about in school this year. You may wish to save the murals to display for next year's incoming students.

### • *PICNIC*

Read aloud *The Teddy Bears' Picnic* by Jimmy Kennedy (Green Tiger Press, 1983). Decide what Teddy bears might like to eat and do at a picnic. Plan food and activities together. Invite students to bring their stuffed Teddy bears to help celebrate the end of a wonderful and successful year.

### • *WATER PLAY DAY*

Bring plastic kiddie pools, buckets, or hoses and sprinklers for students to play in water. Invite students to bring their bathing suits, towels, and a change of clothes for a Water Play Day. Allow them to also bring a variety of water toys and work together to determine how the toys could be classified into groups.

### • *TIME CAPSULE*

Write the letters of the alphabet on the chalkboard or refer to the letters shown on the key pictures of the alphabet line-up. Have students pick one object to represent each letter. Place those objects in a waterproof container and seal it. Get permission from a school administrator to bury the time capsule on the school grounds. Have next year's students retrieve the time capsule and try to determine which object represents each letter.

### • *CHARACTER DRESS-UP DAY*

Have students name their favorite book characters. On Dress-Up Day, encourage them to dress and act like those characters.

### • *GOAL SETTING*

Have a conference with each student. You may wish to invite parents to come to these conferences. During the conferences, help students determine their strengths and weaknesses, behavioral and academic. Then ask them to set goals for next year. Write the goals on paper. Make copies for the parents and next year's teachers.

### • *SUMMER FUN*

Invite students to talk about the things they are going to do to have fun during the summer. You may wish to classify these activities by letters of the alphabet.

### • *SUMMER READING LIST*

Provide parents with a list of books for them to read with their children over the summer. You may wish to reproduce the bibliographies in this book for that purpose. Strongly encourage parents to take their children to the public library.